INTERNATIONAL SERIES OF MONOGRAPHS IN

EXPERIMENTAL PSYCHOLOGY

GENERAL EDITOR: H. J. EYSENCK

VOLUME 12

PERSONALITY AND NATIONAL CHARACTER

Personality
and
National Character

R. LYNN

PERGAMON PRESS

OXFORD · NEW YORK · TORONTO
SYDNEY · BRAUNSCHWEIG

Pergamon Press Ltd., Headington Hill Hall, Oxford

Pergamon Press Inc., Maxwell House, Fairview Park, Elmsford, New York 10523

Pergamon of Canada Ltd., 207 Queen's Quay West, Toronto 1

Pergamon Press (Aust.) Pty. Ltd., 19a Boundary Street, Rushcutters Bay, N.S.W. 2011, Australia

Vieweg & Sohn GmbH, Burgplatz 1, Braunschweig

First edition 1971

Library of Congress Catalog Card No. 71-149707

Printed in Great Britain by A. Wheaton & Co., Exeter

08 016516 8

CONTENTS

v

CONTENTS

PREFACE

IN THIS book I attempt to analyse the problem of national character from the point of view of contemporary psychology. The thesis presented is that among the advanced nations there are differences in the level of anxiety in the population. The anxiety level manifests itself in various ways, such as the incidence of suicide, mental illness, accidents, tobacco consumption and so forth. The thesis demands that all these supposed manifestations of the anxiety level should be associated together so that they form a pattern, and the existence of this pattern is demonstrated in the body of the book.

It may be appropriate here to indicate briefly the scope of the argument. Three limitations are particularly important. First, this book does not aim to present a complete description of the national character of the people of every country, or indeed of any country. It is concerned only with the trait of anxiety. The thesis should be regarded as a simple model of one aspect of the real world. This simplification of reality is of course one of the hallmarks of scientific method, and in this respect the thesis to be presented follows the canons of scientific procedure.

Secondly, neither does this book purport to present a complete explanation for suicide, mental illness, accidents and the other phenomena which are interpreted as indices of national anxiety level. For all these things there are no doubt many determinants. But they are irrelevant for our purpose, which is only to abstract the significance of anxiety from the complexities of reality.

Thirdly, although anxiety appears to be an important determinant of a number of epidemiological and other national differences among contemporary advanced countries, it should not be supposed that anxiety need always, in other circumstances, be equally important or significant. Where phenomena have several causes, the contribution of any particular cause depends upon its variability among the set of cases, and also upon the variability of the other causes. Thus there may well be other sets of countries where anxiety is not a significant cause of national differences in the epidemiological and other conditions discussed in this book. The principle here can be illustrated by a simple example. Consider two pieces of metal of equal length. Now heat one and it becomes longer than the other. Why is it longer? Because it has been heated. But this does not mean to say that whenever one piece of metal is longer than another it is because it has been heated up. The same is true of the significance of anxiety as a cause of national differences among contemporary advanced nations. The thesis does not imply that anxiety is always a significant factor in national differences.

It remains for me to mention my appreciation of the help I have received from others in writing this book. I am particularly indebted to Professor Sir Cyril Burt and to Professor H. J. Eysenck for their critical comments on an early draft of this book. My debt to them is also great because the thesis I present rests on the foundations of their work on factor analysis and its application to personality. Mrs. B. O'Sullivan and Miss S. Hampson have given me much assistance in the collection of data. I am indebted to my wife for her translations of the Russian psychiatric literature.

Economic and Social Research
Institute, Dublin

INTRODUCTION

By Sir Cyril Burt

I GLADLY respond to the suggestion that I should write a brief psychological introduction to this book. I do so all the more willingly because I believe, as Professor Lynn does, that the problems he has raised are of urgent importance, and have been unduly neglected. The wars that so unexpectedly overtook us during the first half of the century, the vastly increased facilities for travel, the waves of migration from one country to another, and the frequent racial conflicts within the same country, have all rendered us more and more aware of the wide divergences between people of different national origin. What, Professor Lynn asks, is the precise nature of these national or racial differences, how far are they innate and how far the result of cultural or educational influences? Why, to use the current phraseology, are some nations comparatively "undeveloped" and others "advanced"? What in short are the principal causes at work?

It is curious that hitherto there have been so few attempts to study these questions by strictly scientific procedures. Politicians, social reformers and the writers who discuss such topics in our popular weeklies and monthlies, are ready to dogmatise and to contradict each other with supreme self-confidence. But their conclusions are manifestly based on little more than subjective impressions, armchair speculation and their own personal ideologies. During the present century almost the only British investigator who has attempted anything like an objective and systematic study is William McDougall. Yet when we turn to his book on *The Group Mind*, a work which claims to "apply psychological principles to the interpretation of national character", all we find is a purely descriptive and theoretical treatment, differing but little from that of Buckle, Bagehot, Kidd and their French contemporaries, a hundred years ago. In his later volume on *National Welfare and National Decay* he compares Morselli's maps of divorce and suicide with Ripley's map of hair-colour (as a clue to race), and refers incidentally to a few results obtained with mental tests by his own research-students and by American army psychologists; but the actual data have manifestly had little to do with shaping the author's own convictions.

The reader has only to glance at the first of Professor Lynn's chapters to see how very different is the treatment he has here adopted. Instead of mere personal impressions varying from one individual to another, we have tables of quantitative data based on detailed references which anyone who wishes can verify for himself. These are subjected to the same statistical techniques as those already applied with such fruitful effect to the study of individual differences—the calculation of correlation coefficients and a subsequent factor analysis. No doubt there will be critics who demur to the choice of the initial data or of the factorial procedures; so much the better if it provokes other pioneers to try their hands with a different set of facts and some other statistical method. The real merit of Professor Lynn's work is to have pointed out the direction which future investigators must follow—the collection of objective data and the application of scientific techniques.

The lists of variables set out in the graphs and tables that follow and the numerous references in the bibliography show how broadly Professor Lynn's preliminary inquiries have ranged. And for that very reason his book should have an equally wide appeal. It should interest not merely sociologists, anthropologists and economists, from whose several fields he has culled much of his data, but also educationists, physicians and psychiatrists, and indeed all who appreciate the importance of studying human progress and welfare.

To appreciate the reasons for the unexpectedly disparate kinds of data that Professor Lynn has collated it will perhaps be helpful to fall back on the analogous type of inquiry that I have already mentioned. How does the psychologist proceed when he is investigating the influences that are responsible for differences—between different persons—the differences, for example, between the gifted child on the one hand and the dull or backward on the other?

In compiling his case-history for a given individual the psychologist commonly starts with what seem to be the relevant environmental conditions. He then proceeds to examine both physical and mental characteristics, the latter including not only intellectual deviations, but also peculiarities of temperament and character. Similarly, in studying the differences between nations, we naturally think first of the geographical, geological, and climatic conditions under which the inhabitants live—the mineral resources, the fertile or mountainous character of the land, the presence of a sea-board with natural harbours along contemporary trade-routes, the temperature, the humidity, and the rapidity of meteorological changes. These were the causal agencies on which pre-Darwinian writers laid great stress, and which later writers held to be indirectly responsible for the adaptive variations produced by natural selection during what Bagehot called the race-making stage. They may be necessary conditions for economic growth; but they are not sufficient conditions. Human factors— the arrival or emergence of a people with adequate physical, intellectual, and motivational characteristics are essential.

The physical characteristics would include not only bodily health and vigour, but also the distinctive features associated with different racial types, not forgetting one of the most significant of all—the so-called "blood group". Mental characteristics are commonly divided into cognitive (practical as well as intellectual) and motivational (temperament and character). And each of these can be subclassified into tendencies that are presumably innate and those that are acquired by tradition, education, and various cultural influences. Of the cognitive characteristics the most frequently discussed and studied is innate general ability, popularly termed "intelligence". Unfortunately, nearly all current tests of intelligence are appreciably influenced by variations in culture; they are therefore far less useful in studying racial differences than in studying individual differences. There are marked differences between the means obtained for different races; but, with few exceptions, they are relatively small as compared with the individual differences within each racial or national group. What appears to be far more important is the range of individual variation, particularly in the upper direction. During the periods of their greatest advance—the Periclean age in Athens, the Augustan age in Rome, and our own Elizabethan and Victorian eras—each nation has been exceptionally prolific of gifted individuals emerging in various walks of life. It seems highly likely that isolation makes for relative homogeneity, while the mingling of different racial stocks in consequence of migration, conquest, or the like, and the recombination of genes that ensues, makes for richer variations.

Motivational characteristics are still more difficult to assess. And yet, as Professor Lynn's results reveal, they are probably much more influential. The early investigations of mine, which he cites with approval, have frequently been misquoted and misunderstood. So may I briefly explain what was the evidence on which I relied? I endeavoured to pick out representative individuals, children as well as adults, who exhibited most conspicuously those physical characteristics which Ripley and others had described in their classification of European races. Judged by observations, interviews and tests of personality, there appeared to be a well-marked contrast between the South European (or "Mediterranean") type and the North European (or "Nordic") type. The former seemed more sociable, loquacious, vivacious, and impulsive; their emotions were promptly and freely expressed, and as quickly subsided. The latter seemed to be more reserved, self-sufficient, self-assertive, and self-controlled; they were characterised by greater independence and individuality—eager to explore, investigate, and decide for themselves; their emotions were equally strong, but more firmly repressed and far more persistent. The mid-European (or "Alpine") type seemed on the whole more phlegmatic than either of the other two—slower and more conservative, yet at the same time shrewd and secretive, and (in many of my own cases) marked by strong aesthetic interests—a love of art and music. These differences are, of course, no more than average tendencies; and no doubt the scheme is oversimplified. But the suggestion that they are in part the effect of innate physiological and biochemical differences, surviving from an earlier race-making stage, seems in some measure confirmed by the way they will continue to reveal themselves when children of one type are adopted by foster-parents of a different type—e.g. Irish children adopted by English foster-parents, English by Welsh, and so on. However, among present-day populations the more conspicuous differences in character and daily habits would seem to be chiefly the result of differences in type of culture and traditional ideals of behaviour, transmitted by parents and older companions. Moreover, within the same nation these qualities may vary widely from one social class to another, and have often undergone considerable modification during the past phases of the nation's history. This means that a favourable social environment is even more important than the physical. The exceptionally able and enterprising members of the nation who should form its more effective leaders can exercise their powers to the full only in periods of peace and security and within a community that is free, tolerant and politically well organised. Extremes of individualism and of self-assertive motivation in the general mass of the population, coupled with an unwillingness to accept the authority of competent leaders, ultimately issue, as history all too plainly testifies, not in progress but in chaos.

In the field of individual psychology what is so remarkable is the fact that, as numerous correlational studies have shown, favourable conditions under each of these widely divergent headings—mental and physical, cognitive and motivational, environmental and hereditary—tend to go together; and now as Professor Lynn's results show the same holds true of national characteristics. "The aim of a genuinely scientific generalisation", so Eddington has assured us, "is not just to produce a plausible hypothesis and confirm it by collecting relevant facts, but rather to reduce to a single, relatively simple, and comprehensive formulation the widest possible variety of observations, and at the same time suggest further inferences and fresh problems which may provide starting-points for future research." This has been the bold and far-reaching aim which Professor Lynn has set out to fulfil; and, if we can accept his conclusions as they stand, we must agree that he has gone far towards accomplishing it. He has compiled from the scattered literature a vast array of quantitative data from seemingly unrelated areas, symptomatic of the various aspects I have just enumerated; and on applying the methods of factorial analysis used in individual psychology, has shown that "one common underlying factor" pervades almost all of them. This he identifies with an emotional drive which he tentatively labels "anxiety". "Anxiety", as he defines the concept, is in his view one of the most powerful incentives for prolonged and purposeful activity.

Perhaps the most interesting of Professor Lynn's chapters are those in which he adduces evidence to show that the basic factor which he has thus demonstrated forms the main agent making for rapid economic growth. From Weber onwards several economists and sociologists have attacked this problem. Professor McClelland, for example, who has also used correlational techniques, concludes that the distinctive quality characterising "achieving societies" is the "achievement motive". This conclusion has been criticised as "an example of the old faculty fallacy, long ago pilloried by Molière". But in point of fact Professor McClelland endeavoured to estimate the achievement motive by independent tests. Professor Lynn has gone one better—he has devised a questionnaire for directly assessing the achievement motive, and finds that it is apparently uncorrelated with the more general factor that he names "anxiety". Certain critics no doubt may reject both the specification and the simplification;

others may argue that some of the items in his table (e.g. "car-deaths" and "suicide") indicate the effects of economic growth rather than its causes. But once again let us remember Eddington's description of a scientific generalisation as one which not only professes to solve old problems, but also provokes new ones for further research.

For the most part Professor Lynn's data relate to conditions obtaining in his selected set of countries during the post-war period—the period which for us is of greatest importance in view of the practical issues with which we are confronted at the present time. Let us hope he will extend his studies to earlier stages in world-history, so that his theory may be tested by the light thrown on economic development and the progress of civilisation in the past. His conclusions, as he himself has emphasised, are tentative and provisional. What I should like chiefly to commend are the methods he has adopted. Only by the collection of objective and quantitative data and the application of modern statistical techniques can the illuminating theories he has advanced be verified, amplified, criticised, or amended.

CHAPTER 1

NATIONAL DIFFERENCES IN MENTAL ILLNESS AND CALORIE INTAKE

THE idea of national character is in some disrepute among social scientists. Still less favoured is the view that there are innate racial differences in personality which contribute to the national character of a people. Such theories are widely regarded as "racism" and *ipso facto* erroneous. For all that, it is the thesis of this book that important national personality characteristics do exist and that racial differences are one of the factors underlying them. It is argued that only the assumption of national character can explain the differences between countries in the prevalence of such things as suicide, mental illness, alcoholism, calorie intake, accident proneness and other matters with which this book is concerned. The attribution of such differences to an underlying racial factor is, of course, a further step and one which can be less securely made. Both theses will no doubt be unpalatable in some circles. Nevertheless, I believe the facts to be considered presently point to the truth of both these propositions.

Consider first the case of Ireland. The Irish Republic has a number of remarkable epidemiological features, of which two of the most well known are the exceptionally high rates of mental illness and calorie intake. The proportion of mental hospital patients (principally psychotics) in Ireland, which stood at 7·3 per 1000 of the population in 1961, is 50 per cent higher than that of any other European country; and is several hundred per cent higher than that of some countries, such as West Germany which has a rate of only 1·7 per 1000. How is such a difference to be explained? One possibility is to assume that psychosis is an extreme manifestation of some personality characteristic which is generally distributed throughout the population, and that this characteristic has a high mean in Ireland. Evidence for the existence of such a characteristic has been presented by Eysenck (1952), who has called it "psychoticism". This theory does not assume that psychosis is to be explained solely in terms of a high level of psychoticism. It assumes only that this is one component of the disorder, to which other specific causal influences affecting the symptoms of the disorder may also contribute (Eysenck, 1967). Now if the population of one country had a higher mean on psychoticism than that of another, there would (other things being equal) be more individuals at the extreme and hence more psychotics. This is a possible explanation of the national differences in hospitalised psychosis rates.

Other explanations are, of course, possible. It could be that the spread (i.e. standard deviation) of the personality dimension is greater in Ireland than in other countries, giving rise to a higher proportion of psychotics and also of extreme non-psychotics, whatever they may be. Or it could be that national statistics of hospitalised mental patients reflect some spurious factor such as the readiness of doctors to send people to mental hospitals, the use of mental hospitals as dumping grounds for old people and unemployables and so forth. If this were so, the national statistics would be devoid of psychological and psychiatric interest. We shall see in due course that these alternative explanations can be ruled out with a reasonable degree of confidence when we examine them in closer detail. In the meanwhile, the possibility that there is a personality dimension, perhaps Eysenck's psychoticism, which has a high mean value in Ireland and is low in West Germany is one interpretation of the data.

Let us now consider the exceptionally high calorie intake in Ireland. Like the mental illness rate, the Irish calorie intake is the highest in the world except for New Zealand, which stands at about the same level. The mean daily intake in Ireland is 3490 calories (1960), approaching 20 per cent higher than some other advanced countries, notably West Germany where the mean intake is around 2960. Thus we have two characteristics—the prevalence of mental illness and the calorie intake—which are exceptionally high in Ireland and rather low in West Germany. The question now arises of whether this is just a matter of chance, or whether there could be some underlying personality factor which has the effect both of making the Irish eat a lot and particularly vulnerable to mental illness.

Fortunately there is a well-established method for answering this question. It rests on the logical principle enunciated by J. S. Mill that if two entities are correlated, then either one causes the other, or they are both caused by some common factor. This principle has had extensive application in psychology and is the basis of factor-analysis, where a number of intercorrelating measures are assumed to reflect some underlying factor. For example, in the field of intelligence testing it was first discovered that a number of measures of intellectual ability are fairly well intercorrelated, and from this the inference is drawn that there is a single underlying factor of general intelligence which enters into the performance of a great variety of intellectual tasks. The presence of the intercorrelations allows us to infer the existence of the single common factor.

This is the logic of the method which we now apply to the problem of the high Irish mental illness rate and calorie intake. To find out whether they both reflect a single underlying factor we need to know whether they are correlated. To determine the solution to this question we need to consider other countries in addition to Ireland. What we are essentially asking here is whether the same pattern of high mental illness together with high calorie intake—or the reverse, low mental illness with low calorie intake—is also found in other countries sufficiently often for a chance association to be ruled out. If the pattern is widespread it will give rise to a correlation of the two measures when a number of countries are considered.

The next step is to select the group of countries among which the possibility of a correlation between mental illness rates and calorie intake can be examined. In making this selection it would not seem fruitful to include underdeveloped countries. For example, it could be shown easily enough that a country like Burma has a much lower proportion of hospitalised mental illness and also a much lower calorie intake than Ireland. There would also be a rather obvious explanation for this, namely that the poverty of Burma is responsible both for the low level of psychiatric services and the low calorie consumption. Such an obvious explanation in comparing Burma and Ireland would make the postulation of some personality factor distinguishing the populations of the two countries distinctly implausible.

To rule out the effect of national wealth it is necessary to take as homogeneous a group of countries as possible. The natural group seems to be the nations of the advanced western world, i.e. Western Europe itself, the white Commonwealth, the U.S.A. and Japan. Broadly, this is the western community of nations as distinct from the communist block and the third world. Naturally in the selection of any group of nations there must be borderline cases whose inclusion or exclusion can only be determined by some arbitrary procedure. To obtain a reasonably homogeneous sample the rules adopted were that for inclusion a country should have a *per capita* income (G.D.P.) of at least 450 U.S. dollars in 1961, a population of over one million, and belong to the group of nations which are broadly regarded as advanced Western countries. On these criteria, Japan is included (*per capita* G.D.P. 464), and Ireland (583), but Spain (296) and Portugal (260) are excluded. Also excluded are Israel and Venezuela, as falling outside the group normally regarded as advanced Western countries. South Africa is also excluded (*per capita* G.D.P. of 414, which conceals an exceptional range of incomes from the affluent white population to the poor black majority). On the criteria of size we have excluded Luxembourg, Iceland, Liechtenstein, Monaco and other small countries which can hardly be regarded as comparable with major powers. This leaves a group of eighteen countries consisting of the countries of Northern Europe, Italy, the old Commonwealth, the United States and Japan. While there is necessarily an element of arbitrariness in including or excluding certain countries at the borderline, it is doubtful whether a slightly smaller or larger group would make any substantial difference to the correlations which will presently be reported. This group of eighteen countries is the set with which we are concerned throughout this book. All data are taken for the year 1960, or 1961 if the data could not be obtained for the earlier year. This year was arbitrarily chosen, but the data with which we are concerned fluctuate little from year to year and hence data taken from any individual year yield much the same results.

Having decided upon the sample, we can now revert to the question of whether national differences in the prevalence of mental illness is correlated with the *per capita* calorie intake. The (product moment) correlation is $+0.58$, which is statistically significant at the 2 per cent level.* The relationship between the two measures is shown in Fig. 1.

The existence of this correlation suggests that the two national characteristics with which we are concerned are indeed causally related (following the logical principle set out by Mill). How they are causally related is a problem requiring much interpretation. But to begin with, it would seem doubtful whether either could be a direct cause of the other. It could hardly be that the excessive calorie intake in Ireland is a direct cause of the high mental illness rate, since although there are numerous theories of the

*It is a moot point whether the use of a criterion of statistical significance is appropriate. It would not be if the group of countries is regarded not as a sample but as the whole universe of advanced Western countries. On the other hand, the view may be taken that the measurements are a sample of one particular year from a number of possible years. The statistical significance of the correlations is given for those who prefer to take the second view.

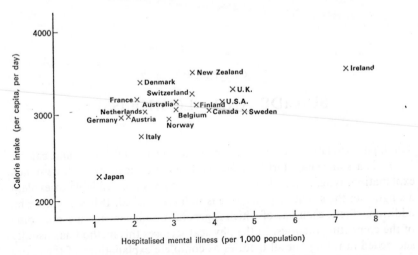

F‍ig. 1. Relationship between calorie intake and mental illness in eighteen countries ($r = +0.58$, sig. at 2 per cent).

causation of mental illness, overeating is not among them. Nor could it plausibly be argued that the rate of mental illness in a country could be directly responsible for the rest of the population's eating habits. It seems, therefore, that there must be some common cause responsible for the co-variation of these two national characteristics. Several hypotheses will no doubt suggest themselves and will require examination. Among these, a national personality characteristic is a possibility. There could be a personality characteristic which tends to increase calorie intake and at the extreme renders people vulnerable to mental illness. Such a model would explain the correlation by assuming a high mean value of this personality characteristic in Ireland and a low mean value in Japan. To make such a thesis convincing would seem to require firstly the exclusion of other plausible interpretations, and secondly the discovery of a personality factor which could be reasonably supposed to have such effects. These are problems to which we now proceed.

CHAPTER 2

SUICIDE AND ALCOHOLISM

THE high correlation between national rates of mental illness and calorie intake is a somewhat startling and challenging discovery which demands explanation. Where several alternative hypotheses are available to explain a single fact the scientific procedure is well established. It lies in gathering additional facts, each one of which is generally sufficient to rule out some of the competing theories. In the physical sciences this method has usually succeeded in ruling out all theories as complete explanations of the entire set of the facts, so that, for example, even Einstein's reformulation of Newton's theory cannot explain all the observations it should account for if it were a perfect theory. Thus the physicist has to be content with a theory which explains as many of the facts as possible. In the social sciences the task is more difficult because of the problems of deciding exactly what the implications of any particular theory are. Nevertheless, the procedure of collecting more facts as a means of distinguishing between alternative theories is well established.

We therefore turn now to inquire whether there are any other national characteristics which are associated with mental illness rates and calorie intake. There are two: the prevalence of suicide and alcoholism. These, however, are *negative* correlates of mental illness rates and calorie intake, i.e. countries with high rates of mental illness and calorie intake tend to have low rates of suicide and alcoholism. At one extreme lie countries such as Ireland and the U.K., with a pattern of high mental illness, high calorie intake, low suicide and low alcoholism. At the other extreme lie countries like Japan, France, West Germany and Austria, where the pattern is reversed. The remaining countries tend to lie in the middle range on all four variables. The data are shown in full in Table 1, and the intercorrelations in Table 2.

Table 2 shows that all four characteristics are well intercorrelated, with the single exception of calorie intake and alcoholism. However, where a

TABLE 1. PREVALENCE RATES OF CALORIE INTAKE, SUICIDE, ALCOHOLISM
AND HOSPITALISED MENTAL ILLNESS

Country	Calorie intake[a]	Suicides[b]	Cirrhosis and alcoholism deaths[b]	Hospitalised mental illness[c]
Australia	3140	10·6	6·3	3·1
Austria	2970	23·1	23·3*	1·9
Belgium	3040	14·6	10·7	3·1
Canada	3020	7·5	6·8	3·9
Denmark	3370	20·3	8·5	2·2
Finland	3110	20·5	3·5	3·6
France	3190	15·8	40·4	2·1
Germany	2960	19·5	18·8	1·7
Ireland	3490	3·0	2·1	7·3
Italy	2720	6·3	18·3	2·2
Japan	2260	21·6	10·2	1·1
Netherlands	3030	6·6	3·8	2·3
New Zealand	3490	9·7	3·2	3·5
Norway	2930	6·5	4·5	2·9
Sweden	3000	17·4	5·5	4·8
Switzerland	3220	19·0	14·9	3·5
U.K.	3280	10·6	3·0	4·5
U.S.A.	3110	10·6	12·5	4·3

(a) *Per capita*, per day 1960–2: *U.N. Statistical Yearbook 1966.*
(b) Per 100,000 population: *U.N. Demographic Yearbook 1966.*
(c) Number of psychiatric patients per 1000 population 1961. Commission of Inquiry on Mental Illness, Dublin, 1966.

*   Cirrhosis deaths only.

number of variables intercorrelate fairly highly the existence of an occasional low correlation must be expected. This is, of course, due to various contaminating extraneous influences on all measures, which will normally not reduce correlations too much but which from time to time occur together and pull a particular correlation down. Taking the correlation matrix as a whole, the intercorrelations are of a fairly high order and the pattern suggests the existence of a single underlying factor. This inference is simply an extension of Mill's principle of causation discussed in Chapter 1 and also used extensively in factor analytic work on intelligence and personality, where the existence of a number of intercorrelating measures has led to the inference of a single underlying factor. The approach here is

TABLE 2. INTERCORRELATION MATRIX OF THE FOUR VARIABLES

	1	2	3	4
1. High mental illness		0·50*	0·58†	0·49*
2. Low suicide			0·26	0·37
3. High calorie intake				0·17
4. Low alcoholism				

*$P < 0·05$;   †$P < 0·02$.

to extend the same method to the intercorrelations of national character-istics. Just as among individuals the discovery of a number of inter-correlating measures leads to the inference of a single intellectual or personality factor, so here the discovery of a number of intercorrelating national characteristics suggests an underlying national factor. With a large number of variables a factor analysis would be the appropriate method of treating the data, but with only four the existence of a single cluster is clear enough simply from inspection of the intercorrelations.*

The measures of suicide and alcoholism may require some explanation. National suicide statistics are straightforward, being simply the official returns collated in the United Nations *Demographic Yearbooks*. It is sometimes argued that national suicide rates reflect the strength of Roman Catholicism in a country. Two arguments are commonly put forward. One is that suicides are reduced by the presence of a strong Roman Catholic church and the other that they are falsified by incorrect certification of the cause of death by doctors and coroners. These are quite different hypo-theses. The first maintains that the suicide rate is genuinely low in Catholic countries and attributes this to the influence of the church. The second that suicide may not be particularly low, but is merely a reflection of the attitudes of doctors and coroners who tend to understate suicide where there is some degree of doubt.

As far as the first argument is concerned, it may be doubted whether there is any strong tendency for suicide to be low as a general rule in Catholic countries. As may be seen in Table 1, suicide is high in Austria and France, both of which have substantial Roman Catholic populations. This makes it doubtful whether Roman Catholicism can be regarded as a decisive factor. To estimate the significance of Catholicism the proportion of Roman Catholics in the population of the eighteen countries has been taken from the Catholic Directories. These figures are shown in Table 3.

* A factor analysis of the date is given in Chapter 13.

The product moment correlation between these and the suicide rates is
−0·17 indicating a small and statistically insignificant tendency for
suicide rates to be lower in strongly Roman Catholic countries. Evidence
for the existence of such an association was marshalled some decades ago
by Durkheim (1897), but it would seem that among the group of countries
we are considering and at the present time, Roman Catholicism must be
regarded as at best a minor factor affecting national suicide rates.

TABLE 3

Country	Percentage of Roman Catholics in population
Australia	22·4
Austria	91·4
Belgium	94·4
Canada	41·3
Denmark	0·6
Finland	0·1
France	80·3
West Germany	49·0
Ireland	94·9
Italy	95·1
Japan	0·3
Netherlands	41·0
New Zealand	16·2
Norway	0·2
Sweden	0·6
Switzerland	45·9
U.K.	9·9
U.S.A.	27·3

Even if this non-significant correlation is admitted as indicating a
minor influence of Roman Catholicism in lowering suicide rates, such an
effect would not, of course, preclude the operation of other influences
such as a national personality factor whose existence we have hinted at.
Naturally it is unlikely that any national statistic would be a reflection of
the operation of a single cause, so that the presence of some causal factors
other than the one we are concerned with is not a crucial objection to our
approach.

The other argument commonly suggested about suicide rates in Roman
Catholic countries is that coroners tend to understate suicides. This

possibility has been investigated by Sainsbury and Barraclough (1968). They considered the suicide rates of immigrants from a number of countries into the United States. If national suicide rates are genuine reflections of national character the same rates should be found among immigrant groups. If, on the other hand, suicide rates merely reflect the vagaries of national statistics collection, coroners' idiosyncracies and so forth, there should be no tendency for the national differences in suicide to be preserved among immigrant groups in the U.S.A. In fact, the rank order of suicide rates of countries is almost exactly the same among immigrant groups in the U.S.A. as in the countries from which they emigrate. These figures are shown in Table 4. This result clearly constitutes a powerful argument that national suicide rates reflect some genuine national characteristic.

Turning now to alcoholism, the problem of measurement is more difficult than in the case of suicide. The commonest measures of the national prevalence of alcoholism are deaths from alcoholism and from cirrhosis of the liver, and the measure used here is simply the addition of these two. Deaths from liver cirrhosis are very much more common in all countries, so that essentially the same results would be obtained by using these alone and ignoring alcoholism deaths, which are so few that they have little effect on the total. The reason for taking deaths from liver

TABLE 4. SUICIDE RATES IN 1959 OF FOREIGN-BORN U.S. CITIZENS, COMPARED WITH THOSE OF THEIR COUNTRIES OF BIRTH

The correlation is 0.88 ($P < 0.001$).

Country	Suicide rate of foreign born in U.S.A. per 100,000	Suicide rate of country of origin per 100,000
Sweden	34·2	18·1
Austria	32·5	24·8
Czechoslovakia	31·5	24·9
West Germany	25·7	18·7
Poland	25·2	8·0
Norway	23·7	7·8
England	19·2	11·5
Italy	18·2	6·2
Canada	17·5	7·4
Ireland	9·8	2·5
Mexico	7·9	2·1

cirrhosis as an index of alcoholism is that it is frequently the result of excessive alcohol intake. As Leitch (1961) puts it, "alcoholism is by far the commonest cause of liver cirrhosis". Cirrhosis of the liver is a condition in which the liver hardens as a result of the development of new fibrous tissue. This is due to two main causes, namely damage to the liver cells produced by virus, microbes or toxic substances and dietary deficiencies interfering with the nutrition of liver cells. The second is often the result of excessive drinking. Since cirrhosis of the liver frequently results from excessive intake of alcohol, the two indices should tend to be associated both over time and between countries or regions within countries. Popham (1966) has shown that this is so in twenty-one instances, drawn from most European countries and North America. The correlations are high, ranging from $+0\cdot45$ to $+0\cdot89$.

Epidemiological evidence for the use of cirrhosis of the liver as an index of alcoholism is available from studies of the effects of prohibition in the United States. During the years of prohibition (1921–32), deaths from liver cirrhosis fell by $42\cdot2$ per cent from the 1910 base, while general mortality fell by $7\cdot1$ per cent (Piedmont, 1961).

As with the suicide rates and, for that matter, the rates of mental illness and calorie intake, the index of alcoholism taken is not a perfect measure of the actual number of alcoholics in a country. The problem we are touching on here is the reliability of the statistics. Generally, it may be said that measures are rarely, if ever, completely accurate reflections of the underlying reality they purport to represent. This is true even in the physical sciences. In the social sciences the amount of distortion is no doubt greater, though the difference is one of degree. I do not propose in this book to pursue in great detail the question of the reliability of the statistics for each individual country. Such a task would clearly involve a considerable search through the literature of all eighteen countries and would be beyond the resources of a single researcher. I have reviewed the question of the reliability of Irish data elsewhere and shown that it is essentially accurate (Lynn, 1971). To delve into the question in detail for each country would fortunately be an irrelevance for our present purposes. The very fact that the measures with which we are concerned are in a number of instances significantly intercorrelated indicates that the figures themselves must have some degree of reliability. If the figures were meaningless such intercorrelations would not occur, since meaningless figures cannot be expected to correlate with anything except as flukes. Furthermore, once it is conceded that the existence of significant correlations itself substantiates the reliability of the data, demonstration that the data are contaminated only serves to make the correlations more impressive. The reason for this is, of course, that it is more difficult to get significant correlations with contaminated data than with pure data. Thus arguments designed to show that the variables with which we are concerned are partly affected by other factors (e.g. the suicide figures by Roman Catholicism and so forth) merely serve to show that the true correlation (if such factors could be partialled out) is really higher than the one presented. Paradoxically, therefore, such arguments drawing attention to contaminating variables, which are sometimes thought to weaken a correlation, actually strengthen it.

Thus we have suggested the existence of a pattern of four intercorrelated national characteristics: high mental illness and high calorie intake associated with low suicide and low alcoholism is the pattern found in Ireland and also in the U.K., while the reverse of the pattern is found in Japan, France, West Germany and Austria. The existence of such a pattern suggests the presence of some underlying factor, and it is to a consideration of what this factor could be that we now turn.

*   *   *   *   *

The problem now is to consider what single factor could be responsible for this pattern of high mental illness and high calorie intake together with low rates of suicide and alcoholism. It could be that the explanation lies in some economic effect. Perhaps the most obvious hypothesis would be the level of affluence, since it is often maintained that psychological problems and also excessive eating increase as countries grow more affluent. Closer inspection of the hypothesis, however, produces the difficulty that two of the undesirable features of society are *negatively* correlated with the other two, so that an affluence hypothesis would have to maintain either that with increasing affluence mental illness and calorie intake rise while suicide and alcoholism fall, or vice versa.

To determine the truth of this line of explanation the best procedure seems to be first to assemble the countries in a rank order on the factor, and secondly to see whether this rank order is associated with affluence. This method can then be extended to any other hypotheses we care to entertain. Assembling the countries in a rank order on the factor is a straightforward matter, consisting simply of ranking the countries on each of the four variables, adding the ranks, and then reranking on the basis of the totals. This puts the countries in the rank order shown in Table 5. Also included in this table are the *per capita* incomes in U.S. dollars for the year 1961. Consideration of this table makes the affluence explanation of the factor appear unpromising. Japan is the least affluent country but has the high rate of suicide–high alcoholism pattern, often thought to be associated with affluence. On the other hand, the second least affluent country is Ireland with the reverse pattern of Japan, a low suicide–low alcoholism pattern. At the other extreme, the most affluent country is the United States, which comes in the middle range on the factor. Thus there appears to be no clear relationship between the factor and affluence. The rank correlation between the two is -0.37, which is not even statistically significant at the 10 per cent level. It seems evident that the factor is not a function of the degree of affluence.

In point of fact this result should not be particularly surprising since the popular belief that advanced affluent societies generate psychological disturbances has little factual basis. Suicide rates, for example, have remained fairly constant in almost all the countries of our sample from 1900 to the present day (see Table 25 below). Mental illness statistics are

TABLE 5

Country	Factor ranks	*Per capita* incomes (1961 dollars)
Austria	1	831
Japan	2	464
Germany	3	1232
France	4	1149
Italy	5	618
Belgium	6	1198
Denmark		1256
Switzerland	8	1571
Norway	9	1208
Finland	10	982
Sweden	11	1592
U.S.A.	12	2572
Australia	13	1380
Netherlands	14	939
Canada	15	1774
New Zealand	16	1439
U.K.	17	1244
Ireland	18	583

less reliable, but do not suggest any general tendency to increase in affluent societies. In a study covering the years 1926–55 in Norway, for example, the incidence of psychotic breakdown has remained virtually constant throughout the period (Ødegaard, 1961).

A second possible economic explanation of the factor is the amount of urbanisation in different countries. It is sometimes argued that the pressures of city life, rather than affluence as such, are responsible for a variety of psychological disturbances. For instance, Russell and Russell (1968) have noted that when rats living in compounds become overcrowded they begin to kill each other, and suggest that human beings may do the same kind of thing.

Two possible measures of the degree of urbanisation can be taken, consisting of the density of population and the proportion of the population engaged in agriculture. Both sets of data are shown in Table 6. The density of population suffers as an index because it does not take into account the spread of the population over a country's total area. Thus a country could consist of one city and a large desert and yet have a low density of population. Nevertheless, inspection of the table suggests that in practice the figures are reasonably reliable, with Japan and Holland having very high densities and Australia and Canada comparatively low. The rank correlation between population density and the factor is $+0.37$ and between the factor and the percentage of the labour force engaged in agriculture, $+0.35$. Neither correlation is statistically significant even at the 10 per cent level. We must conclude that moving from a rural, agricultural and uncrowded life to a high degree of urbanisation and industrialisation does not greatly affect the factor with which we are concerned.

Now that we have ruled out the most obvious economic and demographic explanations of our factor, we can turn to the possibility of a psychological interpretation. It is suggested that sense can only be made of the factor by the assumption that there is some personality characteristic which varies from one population to another, at one extreme producing a population prone to high suicide and alcoholism together with low mental illness rates and low calorie intakes and at the other extreme producing the reverse of this pattern. It is further suggested that this personality characteristic is anxiety. The thesis to be advanced is that where the anxiety level in the population of a country is high, there are high rates of suicide and alcoholism together with a low rate of mental illness and a low calorie intake. In developing this thesis our strategy will

TABLE 6

Country	Population density (per sq. kilometre)	% population in agriculture
Australia	1	10·9
Austria	86	22·8
Belgium	307	7·2
Canada	2	12·1
Denmark	110	17·5
Finland	14	35·5
France	88	19·8
Germany	226	13·4
Ireland	41	35·2
Italy	170	28·2
Japan	262	32·6
Netherlands	361	10·7
New Zealand	10	14·4
Norway	11	19·5
Sweden	17	13·8
Switzerland	142	11·2
U.K.	228	3·8
U.S.A.	21	6·5

be as follows. We shall first present a brief outline of psychological work on the nature of anxiety (Chapter 3). We shall then argue that national rates of mental illness can be understood as an inverse function of national anxiety levels (Chapter 4) and that suicide, alcoholism and calorie intake are also functions of anxiety (Chapter 5). In the succeeding chapters we shall examine further implications of the thesis for national differences in accident proneness, coronary heart disease, duodenal ulcers, hypertension, smoking, celibacy and economic growth. Finally, we consider the causes of national differences in anxiety and advance the thesis that climate and race are significant factors.

CHAPTER 3

ANXIETY

THE task of labelling a factor is apt to give rise to difficulties. For our present factor, anxiety seems the best term on the grounds that it commands the most widespread acceptance among psychologists. There are a number of schools in psychology which use the concept of anxiety in roughly (though not always exactly) the same sense. Although there are differences between these schools, there is agreement in broad outline about what anxiety is and on its significance as an important personality characteristic. The disagreements are principally matters of detail and are on a different plane from that on which we are working in this monograph. For instance, Eysenck (e.g. 1967) regards anxiety as a product of the two more fundamental personality traits of neuroticism and introversion. This does not mean that Eysenck does not regard anxiety as an important and useful concept. He is simply saying that where something (e.g. suicide) is ascribed to anxiety, it is possible to make a further refinement in terms of neuroticism and introversion.

Where Eysenck breaks anxiety down into two subfactors, Cattell breaks it down into the five subfactors of guilt, ergic tension, poor ego-strength, suspiciousness and poorly developed self-sentiment. Many others, such as Gellhorn (1957), think of anxiety as a unitary trait dependent largely on the dominance of the sympathetic nervous system. Others again, such as the Spence (1960) school, think of anxiety as a single drive in terms of Hull's behaviour system. But these are differences within the family, that is to say there is broad agreement on the nature of anxiety and its significance. While in my own view there is much to be said for the Eysenck and Cattell approaches of breaking the concept down into its components, there are circumstances where the data are only sufficient to enable us to work in terms of the broad concept and this seems to be the case with our own data. In short, I suggest that there is sufficient evidence to posit a national personality factor of anxiety, the strength of which is responsible for the national patterns with which we are concerned; but I doubt whether at this stage it would be fruitful to push the analysis further and make any judgements about whether the national differences lie in neuroticism or introversion, or any of the subfactors of the Cattell system.

Furthermore, neither the Eysenck analysis of anxiety in terms of neuroticism and introversion, nor the Cattell analysis or indeed any other approach, is universally accepted. Which of the personality constructs eventually emerges will probably depend on the identification of their physiological bases. It may be, as Eysenck (1967) persuasively suggests, that the level of excitation in the brain stem reticular formation gives rise to introversion and that in the thalamic reticular formation underlies neuroticism, and that when there is a high level in both they tend to augment each other, giving rise to a correlation between the two personality factors and a joint factor of anxiety. However, from our own point of view these possibilities are beyond the range of our data and it seems best to interpret our factor in terms of the broad concept of anxiety. When personality theory has sorted out the details of the structure of anxiety, our own factor should easily fall into place with whatever personality system finally emerges.

Although anxiety has seemed the best term for the factor with which we are concerned, it must be admitted that it is not perfect. There is much to be said for the term *emotionality*, which was suggested as a general factor some decades ago by Sir Cyril Burt (1915). The advantage of emotionality is that it is a fairly neutral term, whereas anxiety has come to have pejorative connotations. This flavour has been acquired comparatively recently, largely as a result of Freud's theory of anxiety as the underlying condition in neurosis. Before Freud's work became popular, however, the association of anxiety with neurosis was less strong and it was more commonly used in the sense of "earnestly desirous" or "strained or solicitous desire". Thus Nelson is said to have written in 1794 that "the general seems as anxious as anyone to expedite the fall of the place". Similarly, W. S. Gilbert wrote

> If you're anxious to shine
> In the high aesthetic line . . .

This usage still exists today, although it has possibly become overshadowed by the associations of anxiety with maladjustment.

As used in this book, the term anxiety is intended to convey both the implications of worry and strong motivation. Which is predominant depends on its intensity. At a low level of anxiety an individual is exceptionally emotionally stable and free from all kinds of worry and nervous tension. In its middle range, anxiety manifests itself as nervous energy or "strained or solicitous desire", and it is here that it is used in the sense of a person being anxious to achieve something. This usage has a slight connotation of worry, but the chief implication is one of strong motivation. It is only when anxiety becomes intense that it takes on the Freudian associations of angst and becomes a neurotic condition which both induces unhappiness and interferes with endeavour. It is probably advantageous to have the moderate level of anxiety where it manifests itself as strong motivation, although disadvantageous for the anxiety to be so high that it turns into neurosis. Thus anxiety can be either useful or otherwise, depending on its degree of intensity.

The remainder of this chapter is concerned with sketching briefly the principal schools in psychology and psychiatry which have been concerned with the concept of anxiety. It is intended for anthropologists, sociologists, epidemiologists and others who may be interested in the psychological approach to national differences but not familiar with psychological work on anxiety. For psychologists the ensuing account will contain little they do not know already (except possibly for the Moscow work on the strength of the nervous system), and they would probably do best to turn now to Chapter 4.

Pride of place for the establishment of anxiety as a central concept in both psychiatry and psychology should probably be given to Freud (e.g. 1936), who regarded it as the underlying condition responsible for many neurotic and psychotic states. He took the view that the person with high anxiety develops "defence mechanisms" for alleviating the anxiety, and these may take the form of neurotic or psychotic symptoms. For instance, someone who is excessively anxious about what he might meet in the street might develop a phobia about going out of doors. While not all of Freud's formulations have been universally accepted, his view of anxiety as a concept of fundamental importance in psychiatry and psychology has undoubtedly met with widespread if not universal agreement.

Among psychiatrists anxiety is generally assessed in a qualitative or "clinical" manner, that is to say an overall judgement is made of the significance of anxiety in a patient's symptomatology. The approach of psychologists has been to try to put the concept on a more objective basis by devising tests by which a person's level of anxiety can be measured. The model followed has been the concept of intelligence, which has been successfully lifted from the level of subjective assessment to that of objective measurement by intelligence tests. Psychologists have endeavoured to do the same thing with anxiety.

Three schools of psychologists have been particularly prominent in these endeavours. The first may be called the London school and has its origin in the work of Professor Sir Cyril Burt, who drew attention early in the century to a factor which he called "general emotionality" (Burt, 1915). This factor has many similarities to anxiety, since Burt suggested that people who are high on "general emotionality" tend to be neurotic.

This approach has been pushed further by Eysenck (1947, 1952), a pupil of Sir Cyril Burt. He too has formulated a general personality trait or "dimension", as he has preferred to call it, of emotionality, and for this he has suggested the term "neuroticism". This is conceived as a personality scale, continuum or dimension on which an individual can be placed and on which neurotics form an extreme group. Hence the labelling of the scale. One of the chief contributions of Eysenck is that he has devised a number of tests, including questionnaires, for measuring a person's position on this scale. We therefore have a scale which resembles intelligence in that a person's position on it can be measured by psychological tests.

A similar approach to that of the London group has been taken by Cattell (1957) at the University of Illinois. He has used the term anxiety and devised scales for its measurement in the general population. The distinctive contribution of Cattell is that he has analysed the general anxiety factor into a number of subfactors, such as guilt, suspiciousness, nervous tension and so forth. These subfactors correlate with one another, but the correlations are sufficiently low (they are generally of the order of around $0 \cdot 3$) for it to be useful to consider them as distinct subfactors. Once again, an illustrative parallel can be drawn with general intelligence. This too can be broken into a number of positively intercorrelated subfactors such as verbal ability, mechanical aptitude, memory and so on. For some purposes it is useful to consider these as separate entities; for others, to combine them into one broad factor of general intelligence. Both usages are possible and neither precludes or invalidates the other. The same is true of anxiety: one can work with the subfactors isolated by Cattell, or with the general factor considered as a single entity.

A third group which has isolated a factor resembling anxiety has worked in Moscow under the direction of the late B. M. Teplov (1964) and V. D. Nebylitsyn (1964). This group has carried on the conceptual framework formulated by Pavlov. In his work on experimental neurosis Pavlov was interested in the question of why some dogs break down when subjected to stress more easily than other dogs. He suggested that the answer lies in a constitutional factor which he called "the strength of the nervous system". The nervous system's strength is the degree to which it can withstand stress. If the nervous system is weak, then a comparatively minor degree of stress is sufficient to precipitate the dog (or human being) into nervous breakdown. This concept has something in common with the Western concept of anxiety, because anxiety is also conceived of as a general trait whose extreme is characterised by susceptibility to neurotic breakdown.

Pavlov's successors in Moscow have established measures of the trait, consisting principally of tests of perceptual sensitivity and nervous exhaustion. There are some dozen measures which intercorrelate positively, thereby defining a general underlying factor. Some are simply tests of absolute sensory thresholds. Others are more complex. For example, one measure is the conditioned photochemical reaction. The subject is first dark adapted and his absolute visual threshold measured. A flash of light is then presented, which has the effect of decreasing the subject's sensitivity. This reduction in sensitivity can be conditioned by presenting a neutral stimulus before the flash. With continued reinforced trials the conditioned stimulus has less and less effect in evoking a response. The percentage reduction in the strength of the conditioned reaction is taken as a measure of the weakness of the nervous system. This is justified statistically by its positive intercorrelation with other measures of the factor, and theoretically because it reflects the exhaustion of the nervous system under the stress of repeated stimulation. Nebylitsyn (1964) has himself drawn attention to the similarity between the Pavlovian concept and the Western concept of anxiety. It should perhaps be noted that Eysenck (1967) has argued that the strength of the nervous system could be identified with introversion rather than anxiety or neuroticism. It is possible that this may turn out to be right, but this would not embarrass the present argument. Anxiety is partly a function of introversion (see, for example, Eysenck, 1957, for detailed evidence of this association), so that up to a point the Eysenck position overlaps with the present one, although admittedly anxiety is more strongly associated with neuroticism than introversion in Eysenck's system. But in any case, our purpose here is only to show that in addition to several schools in the West, the Russian workers have also arrived at a concept resembling anxiety. If this should eventually turn out to be mistaken, the thesis of the monograph—to the effect that there are national differences in anxiety level among the advanced nations—is not severely damaged.

Thus there are four schools which have stressed the importance of anxiety: the psychoanalytic group derived from Freud; Sir Cyril Burt and Professor H. J. Eysenck in London; Professor R. B. Cattell in the U.S.A.; and the Pavlovian group in Moscow. As we have noted, it cannot be said that all these groups are in complete agreement on the details of their theoretical formulation of the structure of personality. But their differences are primarily matters of detail and for our own purposes it is sufficient to draw attention to the importance which all give to anxiety or to a concept resembling it.

There is also a long-standing tradition of a similar concept in physiology and physiological psychology. Over the course of the century it has appeared and reappeared in different guises. Creed *et al.* (1932) held the concept of a "central excitatory state", whose level of activity augmented or diminished reflex actions. At about the same time Duffy (1930) advanced the concept of excitation, which she has later identified with the similar concept of activation. She defined excitation as "the extent to which the organism as a whole is activated or aroused", as assessed by a number of physiological measures such as skin resistance, muscle tension, cardiovascular measures and EEG frequency and amplitude. Cannon (1929) put forward a similar view in his theory of a general emotional state arising from excitation in the thalamus and hypothalamus and manifesting itself in fear or aggression.

In the post-1945 period these theories were restated. Lindsley (1951) put forward an "activation" theory of emotion. He accepted the hypothalamus as the primary locus for emotional expression, but drew attention to the recent work of Moruzzi and Magoun demonstrating that the brain-stem reticular formation also plays a part in maintaining the level of activation. A few years later Morgan (1959) formulated a physiological theory of drive in terms of a "central motive state", which determined the amount of motivated behaviour. Beach (1958) has also suggested a central arousal mechanism.

There are therefore a number of workers primarily in physiology who have suggested the existence of a general emotional factor, for which activation or arousal is now the commonest term. It seems probable that this is the physiological basis of anxiety. The physiology of anxiety is now reasonably well understood, at least in broad outline, and it has much in common with the physiologists' concepts of activation and arousal. The maintenance of anxiety depends to a considerable extent upon the level of neural activity of the frontal lobes, the hypothalamic centres of the sympathetic nervous system, and probably also the brain-stem reticular formation. The part played by these areas can be demonstrated in a number of ways. For instance, the frontal lobes can be severed from the rest of the brain by the surgical procedure of prefrontal leucotomy. This operation is sometimes performed to reduce anxiety or other neurotic conditions in which anxiety plays a prominent part. The inference is that the frontal lobes normally maintain anxiety, so that rendering them inactive reduces a person's anxiety level. The effectiveness of the operation in reducing anxiety has been established by psychological tests given before and after the operation (Petrie, 1952). These show a reduction in anxiety after the operation has been completed.

The sympathetic nervous system also plays an important part in the maintenance of anxiety. The sympathetic system is activated by novel or significant stimulation and threat. It mobilises the body for action by increasing the blood supply to the head, accelerating the respiration and heart rate and other physiological changes, and increasing the sensitivity of the sense organs. These are the physiological concomitants of anxiety. It is probable that anxious people have sympathetic nervous systems which are exceptionally responsive to stimulation. There is considerable evidence in favour of this view. For example, Runquist and Ross (1959) showed a positive correlation between subjects' anxiety scores on a questionnaire (the Taylor Manifest Anxiety Scale) and the amplitude of the heart rate acceleration and psychogalvanic reactions to stimulation. The evidence for an association between the psychological and physiological concepts of anxiety has been reviewed and argued in detail by Eysenck (1967). In terms of Eysenck's two-dimensional theory of neuroticism and introversion–extraversion, anxiety could be regarded as a higher order factor which is principally a function of neuroticism but also to a lesser degree a function of introversion. But this is a refinement which belongs to a different level of discussion from that of the national epidemiological questions with which we are concerned and for our present purposes anxiety and Eysenck's neuroticism can be regarded as broadly the same concept. It has several times been shown that the two are highly intercorrelated (e.g. Franks, 1957).

Thus anxiety can be defined as a personality trait or dimension, measurable both by psychological tests, such as questionnaires, and by physiological tests of the reactivity of the sympathetic nervous system. This is the factor which it is suggested varies in different countries and underlies the intercorrelations between national indices of mental illness, suicide, alcoholism and calorie intake.

CHAPTER 4

ANXIETY AND PSYCHOSIS

THE next step required is the demonstration that all four conditions—mental illness, suicide, calorie intake and alcoholism—can be understood theoretically as manifestations of anxiety. In this section we argue the case for mental illness, which is probably the most controversial and to which most attention will be paid, leaving the other three for briefer consideration in Chapter 5.

Hospitalised mental illness is virtually synonymous with psychosis, and the principal categories of hospitalised psychosis are schizophrenia, psychotic depression and senile psychosis. The thesis advanced in this chapter is that the majority of hospitalised psychotics are characterised by low anxiety. As far as schizophrenics are concerned, the word itself was coined to describe an emotional state which approximates to a low level of anxiety. The "split" refers to the apparent division between the intellectual faculties, which are tolerably well preserved so that the patient can understand and converse with reasonable intelligence and coherence, and the emotional faculties which seem to have atrophied, so that the patient has none of the normal emotional reaction to stress or stimulation. This is the classical state of chronic "burnt-out" schizophrenia in which the patient appears emotionally unresponsive or, in our terms, lacking in anxiety.

This is the typical symptomatology of classical chronic schizophrenia, described and named at the beginning of the century by Bleuler. The phrase "lack of affect" is often used for such cases, which are described in much the same terms today. For example, Hofling (1963) in his *Textbook of Psychiatry for Medical Practice* writes: "While schizophrenic patients may, at times, give way to strange and even violent expressions of emotions, the commonest form of affective deviation from the normal seen in this condition is pervasive apathy." Similarly Mednick (1958) in a review of the literature writes of "the lack of anxiety of the schizophrenic, often considered an aspect of 'flat affect' or emotionlessness".

In psychotic depression the level of anxiety is more difficult to determine. Patients suffering from psychotic depression should be distinguished from cases of neurotic depression, in which anxiety is more commonly present. In psychotic depression the patient has feelings principally of despair and hopelessness. These are sometimes regarded as signs of anxiety. But it should be noted that one of the most prominent symptoms of psychotic depression is the lack of energy, which is often so pronounced that the patient sits doing nothing for long periods of time. This inertness can be regarded as a lack of anxiety, and has frequently been interpreted in this manner. But as long as we are in the world of clinical description there is inevitably disagreement about the precise meaning of the term anxiety and whether or not a particular patient has it. We therefore turn now to more rigorous measures of the anxiety level in psychotics. Four approaches will be discussed: physiological; Pavlovian; factor analytic; and epidemiological.

1. *Physiological*

One of the most extensive investigations of the physiology of psychosis is that of Gellhorn (1956, 1957). His theory is that in chronic schizophrenia and depressive psychosis sympathetic tone and reactivity are reduced. This is itself a result of lowered activity and responsiveness of the sympathetic centres in the posterior hypothalamus. Since the sympathetic system is associated with the maintenance of anxiety, Gellhorn's theory is essentially a low anxiety theory of psychosis.

The verification of the theory involves taking measures of sympathetic tone and reactivity in psychotics, and Gellhorn has reported low tone or diminished reactivity on the following measures. Taking psychotics as a whole, they tend to show (a) low systolic and diastolic blood pressure and minimal rise in blood pressure following stimulation; (b) reduced rise in blood-sugar level following stimulation; (c) poor generation of heat after exposure to cold; (d) minimal lymphopenic response to stress; (e) reduced psychogalvanic reactions to stimulation; (f) reduced EEG desynchronisation of the alpha-rhythm in response to stimulation; (g) poor rise in blood pressure following the injection of mecholyl.

Gellhorn has shown that various shock therapies increase sympathetic tone and reactivity, which accounts for their success in chronic schizophrenia and depression. For example, electro-convulsive therapy induces a sympathetically mediated rise in blood pressure, an increase in adrenaline, an increase in blood sugar and a rise in body temperature. Other shock treatments stimulating the sympathetic system include insulin hypo-glycaemia, sleep therapy, nitrogen and carbon-dioxide inhalation, fever therapy and the amphetamines. The same argument has been presented by Rubin (1962) to account for the successful treatment of depressives by iproniazid (Marsilid). This drug is a sympathetic stimulator and improves depressives by raising sympathetic tone and reactivity. A similar theory is put forward by Claridge (1967) to account for the therapeutic effect of imipramine (another stimulant) for depression. Sargant and Slater (1963) advance the same argument for the beneficial effects of ECT on depressed, apathetic and retarded schizophrenics.

Gellhorn's work indicates that depressives have poor sympathetic tone and reactivity and that schizophrenics fall into two groups, the majority being under-reactors (like depressives) and a minority being over-reactors (Nelson and Gellhorn, 1957). This finding of two groups of schizophrenics has been duplicated by a number of other investigators (see, for example, Claridge, 1967). Neurotics tend to have enhanced sympathetic reactivity, indicating that they have high anxiety and are in this respect the opposite of the majority group of schizophrenics. Gellhorn has also found that among normal people there is a reduction of sympathetic reactivity with age. This finding is consistent with the well-known increase in the incidence of psychosis among older people and it may be assumed that with general lowering of sympathetic reactivity accompanying ageing a higher proportion of people become prone to psychotic breakdown (Lynn, 1962).

Results similar to those of Gellhorn have been reported by a number of investigators. Funkenstein et al. (1951) have worked principally with the mecholyl test. Mecholyl is injected inducing a fall in blood pressure which stimulates the sympathetic centre in the hypothalamus; this in turn induces a rise in blood pressure. Schizophrenics give only small blood-pressure increases, indicating reduced sympathetic reactivity. Altman et al. (1943) have reported the same results. Poor reactions in depressives have been reported by Alexander (1955) and Jones (1956).

The work of Alexander (1959, 1961, 1962) on conditioning in normals, anxiety neurotics and depressives points to a similar conclusion. Electric shocks were given to the finger as unconditioned stimuli, and tones of different frequencies served as positive and negative conditioned stimuli. The effects of the conditioned stimuli on the EEG and the PGR were recorded. Normal subjects discriminate properly, giving conditioned reactions to the positive conditioned stimuli but no reactions to the negative conditioned stimuli. Anxiety neurotics give reactions to both positive and negative conditioned stimuli. This "overgeneralisation" phenomenon in highly anxious subjects has been reported by others (e.g. Mednick, 1957). On the other hand, depressed patients give a weak response to the positive stimulus, or even no response at all. This suggests low anxiety, and that anxiety neurotics and depressives are at the opposite ends of an anxiety continuum.

There is also some work on the excretion of 17-ketosteroids in schizophrenics, which points in the same direction. A high excretion of these steroids has been identified as part of an anxiety factor by Cattell and Scheier (1961) and also by Damarin (1959), so that according to our thesis there should be an abnormally low excretion in psychotics. This result has been found for schizophrenics by Hoagland et al. (1946). They subjected their schizophrenic patients to various stresses and found a greatly subnormal 17-ketosteroid secretion. This team has also found that the excretion of steroids on awakening, which increases by about 50 per cent in normal subjects, only rose by around 3 per cent in psychotics.

17-ketosteroids are secreted from the adrenal cortex, so that the finding of a low rate of steroid secretion in psychotics suggests that the adrenal cortex may be under-reactive. This interpretation fits in with a good deal of other work reporting that the reactivity of the adrenal cortex to ACTH (adrenocorticotrophic hormone) is subnormal in schizophrenics (Hoagland and Freeman, 1959; Nandi and Banerjee, 1958; Sheard, 1958). Gellhorn and Loofbourrow (1963) take the view that this diminished reactivity of the adrenal cortex is a consequence of reduced activity in the hypothalamus. This interpretation naturally has much in common with our own theory of a low anxiety level in schizophrenics, since the hypothalamus plays an important role in the maintenance of anxiety.

Further evidence for this view is available from investigations of hippuric acid secretion. This is higher in anxiety neurotics than in normals (Basowitz et al., 1955, p. 118), whereas in schizophrenics it tends to be lower than in normals (Quastel and Wales, 1938). Grinker's group have shown that exposing subjects to stress brings about an increase in hippuric acid secretion, which is what would be expected from its high level in anxiety neurotics. Cattell and Scheier (1961, pp. 200 ff.) discuss the matter in some detail and conclude that "hippuric acid excretion is a highly specific physiological indicator of true anxiety". Thus once again we seem to have a measure of anxiety on which schizophrenics appear abnormally low and, as Cattell and Scheier conclude, this "fits the concept of schizophrenia as a state of absence of drive" (p. 201).

Many investigators have distinguished between acute schizophrenics characterised by abnormally large sympathetic reactions (suggesting high anxiety) and chronic schizophrenics and depressives with minimal sympathetic reactions. Such investigators include Monroe *et al.* (1961), Earle and Earle (1955), Venables (1960, 1964), Shagass (1957), Shattock (1950) and Rubin (1960). The literature is now so extensive that Claridge (1967, p. 147) in a useful review wrote of the "somewhat obvious conclusion that both hypo- and hyper-reactors were more frequent among psychotics than in control groups". The weight of the evidence seems to suggest that the hypo-reactors, i.e. the low-anxiety group, is the larger of the two.

Taking the literature as a whole, the results suggest that psychotic depression and chronic schizophrenia are characterised by poor sympathetic tone and reactivity or, in psychological terminology, low anxiety. There is also a smaller group of acute (and possibly largely paranoid) schizophrenics characterised by high sympathetic reactivity and high anxiety. It should be noted that acute schizophrenics are generally more responsive to treatment (e.g. Henderson and Batchelor, 1962), so that a country's statistics of hospitalised schizophrenia will tend to reflect predominantly the chronic low-anxiety patients. This means that even if Gellhorn and others are incorrect in their view that the majority of schizophrenics are low on sympathetic reactivity, these are still likely to be the majority in mental hospitals since the high reactors are more likely to have been discharged. Thus if we accept that low anxiety is a significant element in psychosis, we should expect that the lower the mean anxiety level in a country, the higher the proportion of hospitalised psychotics.

2. *Pavlovian Work on Psychosis*

Results similar to those of Gellhorn have been reported by a number of psychiatrists in the Soviet Union. The Russian theoretical framework in psychiatry is derived from Pavlov, who explained the apathy and lack of energy of many hospitalised psychotics in terms of his concept of protective inhibition. According to this theory, in the development of psychosis protective inhibition is first generated in the cerebral cortex. Its effect is to weaken the cortical functions, including their tonic inhibitory control over the subcortical centres. This releases the subcortical centres and accounts for the outbursts of emotional excitement which sometimes accompany the early stages of psychosis. But with further development of the illness, the protective inhibition spreads downwards to the subcortical centres and reduces their activity. This is responsible for the listless apathy and lack of reactivity which the patients typically display.

The area Pavlov described rather generally as the subcortex is now known as the arousal system, consisting principally of the reticular formation and the sympathetic centres of the hypothalamus. Attempts to test Pavlov's theory have centred on devising experimental measures of reticular and hypothalamic reactivity. Five types of test have been developed, involving the measurement of orientation reactions, sympathetic reactions, EEG responses, conditioning and word association tests.

A considerable volume of work has been done recently in Russia on the so-called orientation reaction. The orientation reaction covers what is sometimes called in the West the arousal reaction, i.e. the reaction by which the organism pays attention to new stimuli and is mobilised to deal with them. It has three chief components. First, there are changes in skeletal muscles, the animal pricks up its ears, turns its body or head towards the new stimulus, muscle tonus rises, and there is an increase in muscular electrical activity. Secondly, the sympathetic division of the autonomic nervous system is activated: there is an increase in palmar skin conductance and pupil dilation, vasoconstriction in the limbs and vasodilation in the head, and variable changes in heart and respiration rates. Thirdly, the electroencephalogram (EEG) shows an increase in frequency and the alpha rhythm is blocked.

The orientation reaction is distinguished from the defensive reaction which occurs if the stimuli are intense, moderately intense and prolonged, or if the subject is in a state of tension. In the defensive reaction the subject shows signs of being frightened by the stimulus rather than interested in it, and there is vasoconstriction in the head as well as in the limbs.

A number of the components of the orientation reaction in schizophrenics were recorded by Traugott et al. (1958), namely, movements of eyes and head, galvanic skin response (GSR), respiration rates, heart rates, and vascular reactions from the shoulder. The stimuli used were auditory (a tone, bell and whistling sound), visual (lights) and tactile. In chronic deteriorated schizophrenics there were often no orientation reactions of any kind; where reactions were present, however, the autonomic reactions were much weaker than the motor components. In hallucinated-paranoid patients the size of the orientation reaction and its extinction with repeated presentation of the stimulus were very variable, sometimes being stronger and sometimes weaker than in normal subjects. Some patients showed a defensive reaction, while others showed a poor orientation reaction. Reactions to stimulations were also observed during the course of insulin treatment. It was found that in the initial stages of treatment the patients became overactive and gave defensive reactions to the stimuli. Later, with recovery, the stimuli elicited normal orientation reactions.

A similar experiment is reported by Gamburg (1958) on sixty-nine schizophrenics, mainly simple and paranoid. Motor and autonomic components of the orientation reaction were recorded to auditory stimuli and electric shock to the fingers. It was found that very few of the schizophrenics gave normal orientation reactions. Patients diagnosed as simple schizophrenics tended to give no reaction at all, while paranoiacs tended to give defensive reactions. In four out of five catatonic patients the initial stimulus elicited a defensive reaction, but subsequent stimuli elicited no reaction at all. It was also found that when the schizophrenics did give an autonomic reaction, the autonomic disturbance continued much longer than is usual in normal subjects. In those patients who had not given any orientation reactions to stimulation, caffeine restored the reactivity, but bromine and luminal had no effect. The author interprets this finding as supporting Pavlov's theory that the lack of reactivity is a result of excess inhibition, since it is assumed that caffeine dissipates the inhibition but bromine and luminal further increase it.

A number of Russian investigations indicate that there is a depression of the sympathetic nervous system in schizophrenia, both in its level and its reactivity to stimulation (Ekolova-Bagalei, 1955; Stanishevskaya, 1955; Streltsova, 1955; Vertogradova, 1955). Ekolova-Bagalei (1955) investigated eighty-five catatonic patients and reported low sympathetic tone as assessed by pulse rate, respiration rates, blood pressure, pupil diameter, sweating and vasometer tone; there was also little reactivity to stimulation. Similar results using the plethysmograph to measure vascular reflexes to hot and cold stimuli were reported by Vertogradova (1955) on thirty early cases of paranoid and simple schizophrenia.

In an investigation by Streltsova (1955) four studies were made of effects of stimulation on the pupil reaction in schizophrenic patients, the first being concerned with determining how far stimulation produces the normal reaction of pupil dilation in schizophrenics. The patients studied were 136 schizophrenics of different kinds (eighty-five men, fifty women, aged 14–55 years, length of illness 2 months to 25 years). The stimuli used to elicit pupil reactions were hot and cold pricks (at 45° and 15°C), a bell and an olfactory stimulus. In normal subjects it was found that these stimuli elicit pupil dilation of the order of an increase of one-eighth over the initial pupil diameter. Of the schizophrenics, 27·4 per cent reacted normally. The majority of the patients, 65 per cent, showed strikingly subnormal reactions to stimulation; 40 per cent showed no reactions at all and in 25 per cent it was greatly reduced. These patients were long-standing hebephrenics and hallucinated paranoiacs, and simple schizophrenics independent of the duration of the illness. The remaining 7·6 per cent of patients showed other abnormal pupil reactions. An excessively large pupil dilation was shown by 3·9 per cent to the extent of an increase of 40–50 per cent over the original pupil diameter. Streltsova states that increases of this size never occur in normal subjects. These patients were tense and anxious and had confused thought processes. The final group of 3·7 per cent of the patients showed pupil constriction. This reaction is said never to occur in normal subjects except when they are in pain or ill. Streltsova argues that the low reactivity of the majority of her schizophrenics is a result of the high level of inhibition (she does not explain the high reactivity of the small minority of schizophrenics).

In a second experiment, Streltsova (1955) goes on to investigate the extinction of the pupil reaction in schizophrenics using as subjects fifty patients in whom it had been possible to elicit a reaction. In this experiment a bell was used as a stimulus and was presented in two conditions: continuously, and a number of times in short bursts. The results showed that the schizophrenics fell into two groups. Thirty-four out of the fifty patients failed to extinguish the pupil reaction. In normal subjects the pupil reaction is extinguished after an average of 15 seconds when the stimulus is presented continuously, and after four to twenty-five presentations when it is presented successively for short intervals, but in the schizophrenic patients the reaction had not extinguished after 3 minutes in the continuous condition or after fifty presentations in the successive condition. A paradoxical result is now reported. After this failure of extinction the intensity of the stimulus was raised considerably. In normal subjects this procedure increases the size of the orientation reaction, but in the schizophrenics the reaction promptly extinguished and remained extinguished for 40 or more minutes.

The second group of sixteen patients extinguished the orientation reaction as quickly or nearly as quickly as normal subjects, but these subjects took much longer than normal to recover from the extinction procedure and it was not possible to restore the reaction through the presentation of an intense (disinhibiting) stimulus, as it is in normals. In considering her results, Streltsova favours an explanation in terms of the tendency of schizophrenics to generate "protective inhibition". She argues that this accounts for (a) the sudden appearance of inhibition, previously absent, when an intense stimulus is presented; and (b) the length of time schizophrenics take to recover from the effects of extinction once their orientation reaction has been extinguished.

In a third experiment Streltsova (1955) investigated the effects of caffeine on the orientation reaction in schizophrenics. The rationale of this investigation springs from the hypothesis that the absence of reaction characteristic of most schizophrenics is a result of the strong inhibitory state of the nervous system. It is assumed that caffeine dissipates inhibition and hence the hypothesis is advanced that if schizophrenics are given caffeine their orientation reactions should be restored. Fifteen patients who had shown the most persistent failure to give pupil reactions were taken as subjects. They were given doses of $0 \cdot 1$, $0 \cdot 3$, $0 \cdot 8$ and $1 \cdot 3$ millilitres of caffeine and were tested before and at intervals of 15, 30, 45 and 60 minutes after injection.

Thirteen of the subjects showed a normal orientation reaction or pupil contraction after $0 \cdot 1$ and $0 \cdot 3$ millilitre of caffeine. Streltsova argues that this supports her hypothesis that the schizophrenics were previously in an inhibited state. However, only three patients gave orientation reactions after doses of $0 \cdot 8$ and $1 \cdot 3$ millilitres of caffeine, the other twelve failing to respond. This failure to respond with the higher doses is attributed to protective inhibition.

In her fourth study Streltsova (1955) compared the reactivity of patients early in the morning with that obtained later in the day. She based this investigation on the Pavlovian view that protective inhibition accumulates during the day, as a result of the stimulation received, and is dissipated during sleep. If this is so, an implication of the theory that schizophrenics are characterised by high levels of protective inhibition would seem to be that, if patients were tested immediately on waking in the morning, they would not have time to generate protective inhibition to any appreciable extent and should react more like normals. In this connection Streltsova cites an observation by Naumova to the effect that catatonic symptoms are less marked early in the morning and increase in the course of the day. Streltsova tested this theory using the pupil-dilation measure of reactivity. Twenty-two schizophrenics were tested immediately on waking in the morning and again 2–5 hours later. Twenty-one of the patients responded normally immediately on waking, or occasionally with over-reactivity, but later in the day they failed to respond.

An investigation of the characteristics of the vascular system in schizophrenics has been reported by Stanishevskaya (1961). Young simple schizophrenics and anxious hallucinated paranoiacs gave an unusually great number of spontaneous reactions, which is interpreted as indicating a high level of excitation. This in turn is due to the weakening of the cortical inhibitory control over the subcortical areas. In catatonic schizophrenics and in hallucinated paranoiacs who were not anxious, there was very little or no spontaneous activity. When the patients were stimulated, catatonics gave no reactions, hallucinated paranoiacs gave normal reactions, and simple schizophrenics gave generalised vascular reactions but not the local vascular pressor reaction which in normal subjects succeeds the generalised reaction when stimuli are presented a number of times.

Several investigators have reported that sympathetic tone and reactivity are improved in schizophrenics by stimulants including caffeine (Gamburg, 1958; Trekina, 1955), cocaine (Ekolova-Bagalei, 1955) and atropin (Taranskaya, 1955).

The EEG activity characteristic of schizophrenia reported by a number of Russian workers includes low frequency or absent alpha rhythm, a reduction or absence of blocking of the alpha rhythm to light and other stimuli, large latencies in alpha blocking when it can be obtained, and the presence of "constellations" and "overflows" (Belenkaya, 1960, 1961; Frenkel, 1958; Gavrilova, 1960; Segal, 1955; Trekina, 1955). In Gavrilova's experiment ten normal subjects were compared with fourteen schizophrenics (five cases of simple schizophrenia, two catatonic, and seven paranoids; duration of the schizophrenia was 8–12 years). The EEGs were recorded when the patients were relaxed and after the presentation of visual and auditory stimuli. When the patients were relaxed, a low-frequency alpha rhythm was present in the paranoiacs; but in the simple and catatonics the frequency was below that of the alpha rhythm. No reaction to auditory and visual stimuli was obtained in the simple and catatonic patients, but some reaction occurred in the paranoiacs. With auditory stimuli, a low intensity stimulus produced increased EEG frequency, but when the intensity of the stimulus was increased the reaction disappeared. The results are interpreted as indicating the inhibited state of the cortex in schizophrenics, especially in the simple and catatonic forms and to a lesser extent in paranoia. In paranoid patients weak stimuli evoke some EEG reaction, but strong stimuli increase the inhibition and hence no reaction is obtained.

Gavrilova (1960) also notes the presence in her paranoiacs (but not in the simple or catatonic patients) of frequent constellations, i.e. apparently causeless bursts of high-amplitude potentials lasting 0·5–2 seconds from one cortical area accompanied by low-amplitude potentials from another.

These constellations have also been reported in acute, tense and delirious schizophrenics by Belenkaya (1960). The suggested explanation of these constellations is as follows. The development of protective inhibition in schizophrenia attacks both excitatory and inhibiting processes. It first weakens the process of internal inhibition in the cortex, thereby upsetting the balance between excitatory and inhibitory processes and increasing the strength of excitation. Strong excitatory stimuli increase the protective inhibition and prevent any reaction, but weak stimuli can still "get through" in the less advanced (paranoid) forms of schizophrenia. When these weak stimuli do get through they produce a violent effect. The reason for this is that the cortical process of internal inhibition is normally concerned with damping down incoming stimuli, and since this process has been weakened, the incoming stimuli can no longer be contained.

In paranoid forms of schizophrenia the presence of overflows has been reported, i.e. a burst of activity in one cortical area appears to spread and is followed by bursts of activity in other cortical areas. These overflows rarely occur in normal subjects when they are awake; but are present in falling asleep and during sleep, and also occur in epileptic cases and in patients with subcortical tumors. Gavrilova observed that external stimuli can induce overflows in paranoiacs, and argues that overflows are caused by subcortical stimuli acting on the cortex and inducing excitation which spreads to other areas. She argues from the absence of overflows in her groups of schizophrenics that subcortical–cortical relations are impaired. But Belenkaya (1960) reported overflows in all stages of paranoia, from the initial acute delirium to the final "secondary catatonic" stage.

A number of Russian investigators have followed the course of EEG changes during the administration of drugs to schizophrenics. Trekina (1955), working with thirty-five chronic deteriorated schizophrenics, reported absence of alpha rhythym, lack of any reaction to light stimuli, and unsynchronised random oscillations which are interpreted as indicating excitation in the reticular formation. Moderate doses of caffeine brought general improvement and restored the alpha rhythm and the reaction to light stimuli, and abolished or decreased the pathological activity from the subcortex.

A similar experiment by Ekolova-Bagalei (1955) reports the EEG activity of eighty-five catatonic patients (aged 17–45, duration of illness from a few days to several years) before treatment and after administration of cocaine. The cocaine improved the patients' behaviour, so that in the majority of cases they began to move to instructions, speak, and negativism and waxy flexibility disappeared. (In eight cases of very long-standing schizophrenia, no improvement was obtained even with increased and extended dosage.) At the same time the cocaine had the effect of increasing the alpha frequency. In a small number of cases, however, large doses of cocaine made the patients worse than before. The explanation of the findings is that small doses of cocaine reduce the amount of cortical inhibition, but larger doses induce protective inhibition, which further intensifies the inhibited state of the cortex. It was noted that cocaine acted first by increasing alpha frequency, then by increasing sympathetic tone, and finally by bettering the patient's voluntary behaviour. It is argued that this indicates that cocaine acts first on the cortex and that an effective attack on schizophrenia can be made by restoring the cortical excitatory processes.

Two papers of Belenkaya (1960, 1961) report the effects of chlorpromazine and the stimulant meratran on the EEG activity of paranoid schizophrenics. It is argued that there are typically four successive stages in the evolution of paranoid schizophrenia: first, paranoid delirium without hallucinations; secondly, with hallucinations; thirdly, paraphrenic delirium; and fourthly, a state of secondary catatonia with hallucinations. Forty patients were divided into the four groups, and without drugs the increasingly advanced stages showed decreasing EEG activity and lesser reactivity to light (in these experimental conditions normal subjects gave a reaction to light on all testings compared with 24 per cent of the first group of patients and only 5 per cent of the last group). All the groups showed overflows. Both meratran and chlorpromazine had a beneficial effect on the first group and to some extent on the second, improving their general condition and making their EEG records more normal. With chlorpromazine, however, there was a delayed effect. For 2 or 3 weeks the pathological features of the EEG increased, especially the number of overflows. After this time the EEG became normal. Belenkaya explains these results in the following way. Chlorpromazine depresses the excitation in the reticular formation, and during the 2- or 3-week period this depression of reticular excitation allows the internal inhibitory processes to be restored. The increased presence of overflows is a sign of the increasing restoration of the inhibitory processes (assuming the equivalence of inhibition, sleep and the occurrence of overflows). In the next stage, the reticular formation recovers from the effects of chlorpromazine and exerts a normal excitatory effect on the cortex, controlled by the restored inhibitory processes. Patients with the severer forms of paranoia did not benefit from either drug and showed paradoxical reactions to them, viz. after meratran EEG activity decreased and after chlorpromazine it increased.

Fedorovsky (1955) compared the EEG activity of normal subjects and thirty-six schizophrenics (hallucinated paranoiacs and simple) during sleep therapy. He found that the schizophrenic records tended to show slow alpha rhythms when they were awake, but that during sleep they showed lower amplitude slow waves than normals. It is suggested that this indicates that schizophrenics sleep less deeply than normal people. A similar result is reported with catatonic patients by Popov (1955).

Both autonomic and motor conditioning techniques have been used on schizophrenics by Russian investigators (Dobrzhanskaya, 1955; Kostandov, 1955; Saarma, 1955; Sinkevich, 1955; Vertogradova, 1955).

All investigators have found that conditioning is poor or cannot be obtained in schizophrenics. An attempt to condition vascular reactions has been reported by Vertogradova (1955), working with thirty schizophrenics (mainly paranoid and simple, duration of illness 1 month to 3 years). Unconditioned vascular reactions to heat and cold were less than normal. A light was used as a conditioned stimulus and conditioned vascular reactions were typically acquired after two to eighteen pairings of the light with the unconditioned stimuli. However, the conditioning was not stable, i.e. frequently the presentation of the conditioned stimulus did not elicit a response, and generally the conditioned response had disappeared on subsequent days. Firm conditioned responses could not be acquired with up to 100 pairings. It was also observed that in a number of cases the presentation of the light during the conditioning procedure inhibited the vascular reaction, so that it was either reduced or disappeared entirely. Thirteen patients were retested after a course of insulin, and in the ten of these who improved, the vascular reactions became stronger and the inhibiting effect of the light during conditioning disappeared. In the other three patients the lack of behavioural improvement was accompanied by a corresponding absence of increase in the vascular reactions.

A somewhat similar experiment has been reported by Trekina (1955) on thirty-five chronic deteriorated schizophrenics subject to excited outbursts. Plethysmograph recordings were made of the reactions to the unconditioned stimuli of cold, heat, pain, light and touch. Some vascular reactivity was present, and it is argued that this indicates that excitatory processes are present in the subcortex. It was found that on the second or third day of the investigation the unconditioned vascular reactions extinguished much more quickly than is normal, i.e. after four to six presentations. This is taken as evidence for the strong cortical inhibitory processes in schizophrenics. Attempts were then made to condition the vascular reactions to light and to verbal stimuli, but the conditioning was very slow and the conditioned reactions, once established, were very unsteady and kept disappearing and reappearing. This again is taken as evidence for the strong inhibitory processes in the cortex.

A number of experiments use some variety of motor conditioning in which the subject is instructed to give a response to a certain stimulus (e.g. pressing a buzzer to a light) and is given verbal reinforcements when the response is made correctly. This conditioning procedure is then made more elaborate by investigating the discrimination of the stimulus from similar stimuli, extinction of the response through non-reinforcement, effects of extraneous stimulation, and developments of conditioned disinhibition. The findings most commonly reported using these techniques on schizophrenics are as follows:

1. The speed of conditioning is impaired in all schizophrenics, but more in catatonic patients than in paranoiacs. Several investigators have found it impossible to condition catatonics whereas the conditioning of

paranoiacs is possible, but slow. Typically three to five trials are required to condition normal subjects and fifteen to twenty trials in schizophrenics.

2. The associations are very unstable, but can be stabilised with a very large number of reinforcements (100 or more).

3. The conditioned reaction is very easily inhibited by extraneous stimuli, i.e. changes in laboratory conditions, etc., even though these are quite slight.

4. There is a great variability in response latency.

5. Discriminations are very difficult for schizophrenics to make. Many investigators found only a minority of patients would make correct discriminations.

6. Improvements in behaviour following treatment are paralleled by improvement in conditionability.

The impairment of schizophrenics in this type of conditioning is generally interpreted as reflecting the inhibited state of the cerebral cortex. The instability of the conditioned reactions, inhibition by extraneous stimuli and variability in response latencies are regarded as due to the strengthening of cortical inhibition through negative induction from the subcortex. Saarma (1955) reports two further findings consistent with this explanation. When discrimination is attempted the schizophrenic frequently ceases to respond at all. It is inferred from this that inhibition has readily become attached to the stimulus to be discriminated and has spread to the original stimulus. Secondly, when reversal shifts (i.e. the positive stimulus is changed to a negative and the negative stimulus to positive) are attempted on schizophrenics, the positive stimulus can easily be changed to negative, but in many cases it was impossible to change the negative stimulus to positive. A similar finding is reported by Sinkevich (1955).

A possibly unexpected finding from this point of view is that two groups of paranoid schizophrenics, while showing the typical features of poor conditioning listed above, take a large number of non-reinforced trials before the conditioned response is extinguished. This finding has been reported by Dobrzhanskaya (1955) and Kostandov (1955). The explanation advanced by both authors is that the slow conditioning of schizophrenics is due to the protective inhibition. Extinction and discrimination are brought about by the accumulation of internal inhibition and the process of generating internal inhibition has itself been weakened by the protective inhibition. Hence, the slow extinction and discrimination which is characteristic of schizophrenia.

The effect of drugs on motor conditioning has been reported by Taranskaya (1955). Moderate doses of the stimulant atropin improved schizophrenics' performance on a motor conditioning task, increasing speed of conditioning, the stability of the response, and reducing the latency. At the same time hallucinations disappeared. Larger doses produced less beneficial effects on conditioning and increased hallucinations. The inhibitory drug phenamin further impaired conditionability and increased hallucinations.

Apart from conditioning, word association tests are sometimes used in Russian research on schizophrenia. A typical experiment is that of Dokuchaeva (1955). The method consists in presenting a stimulus word, to which the patient has to give a response. The response is scored both for the time taken to give it and for its adequacy, e.g. repetitions of the word, etc., are scored as inadequate. The general findings are that schizophrenics are slow and give inadequate responses. In Dokuchaeva's experiment sixty schizophrenics were given the word association test before and after varying doses of caffeine. It was found that moderate doses of caffeine increased the speed of the response and improved the quality of the associations. This improvement appeared to depend on the reactivation of the sympathetic system, since in cases where caffeine had no sympathetic effect the associative reactions remained unchanged. With large doses of caffeine the speed of reaction became slower and the adequacy of the responses deteriorated.

3. *The Factor-analysis Approach*

One of the most influential approaches of psychologists using factor-analysis techniques is that of Eysenck (1952). He has postulated a personality dimension of "psychoticism" on the basis of three groups of psychological tests measuring perceptual efficiency (e.g. visual acuity, speed of dark adaptation, etc.), speed of reaction, and expressive movements (i.e. amplitude of writing and drawing). These three types of test intercorrelate positively both in groups of normal subjects and in groups of psychotics (Eysenck, 1952; Eysenck *et al.*, 1957; Payne and Hewlett, 1960). Both schizophrenics and depressives score at one end of this dimension, characterised by poor perceptual efficiency, slow reaction times and large amplitude expressive movements.

This factor can be interpreted as a dimension of anxiety. It is known that moderate increases in anxiety from the normal resting level improve perceptual efficiency and reaction times (Samuels, 1959; Lynn, 1966). The improvement in perceptual efficiency is part of a general phenomenon known as intersensory facilitation, in which stimulation of one sense organ leads to an increase in the sensitivity of others. For instance, if a subject's visual threshold is measured and he is then stimulated by a tone, his visual threshold is reduced so that he can perceive a stimulus which he was unable to perceive before. This lowering of threshold is part of the orientation reaction or arousal reaction, in which any new, intense or significant stimulus gives rise to a small increase in anxiety, which in turn is responsible for the improvement in perceptual sensitivity (Lynn, 1966). Thus the poor perceptual abilities of psychotics could be explained in terms of a low level of anxiety.

The same explanation would account for the slow reaction times of psychotics. The classical experiment here was carried out by Lansing *et al.* (1959). They stimulated their subjects and noted a speeding up of reaction times as a result. As we have noted, any stimulation leads to a slight increase in anxiety, so that this experiment also suggests that a low anxiety level could account for the slow reaction times of psychotics.

In addition to perceptual efficiency and reaction times, the Eysenck psychoticism factor also consists of large expressive movements, i.e. large handwriting and drawing. Are these also affected by anxiety? To test this possibility I carried out an experiment in which subjects were asked to write a sentence and to draw three squares, the tests used by Eysenck (1952). They did these tasks when they were relaxed and then when they were put under mild stress by being given instructions to carry out the task as fast as they could. It is assumed that this gives rise to a slight increase in anxiety. There was a highly significant tendency for expressive movements to decrease when the subjects were made anxious, i.e. they wrote and drew smaller (Lynn, 1963). Thus once again the large expressive movements of the psychotic can be interpreted as a sign of low anxiety.

Admittedly, Eysenck regards his psychoticism factor as independent of neuroticism, which is largely a dimension of anxiety (e.g. Franks, 1957). Eysenck regards neurotics and psychotics as extreme groups on two independent dimensions, whereas on the present thesis they are at opposite extremes of an anxiety dimension. These positions are not necessarily incompatible, since psychotics and neurotics could perfectly well be at opposite ends of one dimension (anxiety) but be independent of each other on other dimensions. An amendment to the Eysenck system along these lines has been proposed by Claridge (1967), who takes the view that this model fits the facts better than Eysenck's earlier (1952) formulation of the theory. Claridge has proposed a two-dimensional system consisting of anxiety or arousal corresponding to Eysenck's neuroticism, and "modulation of arousal", a control factor corresponding to Eysenck's introversion and Pavlov's concept of internal inhibition. As formulated by Claridge, anxiety neurotics are characterised by high anxiety and strong

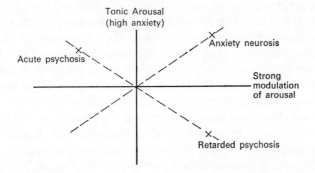

FIG. 2. Model suggested by Claridge for the underlying personality dimensions involved in acute psychosis, retarded psychosis and anxiety neurosis.

modulation, acute psychotics by high anxiety and weak modulation, and chronic retarded psychotics by low anxiety and strong modulation. This system is illustrated in Fig. 2. We are not concerned here with the aptness of Claridge's concept of modulation, but only to show the similarity of his formulation of the anxiety factor to our own conception. Claridge's system posits anxiety neurotics and retarded psychotics at opposite ends of an anxiety continuum and at the same time assumes that anxiety neurotics lie on an independent dimension from psychotics. This allows Claridge to preserve Eysenck's original interpretation of neuroticism and psychoticism as independent dimensions. Hence Eysenck's work showing the independence of psychoticism and neuroticism is not incompatible with the present thesis that psychotics are characterised by low anxiety.

4. *Epidemiological Data*

Finally, certain epidemiological evidence indicates a low level of anxiety in hospitalised psychotics. The evidence here is that in groups with a high proportion of hospitalised psychotics, the proportion of neurotics tends to be low. The most plausible explanation of this relationship would seem to be first that neurosis is a manifestation of high anxiety, an assumption to which virtually all schools of thought in psychiatry and psychology assent. Thus a group with a high level of anxiety should produce a comparatively high number of neurotics. Now if we then find that such groups producing a high proportion of neurotics also produce a low proportion of psychotics, the inference seems to be that a high anxiety level is some kind of antidote to a high prevalence of psychosis or, in other words, a high prevalence of psychosis occurs where there is a low level of anxiety.

There are at least two kinds of groups where an inverse relation between the prevalence of psychosis and neurosis seems reasonably well established. One of these is social class groups and the other is age groups. To take the social class groups first, the prevalence of psychosis is low in the higher social classes and increases progressively down the social scale. But the prevalence of neurosis is highest in the top social classes and falls down the social scale. This is particularly true of anxiety neurosis. Some figures illustrating these tendencies are shown in Fig. 3. The negative relationship by itself would be open to a number of interpretations. But taken in conjunction with our other evidence, it adds further strength to the thesis of an inverse relation between psychosis and neurosis, the one produced by low anxiety and the other by high. We have only to assume that anxiety levels fall as we descend the social scale and the results fall into place.

Much the same pattern occurs when the prevalence of neurosis and psychosis are considered in relation to age. As people get older, the chances of psychotic breakdown become greater. The chances of neurotic breakdown, on the other hand, become less. Some representative results are shown in Fig. 4.

Once again, these results fit in quite well with our thesis. The implication is that anxiety levels fall with ageing from the age of around 35 onwards. Fortunately, there is some evidence that this is so. For instance, older people are less sensitive to pain (i.e. have higher thresholds for pain perception) than younger people (Chapman and Jones, 1944; Critchley,

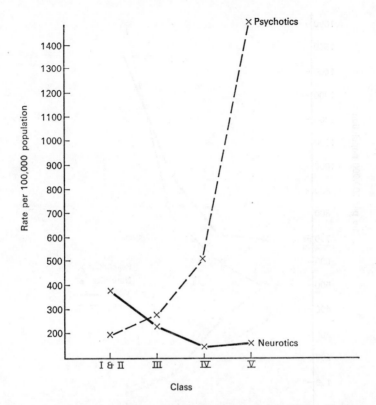

FIG. 3. Prevalence of neurotic and psychotic disorders by class (from Hollings-head and Redlitch, 1958).

1956) and there is some evidence that sensitivity to pain is a function of anxiety (e.g. Lynn and Eysenck, 1961). Gellhorn (1957) has shown that sympathetic reactivity declines with ageing over the span of adult life. However, the most direct evidence comes from Cattell who has shown that his general anxiety factor declines from adolescence into maturity and middle life (1957, pp. 613–15). Thus there is both physiological and psychological evidence to suggest a decline in anxiety as ageing proceeds, which will explain (according to our thesis) the higher incidence of psychosis and lower incidence of neurosis accompanying ageing.

Finally, there is a study by Cowie (1961) in which the personalities of

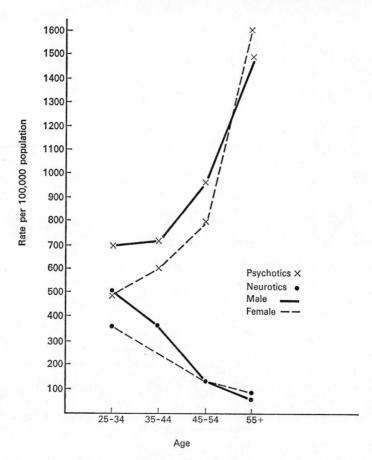

FIG. 4. Prevalence of neurotic and psychotic disorders by age and sex (from Maccoby, Newcomb and Hartley, 1959).

children with psychotic parents were assessed. She found that such children had rather less neurotic symptoms than average. This result would be a puzzling one for many theories of psychosis and neurosis, but for our own it is quite explicable, assuming that these children tend to inherit a low anxiety level from their parents. Since there is sound evidence for the inheritance of anxiety (e.g. Cattell, 1957; Shields, 1962) this explanation should not be objectionable.

Thus the evidence from the physiological, Pavlovian, factor analytic and epidemiological sources all points in the direction of a low level of anxiety in the majority of hospitalised schizophrenics and depressives, notwithstanding that there is probably also a smaller group of schizophrenics characterised by high anxiety. Our contention is that these hospitalised psychotics come principally, though not necessarily exclusively, from the low tail of a general distribution of anxiety throughout the population. If we assume also that the distribution of anxiety is much the same from one country to another, a low average level of anxiety can be inferred from the high proportions of hospitalised psychotics in certain

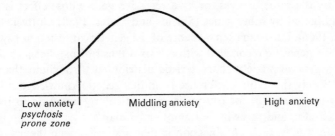

Low anxiety   Middling anxiety   High anxiety
psychosis
prone zone

FIG. 5. Model postulating normal distribution of anxiety in the population with psychosis-prone zone at the low-anxiety tail. If the mean anxiety level is shifted downwards the incidence of psychosis rises.

countries, such as Ireland and the U.K. The model proposed is illustrated in Fig. 5 (which assumes a normal distribution of anxiety although the assumption of normality is not, of course, necessary). The model postulates a distribution of anxiety throughout the population and that those individuals at the low end are psychosis prone. Thus if the mean for the population is shifted downwards, there is a higher proportion of the population in the danger zone for psychosis, and hence a higher proportion of psychotics.

There should be no difficulty about the assumption that anxiety is distributed throughout the population, as against the alternative assumption that lack of anxiety is some kind of disease which marks off psychotics as qualitatively different from the rest of the population. A general distribution of anxiety throughout the population is accepted by all the psychological schools reviewed in Chapter 3, including Freud, who once wrote in his customary dramatic vein that "We are all of us ill" (Freud, 1936) to express the fact that everyone has greater or lesser degrees of anxiety.

It may be objected, however, that the model proposed encounters a difficulty from the evidence on the genetic causation of schizophrenia. Kallman (1951), Shields and Slater (1960) and others have shown that the degree of concordance between identical twins in schizophrenia is much higher than between non-identical twins, and the inference that genetic causes are a significant factor in schizophrenia is now widely accepted. It is widely held that manic-depressive disorders are caused by a dominant gene with reduced manifestation and schizophrenia may be caused by the same process, or by a recessive gene whose effect is sometimes mitigated by other genes (Shields and Slater, 1960; Gottesman and Shields, 1966). How can such evidence of the genetic causation of psychosis by specific genes be reconciled with our own thesis of psychosis as the tail end of a general anxiety characteristic distributed throughout the population? Surely the natural inference from our genetic knowledge is simply that the specific genes for psychosis are particularly common in Ireland, the U.K., etc., and rarer in Germany and Japan?

One answer to such an objection is that a specific gene theory of psychosis is not incompatible with our own thesis of psychosis as the tail end of a normal distribution. Our thesis would imply a polygenic factor of psychotic disposition in addition to the single genes which determine the precise nature of the psychotic breakdown. There could, for instance, be a specific gene for schizophrenic thought disorder which sometimes occurs in association with very low anxiety and in this combination predisposes an individual to schizophrenic psychosis. Possibly the gene for schizophrenic thought disorder by itself merely leads to eccentric thought processes, such as bizarre political or religious beliefs or existentialist philosophies, which are not in themselves certifiable. In addition, very low anxiety may make a person so apathetic as to become hospitalised as a simple schizophrenic. Where the two genetic predispositions occur together (i.e. schizophrenic thought processes and low anxiety), the victim develops the kind of psychosis characterised by both low anxiety and bizarre thought processes.

Such a theory may seem complex but such has been the difficulty of solving the problem of psychosis that it is by now virtually certain that the truth is complicated. Some such theory as the one suggested seems necessary because a simple single gene theory cannot account for all the known facts. For instance, on the basis of this theory alone we should infer that the very high psychosis rate in Ireland is simply a matter of a high proportion of the specific genes for psychosis. But why then should a high psychosis rate occur in conjunction with a low rate of suicide and alcoholism and a high calorie intake? The specific gene theory does not seem able to handle these facts, so that we are forced to hold some kind of general personality trait theory, of which all these conditions are manifestations. We are also forced into this position by Eysenck's psychoticism factor, for which there is good evidence for a general distribution throughout the population. Indeed, Eysenck has himself inferred from his own results that psychosis must be determined, at least in many instances, partly by specific genes and partly by a polygenic factor which is generally distributed (Eysenck, 1967, p. 223). Looked at from this point of view, the epidemiological evidence assembled in this monograph adds further strength to the position which Eysenck has adopted.

The model shown in Fig. 5 is not only applicable to the relation between the national incidence of psychosis and the mean anxiety level. It can be extended also to the incidence of suicide, alcoholism and the calorie intake. In the next chapter we shall argue that suicide and alcoholism can be interpreted as indices of high anxiety and occur among people at the high anxiety tail of the distribution. Thus if the mean anxiety level in a nation is shifted upwards, there is a low incidence of psychosis together with a high incidence of suicide and alcoholism, while if the mean anxiety level is shifted downwards the reverse pattern results. As for the mean calorie intake, it simply varies inversely with the mean anxiety level. Hence the model explains all four measures of the factor. We have argued in this chapter the details of the case for interpreting psychosis in terms of the model, and we have now to show that the other measures can also be plausibly interpreted as functions of anxiety.*

*The discussion of Russian research on psychosis is largely taken from the *Psychological Bulletin*, 1963, to whom the author is indebted for permission to reproduce the material.

CHAPTER 5

SUICIDE, CALORIE INTAKE AND ALCOHOLISM

THE interpretation of the factor we are pursuing demands the theoretical justification of suicide, calorie intake and alcoholism as functions of anxiety. This is the subject of the present chapter.

1. *Suicide*

Anxiety is generally regarded as an important cause of suicide. For example, Stengel (1964) in his book on the subject lists the causes and gives as the first "depression with guilt feelings, self-depreciation and self-accusations, associated with anxiety and tension". Dublin (1965) writes:

> The reasons most often indicated by the person who commits suicide or by the family are ill health, economic distress, the loss of a loved one and domestic discord. Behind all these characteristics are found almost invariably certain emotional attitudes and fears and anxieties, a sense of inferiority and insecurity, hatred, aggressiveness, guilt, frustration or revenge.

This passage indicates that suicide occurs principally in highly emotional, i.e. anxious, people; this is especially the case when they are subjected to stress, such as bereavement or economic crisis, which has the effect of increasing anxiety still further.

A similar view was taken by Rook (1959) in his investigation of suicide among Cambridge University students. He reached the conclusion that over half had an excessive fear of examinations and the majority of student suicides occur around the time of examinations. Although there is a slight tendency for all suicides to occur in the months of April to July, this tendency is much more pronounced among university students. Similar conclusions have been reached about students who commit suicide in Berkeley, California. Seiden (1966) investigated a number of cases and concluded that the principal causes were anxieties about work, health and personal relationships.

The problem of measuring the personality of those who commit suicide presents certain technical difficulties. One way of overcoming these is to test people who attempted suicide unsuccessfully. It must be admitted that some have argued that these have a different personality structure from the successful suicides, but Wilkins (1967) after a thorough review of the literature concludes that successful and unsuccessful suicides probably have a similar personality structure. While this is difficult to prove, it certainly seems worth considering the results of personality tests on unsuccessful suicides. One such study has been made by Philip (1969). He took 100 cases of attempted suicide by poisoning in Edinburgh. This seems a good group to take, since those intent on making a dramatic display rather than on genuine suicide are probably less likely to choose poisoning because of the possibilities of error as compared with, say, putting one's head in a gas oven 5 minutes before someone is known to be coming home. However this may be, Philip administered the Cattell anxiety questionnaire to his hundred attempted suicides and found that they were significantly more anxious than the average population.

One fairly common cause of suicide is some kind of economic crisis such as losing one's job or going bankrupt. For instance, Schmid (1933) investigated suicides in Minneapolis between 1920 and 1930 and concluded that 20 per cent had been experiencing "financial troubles". Further studies confirming a high proportion of financial insecurity in suicides have been carried out in London (Sainsbury, 1955), Philadelphia (Tuckman and Lavell, 1959) and New Orleans (Breed, 1963). There are also several studies which show that suicide rates rise and fall *pari passu* with the percentage of unemployment and thus with general economic prosperity (Swinscow, 1951; MacMahon *et al.*, 1963). The most plausible interpretation of this set of results is surely that financial stress increases the anxiety level, and this in turn tends to motivate the suicide.

It may be felt that there is something paradoxical about our argument that suicide and psychosis are manifestations of opposite extremes of the anxiety personality dimension, on the grounds that suicide and psychosis are sometimes associated. If suicide tends to result from high anxiety and psychosis from low anxiety, how is it possible for an individual to be psychotic and commit suicide at the same time? There is not much doubt that psychotics, especially depressives, do sometimes commit suicide. Six studies of depressives suggest that around 13 to 16 per cent subsequently commit suicide (Robins *et al.*, 1957; Pitts and Winokur, 1964, p. 179), and this is naturally a much higher percentage than occurs in the general population. Such an association is not, however, an embarrassment to our thesis. We have already argued that a minority group of psychotics are highly anxious and these may be the ones who commit suicide. Alternatively, it may be that while the majority of suicides are anxious, there is a minority group who are excessively unanxious and depressed; if these are taken together there would still be an overall association between anxiety and suicide. The point is, of course, that the associations embraced by our present thesis are only of a statistical nature (like those elsewhere in the social sciences and, for that matter, in the physical sciences, too), so that particular instances where the association does not hold are not fatal to the theory.

2. *Calorie Intake*

A high calorie intake can also be understood in terms of our theory of a low level of anxiety. People who are emotionally stable normally have a good hearty appetite, while among those who are anxious the appetite tends to be reduced. The reason for this is that eating and the digestive processes are mediated by the para-sympathetic system while anxiety is mediated by the sympathetic system, and these two systems have a reciprocally inhibiting relationship with each other (e.g. Gellhorn, 1956). It is common in general medical practice to prescribe amphetamines to women who wish to slim, and the rationale for this is that the amphetamines are sympathetic stimulators which suppress the appetite. In cases of *anorexia nervosa*, in which there is a high level of anxiety, the patient will not eat at all and dies of starvation unless forcibly fed.

The effect of the amphetamines on reducing the appetite, and hence the calorie intake, is fairly well established. For instance, the *British Medical Journal* stated in 1963 that amphetamine is the most widely used medicine to deal with obesity: "In man and animals amphetamine curbs appetite, leading to weight loss. Weight loss is entirely due to reducing calorie intake and other suggested mechanisms and impaired digestion are of no importance. Recent experimental work supports the long held view that amphetamine has a direct effect on the hypothalamus, by which it inhibits food intake" (*British Medical Journal*, 1963). In the U.K., where around 20 per cent of the population is clinically obese, i.e. is more than 10 per cent over ideal weight, amphetamines are extensively prescribed to reduce the appetite. It has been estimated that in 1967, 100 million tablets were prescribed, and that 64 per cent of these were for the treatment of simple obesity (McKenzie, 1969).

The evolutionary process by which appetite and anxiety have come to have this reciprocally inhibiting relationship is reasonably well understood. It has come about because when an animal is in a state of anxiety it must be prepared for energetic action, which consists normally of either fighting or fleeing. The animal has been made anxious by some danger, and needs to be capable of its best physical performance. The digestive processes consume energy which could be better deployed for these emergency reactions, so that in states of anxiety the digestive processes are inhibited.

Another source of evidence on the inverse relationship of eating and anxiety is derived from the effects of the operation of prefrontal leucotomy. This operation involves severing the neural connections between the frontal lobes and the thalamus, as a result of which the frontal lobes are rendered inoperative. The operation is now mainly performed for the relief of intense anxiety or obsessional neurosis in which anxiety is prominent. One of the effects of the operation which has frequently been recorded is that in addition to reducing anxiety it increases the appetite. For instance, Henderson and Batchelor in their *Textbook of Psychiatry* write of prefrontal leucotomy that "apart from the relief of distress and tension, there has been recorded . . . increased appetite and a gain in weight" (1962, p. 343). Meyer and McLardy (1948) observed that after the operation "a morbidly increased appetite may lead to obesity". Hofling (1963, p. 176) states that "frontal lobotomy . . . also tends to lead to obesity". Increases in calorie intake following prefrontal leucotomy have also been reported quite frequently in animals (e.g. Richter and Hawkes, 1939; Langworthy and Richter, 1939). The effect of these operations is particularly interesting because they are virtually experiments in that they control the time sequence and demonstrate that the reduction of anxiety is followed, as a consequence, by the increase of appetite. Thus where the appetite in an individual or in a whole population is high, the inference is that anxiety is likely to be low.

It might be expected to follow from the negative relationship between calorie intake and anxiety that anxious people would tend to be thin. Evidence confirming this association has been collected by Eysenck (1952) and, independently, by Rees (1950). Measurements of chest circumference, holding height constant, are associated with measures of the neuroticism factor. There may, of course, be other constitutional determinants of this association, but it seems probable that differential calorie intake would contribute to it.

Extreme overeaters have been investigated by Atkinson and Ringuette (1957). They examined twenty-one cases of obesity whose weight was double the normal for their height, a rare condition afflicting around 1 in 10,000 of the population. Their most prominent psychological character- istic was found to be depression, for which one-third of the patients had received psychiatric treatment. Leckie and Withers (1967) have also found that obese patients tend to be depressed. Depression is frequently associ- ated with apathy and lack of energy, so that it would be possible to inter- pret these results as indicating a low level of anxiety among these obese patients. This would be in line with the Gellhorn theory of depression outlined above. But unfortunately the diagnostic category of depression is a loose one and it is impossible to be certain of the anxiety levels of these patients from this description.

It may be felt that in certain circumstances people can eat to reduce their anxiety and that the association between anxiety and calorie intake might therefore be positive. It is probable that this can occur and some investigators have reported that overeaters often tend to be nervous, anxious or worried (e.g. Freed, 1947; Silverstone and Solomon, 1965). It should be noted that many investigators do not use valid psychological tests of anxiety, but go on clinical assessment (i.e. general impression), and it is quite easy to mistake the depression of the insufficiently anxious for genuine high anxiety. However, it is probably true that in certain cases anxiety can motivate excessive eating. The explanation lies in the recipro- cally inhibiting relationship of anxiety and food intake to which reference has been made. Just as anxiety tends to inhibit food intake, so food intake tends to inhibit anxiety. For this reason food intake can be used as an anxiety reducing mechanism. But it seems probable that this only occurs in a minority of cases. This conclusion is supported by an extensive study of the eating habits of 1000 children by Brandon (1968). These were a random sample of 12-year-olds in Newcastle-on-Tyne and it was found that 19 per cent of them had had some "substantial episode of disturbed behaviour". Among the remaining 81 per cent of apparently emotionally stable children, 4·7 per cent had an inadequate appetite, but among the emotionally disturbed children 16·7 per cent had an inadequate appetite. Food fads were also almost twice as common among the emotionally disturbed as among the well-adjusted (34 per cent compared with 18 per cent). The symptoms of the emotionally disturbed were "emotional dependence, shyness, over-activity, undue reliance upon others, excessive reserve, instability of mood and excessive temper". This seems to be the anxiety syndrome and once again shows the association between anxiety and reduced appetite. The emotionally maladjusted also weighed less than the controls, which is perhaps not surprising, and is a further confirmation of Eysenck's work showing an association between the neurotic personality and thinness.

Brandon also examined his sample for voracious eaters, who comprised 8·7 per cent of the total sample. But there was no tendency for the emotionally disturbed children to be more voracious eaters as compared with the controls. Once more, this seems to show that the predominant tendency of anxiety is to reduce the appetite, not to enhance it.

3. *Alcoholism*

Alcoholism is commonly regarded as a reaction to anxiety (e.g. Franks, 1958). Alcohol reduces anxiety, so that when people are in a state of anxiety one of the avenues of relief lies in inbibing alcohol. There is considerable psychological evidence for the anxiety-reducing properties of alcohol, which has been shown to overcome fear in animals and human beings in a variety of situations. For example, Masserman and Yum (1946) carried out an experiment in which they first trained cats to manipulate some apparatus for food. The cats were then given electric shocks when they touched the apparatus. This made them anxious about approaching it, and they refused to touch it. They were then given alcohol, after which they again approached the apparatus. This result was interpreted with apparent plausibility as showing that alcohol reduces anxiety. A further observation of Masserman and Yum was that cats ordinarily prefer plain milk to milk containing 5 per cent alcohol. Yet after the experimental cats had been given the electric shocks, they developed a preference for milk laced with alcohol. At a later stage of the experiment the cats' anxieties were removed, and they then reverted to their preference for plain milk. This seems to show that animals can develop a taste for alcohol when they are in states of anxiety, presumably as a means of alleviating the anxiety.

The physiological basis of this effect lies in the depressant effect of alcohol on the nervous system. Alcohol is one of a group of nervous system depressants which reduce the transmission of neural impulses both at the synapses and in the axons. In addition, depressants seem to have a particularly powerful effect on the reticular activating system in the brain stem (Gooch, 1963). This system plays a part in the maintenance of anxiety through its tonic effect on the thalamic structures, so that this appears to be one of the mechanisms through which the depressants reduce anxiety (Samuels, 1959).

Among many quotations which could be cited for the sedating effect of alcohol the following are representative. Rosen and Gregory (1965, p. 398) write that "contrary to popular belief alcohol is not a stimulant but a sedative. Its immediate physiological effect is to depress the functioning of the higher brain centres. This results in, firstly, impairment of perceptual and intellectual functioning; secondly, relief from anxiety, fear and sorrow". Strange (1965, p. 195) writes that "when in the blood stream, ethyl alcohol even in amounts of one-tenth of 1 per cent of the total blood volume, acts as a depressant or general anaesthetic on the CNS, in an action similar to that of chloroform or anaesthetic ethyl ether". Block (1962, p. 116) writes that "alcohol affects the nervous system as a depress-ant of the higher brain centres concerned with behaviour and speech and memory . . . the early ingestion of alcohol therefore produces initial symptoms that result from depression of centres concerned with worry and anxiety".

As a result of the anxiety-reducing properties of alcohol, people who are highly anxious can alleviate their anxiety through drinking. Thus there tends to be an association between alcoholism and anxiety. This associa-tion has frequently been described. For example, Hofling (1963) writes that "the alcoholic is one who is psychologically ill . . . as one of his defence measures, he comes to rely upon an excessive intake of alcohol". Bleuler (1955, p. 406) writes that: "the typical individual who drinks heavily does so to reduce anxiety". Strange (1965, p. 116) writes of the alcoholic that "he begins to seek out social situations that allow drinking for he has discovered that his tensions are eased whenever he is under the influence of alcohol". Vallance (1965) reported a study of sixty-six male alcoholic patients admitted to Glasgow General Hospital and found that 42 per cent had a history of neurotic symptoms and took alcohol for relief.

Since alcohol reduces anxiety, and is sometimes used by anxious people as a means of reducing anxiety, we should expect that in societies where anxiety levels are high there would be a high consumption of alcohol. This inference has been investigated by Horton (1943). He took fifty-six primitive societies and assessed the incidence of drunkenness and the degree to which the people were exposed to stress from subsistence hazards (crop failures, droughts, etc.) and from aggressive neighbours, which he presumed would increase their anxiety. He found that there was a significant positive correlation: the greater the stress, the more the alcoholism. This suggests that the amount of alcohol consumed in a society is a function of the anxiety level of the people, and runs parallel to our own thesis of the relation between alcoholism and anxiety in advanced societies.

The logic of our procedure with alcoholism (as with suicide and psychosis) has been to infer the anxiety level of the whole population from the prevalence of the extreme condition of death from excessive drinking. This procedure assumes that there is much the same distribution of the underlying personality trait from one country to another. While this is probably reasonable enough, it may be more satisfying for some readers to demonstrate that we could equally well have substituted the mean alcohol consumption of the population for deaths from alcoholism and liver cirrhosis. The two are correlated, as would be expected on the assumption of a fairly uniform distribution of drinking from one country to another. Figures for *per capita* alcohol consumption for sixteen of our eighteen countries have been published by the Canadian Alcoholism and Drug Addiction Research Foundation and are shown in Table 7. It will be noted that there is a high alcoholic consumption in the countries with a large proportion of deaths from alcoholism and liver cirrhosis (see Table 1) especially France, Italy and Switzerland, while both are low in other countries such as Ireland and the U.K. The rank correlation between the two measures is $+0.41$. The only reason for using the deaths figures in preference to the *per capita* consumption figures is that the latter are not complete for our eighteen countries. The interest of this correlation between alcoholism deaths and *per capita* intake is that it demonstrates that inferences about the population as a whole can be made legitimately from the incidence of an extreme condition.

Before concluding this discussion of alcoholism it may be of interest to note that just as the incidence of alcoholism and suicide are correlated in nations, so too they are associated in individuals. Many studies have shown this association. Several investigators with an interest in alcoholism

TABLE 7. ALCOHOL CONSUMPTION IN THE
LATE 'FIFTIES

	Gallons of alcohol *per capita* aged 15 and over
Australia	2·03
Belgium	1·83
Canada	1·59
Denmark	1·13
Finland	0·65
France	5·87
Germany	1·66
Ireland	0·96
Italy	3·25
Netherlands	0·70
New Zealand	2·12
Norway	0·68
Sweden	1·07
Switzerland	2·39
U.K.	1·25
U.S.A.	1·61

have reported the high percentage of alcoholics who commit suicide. Kessel and Grossman (1961) and Lemere (1953) found that 8 per cent did so, Norvig and Neilson (1953) put the percentage at 11, Gabriel (1935) at 20 and Dahlgren (1945) at 21. Other investigators have considered the matter from the point of view of suicides and noted the high percentage of them who are alcoholic. Sainsbury's (1955) estimate of 6 per cent is comparatively low. Four investigators have considered that the percentage is 10 (Schmid, 1933; Tuckman and Lavell, 1959; Yessler *et al.*, 1961; Pitts and Winokur, 1964). Three investigators put it even higher. Robins *et al.* (1957) report the figure of 23 per cent; Dahlgren (1945) of 30 per cent and Palola *et al.* (1962) of 31 per cent. All of these figures are higher than would be found in the general population, so that there is a substantial body of evidence for the association of alcoholism and suicide in individuals as well as in nations. This is, of course, what our thesis of anxiety as the common factor underlying both alcoholism and suicide would predict.

CHAPTER 6

ANXIETY IN UNIVERSITY STUDENTS

It would be desirable to strengthen the thesis that the conditions with which we are concerned represent national differences in anxiety levels by further evidence. One possibility is to consider the results of anxiety questionnaires from samples of the population. These questionnaires ask the respondent whether he suffers from various symptoms of anxiety, such as sleep difficulties, restlessness, irritability and so forth. The advantage of using such questionnaires for our present purpose is that they are unambiguous measures of anxiety. On the other hand, they encounter certain difficulties. One of these is the translation problem. The answers people give are affected by fine nuances of wording which are likely to be distorted in translation. Another difficulty lies in obtaining true random samples of the population. This has not yet been attempted and the only extensive data available for national comparisons lie in results from male university students. These do not form ideal samples. Nevertheless, it does not seem altogether impossible that students could be reasonably representative of the populations from which they are drawn. If, for example, one were interested in national differences in attitudes towards eating snails, a comparison of French and English students would almost certainly reflect the beliefs of their compatriots as a whole reasonably well. The same may be true of anxiety.

Scores on anxiety questionnaires have been collected by Cattell and his associates for ten advanced Western countries. Unfortunately, six of the countries were tested with one questionnaire and seven with another, three countries being tested on both. This means that the scores cannot be directly compared. It is, however, possible to put all the countries together into a rank order.

Cattell's first inquiry reported anxiety questionnaire results on male students in France, Japan, Italy, Norway, the U.K. and the United States. The students emerged in the order given above, i.e. the French were the most anxious (Cattell and Scheier, 1961). The second set of data uses Cattell's 16 Personality Factor Test, from which anxiety scores can be derived. This has been given to students in seven countries, which emerge in the following rank order of anxiety: Japan, Germany, Australia, New Zealand, Canada, United States and the U.K. These results are available from the files of Cattell's research laboratory in Illinois.

The results of these two inquiries are broadly consistent, with Japan emerging as a high-anxiety country and the U.K. and the United States as low-anxiety countries in both cases. It will, however, be noted that the positions of the U.K. and the United States differ in the two inquiries. We have therefore taken the second as being more accurate, partly on the grounds of the larger number of subjects involved and partly because it is consistent with Eysenck's (1959) finding of higher American scores on his neuroticism factor.

Our first step was to collect results for Ireland and for this purpose the 16 PF questionnaire was administered to 160 male students at University College, Dublin. The sample was drawn as a random sample from all faculties, and replies were obtained from 152. The Irish students scored between the Australian and the New Zealanders, that is to say in fourth place out of eight countries for which 16 PF results are available.

The next requirement is to integrate the 16 PF results with the Cattell and Scheier anxiety questionnaire results. Several countries can only go into one rank. France must be placed in rank 1 and Japan in rank 2; the United States must go in rank 10 and the U.K. in rank 11. This leaves Italy and Norway to be fitted into the seven ranks 3–9 in the middle of the scale. The most reasonable solution seems to be to put Italy at 4 and Norway at 8. This would give the overall ranking shown in Table 8. While it may be

TABLE 8. RANK ORDER OF COUNTRIES ON THE BASIS OF STUDENTS' QUESTIONNAIRE RESULTS

Country	Anxiety rank	Country	Anxiety rank
France	1	New Zealand	7
Japan	2	Norway	8
West Germany	3	Canada	9
Italy	4	U.S.A.	10
Australia	5	U.K.	11
Ireland	6		

felt that there is an element of arbitrariness in this solution, it should be borne in mind that the ranking is required for correlation analysis and for this the extremes are the most important. The rankings in the middle of the scale make little difference to the size of any correlation with other variables.*

With these results we can consider how the students' anxiety scores compare with the other conditions (suicide, mental illness, calorie intake, alcoholism) which we have interpreted as manifestations of national anxiety level. This has been done by computing rank correlations and the results are shown in Table 9. It will be seen that in all four cases the correlations are in the direction predicted by our thesis. The correlation of -0.80 between psychosis rates and anxiety level is remarkably high and statistically significant at the 1 per cent level. The correlation of $+0.59$ between anxiety level and alcoholism is statistically significant at the 5 per cent level using a one-tailed test, which is legitimate because we are predicting the correlation. The other two correlations are reasonably sizeable, although falling short of statistical significance. But taking the correlations as a whole, the pattern of all four coming out at a reasonable size in the predicted direction gives some further support to the anxiety interpretation of the factor.

TABLE 9. RANK CORRELATIONS OF NATIONAL ANXIETY WITH ALCOHOLISM, PSYCHOSIS, CALORIE INTAKE AND SUICIDE

Anxiety correlated with:	
1. Alcoholism	$+0.59$
2. Psychosis	-0.80
3. Calorie intake	-0.30
4. Suicides	$+0.41$

However, while the anxiety questionnaire results as a whole support the thesis we are advancing, the results from Ireland are something of an exception. The Irish students did not come out as the least anxious, as would have been expected. Such a result need not be regarded as crucially damaging to the thesis. There may be several reasons why the students from any one particular country may not be representative of the national anxiety level. For example, it could be that anxiety in Ireland is rising and is higher in the younger generation than in the population as a whole.

* The rank order was suggested before the present theory was conceived (Lynn, R., *Nature*, 1968, 219, 765–6).

Alternatively, Irish students are in general differently financed from those elsewhere. English students are almost universally on grants, those on the Continent of Europe are more normally on loans, while most Irish students are on neither. Possibly this might increase the anxiety levels of Irish students. These are merely suggestions which it would be difficult to prove conclusively one way or the other and they are put forward to show that the Irish result is not crucially damaging to the thesis being advanced. When the students' results from the countries are taken as a whole it would seem difficult to dispute that they give further support to the interpretation of our factor in terms of anxiety.

At this stage of the argument, it would be helpful if we could turn to other studies and show that there were a number of established national differences which could reasonably be interpreted in terms of the anxiety factor. Unfortunately, very few such investigations have been carried out. Indeed, apart from the Cattell and Scheier collection of students' scores on anxiety questionnaires, it has only proved possible to find one other study which has even some marginal relevance to our thesis. This is an investigation by Morris and Jones (1955), who collected ratings of thirteen possible "ways to live" from university students in India, Japan, China, Norway and the United States over the years 1945–52. Their work is discussed by Cattell and Scheier (1961, p. 275) who suggest that two of the ways of life imply anxiety. One was number 6, which Morris and Jones describe as "Constant activity, striving for improved techniques to control nature and society. . . . We have to work resolutely and continually if control is to be gained over the forces of nature which threaten us." The other way of life suggestive of anxiety was number 13, apparently a submissiveness factor described as "A person should let himself be used. . . . One should be humble, constant, faithful, uninsistent. Grateful for the affection and protection one needs, but undemanding." This way of life seems to cover the neuroticism aspect of anxiety fairly well. The ways of life were put to the students, who were asked to assess how far they subscribed to them. The two anxiety ways were most favoured by the Indians and Chinese, and after that by the Japanese, the Norwegians and finally by the Americans. The Japanese, Norwegians and Americans fall into exactly the same rank order on this result as they do on our own anxiety factor, so that this study gives some corroboration to our thesis.

We have now assembled the evidence in favour of the postulation of anxiety as the common factor underlying national prevalence rates of mental illness, suicide, alcoholism and calorie intake. Nevertheless, other interpretations are always possible, and before proceeding we pause here to consider two alternatives which may have occurred to some readers.

One of these is aggression and is suggested by Rudin (1968) in an investigation which bears some similarity to our own. In this, he collected data for seventeen advanced countries on suicide, liver cirrhosis (as an index of alcoholism) and homicide for the year 1950, and found substantial positive intercorrelations between the three variables. On the basis of this he suggested the existence of a general factor. This might be the same factor as our own. Rudin interprets his factor as "aggressiveness or acting out". This interpretation admittedly fits homicide well enough, but it does not seem particularly convincing as the factor responsible for suicide or alcoholism. The man who commits suicide or becomes an alcoholic is not, in the ordinary sense of the word, behaving aggressively, unless it be held that the aggression has taken a peculiarly masochistic turn.

The other components of the factor throw more doubt on Rudin's interpretation. Does a high level of aggressiveness lead to a low calorie intake or a reduced proneness to mental illness? This seems doubtful and the anxiety interpretation seems to cover the various manifestations of the factor more convincingly. On the other hand, there is some evidence that anxiety and aggressiveness are associated (see below), so that Rudin's interpretation is not entirely alien to our own thesis of anxiety as the underlying factor.

A variant of Rudin's aggression factor is Menninger's (1938) theory that alcoholism and suicide are associated because they are both manifestations of the death instinct. Freud postulated the death instinct to account for the extraordinary aggressiveness of man, so that the death instinct and aggression are closely related concepts. We should presumably infer that the death instinct is rather more powerful, or less effectively deflected, in countries like Austria and Japan than it is in Ireland and the U.K. With some ingenuity this explanation might be extended to cover the lower calorie intake in countries like Austria and Japan. Could this not be an incipient form of self-destruction by starvation? It must be admitted, however, that within the range of calorie intake of the advanced countries, overeating is a more likely way of ensuring an early death than undereating. The death instinct theory seems to encounter difficulties here, and perhaps would get into even greater trouble when it comes to handling psychosis and its negative correlations with suicide and alcoholism. To chase out these possibilities in detail would require more predictive precision than psychoanalytic theory can provide, but there may be some followers of psychoanalytic theory who would like to consider our factor in these terms.

Another possible interpretation of the factor might be that it represents the particular areas into which anxiety is channelled in certain countries. According to this interpretation it might be maintained that anxiety is not low in Ireland, but simply that it is channelled into some areas other than suicide and alcoholism. To become convincing such a theory would require the discovery of some manifestation of anxiety with a high prevalence in Ireland. Some possibilities are discussed in due course, but it may be said now that none fitting the requirement has been discovered. It is, of course, always possible that some manifestation of high anxiety with an exceptional prevalence in Ireland might come to light and lend more weight to such an interpretation. But on the present facts anxiety seems the most promising interpretation of the factor.

In concluding this discussion of the possibility of alternative interpretations, it may be noted that there is much to be said for interpreting our factor in terms of some personality trait which is already established within an existing body of theory. This is where our own interpretation of the factor as anxiety has an advantage over Rudin's interpretation of it as aggression. For what is aggression? There are no widely accepted techniques for measuring aggression, agreed by a large body of research workers who subscribe to a common theory, and thus no general agreement on what is and what is not aggression. Are men displaying aggression when they court women, as Storr (1968) suggests? The absence of an agreed and coherent body of theory on aggression makes it a less useful concept than anxiety, even apart from the difficulties of detail when it comes to interpreting mental illness and calorie intake in terms of low aggressiveness. In contrast, anxiety is a very well-established concept about which a great deal is known and agreed. This means that the analyses presented in this monograph can easily be integrated with an existing body of knowledge. It thus fulfils one of the principal objects of scientific inquiry: the integration of many diverse fields by a small number of theoretical concepts.

The case for the interpretation of our factor in terms of anxiety is now concluded. We turn shortly to consider other matters affected by national anxiety levels. The fact that there are further significant correlates of the factor which can be reasonably interpreted as functions of anxiety strengthens the case for an anxiety interpretation of our factor. Indeed, it would have been possible to have presented all the variables discussed in this monograph in a correlation matrix and then interpreted each of them in turn in terms of anxiety. This approach is presented in Chapter 13. For the present we have followed the alternative of first establishing the anxiety factor and then seeking for further correlates. The difference is simply one of exposition. The method pursued here may be likened to the history of intelligence testing, where the first step was to establish a general factor on the basis of intercorrelating tests; and the next step to discover further correlates of the factor, such as social class, sex differences and so on.

But before closing this discussion of the interpretation of our factor in terms of anxiety, it seems worth asking whether the interpretation is consistent with commonsense. Surely the answer to this must be in the affirmative. At the low anxiety pole lie the Anglo-Saxon countries of the British Isles and the white commonwealth. At the high-anxiety pole lie the Latin countries, France and Italy. Surely this difference is simply putting on a scientific basis the commonly accepted tradition of the Anglo-Saxons as unemotional and phlegmatic? The British are notoriously un-reactive emotionally, slow to respond to crises, have rarely bothered to prepare themselves adequately for war, and, when they become embroiled, traditionally are so slow that they lose every battle except the last. In contrast, the French and Italians are traditionally regarded as excitable and emotional. The low anxiety of the English is expressed in such stories as Sir Francis Drake's sangfroid on being appraised of the approach of the Spanish Armada. The national figure of John Bull, hearty, bullying and corpulent, is hardly suggestive of anxiety or neurosis. Napoleon's description of the English as a "nation of shopkeepers" seems to have implied the widespread presence of solid and stable bourgeois virtues. E. M. Forster in his *Notes on the English Character* considered that the English have "undeveloped hearts" and are slow, cold and unemotional, all of which seem to be layman terms for low anxiety. Forster (1936) cites the following anecdote as typical of the English as compared with the French:

> The Englishman appears to be cold and unemotional because he is really slow. When an event happens, he may understand it quickly enough with his mind but he takes quite a while to feel it. Once upon a time a coach, containing some Englishmen and Frenchmen, was driving over the Alps. The horses ran away, and as they were dashing across a bridge the coach caught on the stonework, tottered, and nearly fell into the ravine below. The Frenchmen were frantic with terror: they screamed

and gesticulated and flung themselves about, as Frenchmen would. The Englishmen sat quite calm.

It is rather unfashionable in contemporary psychological circles even to refer to literary observations and folk stories of this kind. But do they not show that the conclusions we have reached from epidemiological evidence are consistent with common observation? And would it not be surprising if such traditional views of national character did not turn out, on closer scientific investigation, to be roughly correct, since they represent the consensus of countless observers and are thus likely to be moderately accurate approximations to the truth? At its present stage much of psychology is concerned with measuring more accurately things that reasonably well-informed people already know, such as, for example, that middle-class children do well in examinations, neurotics are emotionally unstable, delinquents generally come from slums and so forth. Our own analysis conforms to this pattern and shows in quantitative form and in detail what most people are no doubt already aware of, namely that the Latin peoples are more emotional than the Anglo-Saxons.

CHAPTER 7

ACCIDENT-PRONENESS AND AGGRESSION

WE NOW consider the possibility that there may be other national characteristics which could be explained in terms of the anxiety factor. In this chapter we discuss vehicle accidents and murder. To determine whether these, and other conditions considered later, are related to the anxiety factor we shall make use of the overall measure of national anxiety level for the eighteen countries which was obtained in Chapter 2 by ranking the countries on each of the four conditions (suicide, mental illness, calorie intake and alcoholism). The rank order of the countries on the anxiety factor was shown in Table 5.

It is now possible to determine whether new variables are associated with the anxiety factor. The logic of this step follows the methodology established in intelligence and personality theory, where a personality trait (e.g. intelligence, extraversion, etc.) is first defined in terms of a number of intercorrelating tests, which are then summed to give an overall measure of the trait. Further research then proceeds to establish additional correlates of the trait (e.g. investigations of the relationship between intelligence and social class, sex, personality qualities and so forth). This is the methodology we are following, the only difference being that we are treating populations of countries as if they were individuals.

We turn now to the relation between national anxiety level and vehicle deaths. The data for vehicle deaths, expressed as a percentage of the number of vehicles, is shown in Table 10. The rank correlation between these and the national anxiety level is $+0 \cdot 62$, i.e. there are more accidents in the more anxious countries. The correlation is statistically significant at the 1 per cent level.

Two interpretations can be suggested for this association. In the first place, there is a general association between anxiety and accident proneness, particularly in vehicle accidents (Cattell, 1964). This is partly due to the well-known effect of anxiety in impairing the performance of skilled

TABLE 10. INTERNATIONAL COMPARISON
OF DEATHS IN MOTOR ACCIDENTS PER
1000 VEHICLES (1960)

Australia	0·93
Austria	3·20
Belgium	1·88
Canada	0·71
Denmark	1·34
Finland	2·98
France	1·14
Germany	2·70
Ireland	1·15
Italy	3·60
Japan	7·30
Netherlands	2·80
New Zealand	0·56
Norway	0·89
Sweden	0·83
Switzerland	2·15
U.K.	1·04
U.S.A.	0·52

tasks. It will be recalled that this is the principle underlying gamesmanship, whose object is to raise the opponent's anxiety level by derogatory criticism and thereby impair his performance (Potter, 1947). This effect has frequently been demonstrated by psychologists. For example, Eysenck and Gillan (1964) carried out an experiment on two groups of boys, one of which was led to understand that the task they were about to perform was part of a selection test for a job (the anxious group), while the other merely thought they were assisting some psychologists in an academic inquiry (the unanxious group). The task involved holding a stylus for 15 seconds in a small hole, without touching the sides. Every time the subject allowed the stylus to touch the side an automatic recording was made. The anxious subjects made significantly more mistakes, presumably due to poorer muscular control, than the unanxious. Kellogg (1932) has also demonstrated a relationship between emotional excitement and poor muscular control, and the general relationship between high anxiety and impaired performance in skilled tasks is fairly well established (e.g. Mednick, 1958; Spence, 1960; Kimble, 1961; Eysenck, 1964).

Thus high anxiety is likely to lead to vehicle accidents because it impairs motor control. In addition, anxiety tends to make people aggressive, and this could also lead to driving accidents. Anxiety and aggressiveness have much in common. They are difficult, if not impossible, to distinguish physiologically. Both involve an activation of the sympathetic nervous system entailing an increase in heart rate, respiration rate, and other changes mobilising the body for energetic action (e.g. Morgan, 1965). Indeed, the evolutionary function of anxiety is generally regarded as the mobilisation of the body for dealing with threat, and one of the commonest courses of action in the face of anxiety has been aggression. Hence the similarity between the two conditions.

In recent years the close relationship between anxiety and aggression has been confirmed by anatomical studies. The same parts of the brain seem to control both the anxiety level and aggression. One of these is the amygdala. Rosvold *et al.* (1954) inserted fine wires into this brain area of monkeys and raised the level of nervous excitation by electrical stimulation. The effect on the monkeys is to make them more fearful and aggressive, a preponderance of one or the other depending upon the exact site of stimulation. Conversely, when the amygdala is damaged and thereby rendered partly or wholly inoperative, monkeys become placid and docile, and it is difficult to obtain either anxiety or aggressive reactions. This seems to indicate the close physiological relationship between anxiety and aggression.

In a related experiment Rosvold *et al.* set up eight male monkeys in a colony. They rapidly established themselves in a dominance hierarchy. The investigators then destroyed the amygdala of the top monkey, and as a result he dropped to the bottom of the hierarchy. To attain and keep the top position requires quite considerable powers of aggression, so that in this experiment the destruction of part of the brain which is involved in maintaining anxiety has the effect of reducing an animal's aggressiveness in a real life situation.

A somewhat similar experiment was carried out by Brody and Rosvold (1952). They also set up a monkey colony and took out the most dominant male for surgical treatment. They severed the frontal lobes and found that the effect of this operation was the same as in the previous experiment: the dominant male lost his position and fell to the bottom of the hierarchy. The significance of the experiment is that the frontal lobes play an important part in the maintenance of anxiety (e.g. Petrie, 1952). Indeed, they are sometimes deliberately severed in human beings who suffer from intense anxiety. This is done in the operation of prefrontal leucotomy, whose effect is to reduce anxiety. Thus in these experiments there were surgical operations which impaired the brain mechanisms in the maintenance of anxiety, and the effect was to reduce the animals' aggressiveness.

To revert now to driving accidents, in view of the association between anxiety and aggression we might expect that anxious people would tend to drive aggressively. This in turn would be likely to result in accidents. The aggressive element in driving has been investigated by Parry (1968), who has devised a questionnaire consisting of questions like "Do you flash your lights in anger?" and "Do you make rude signs at other motorists when you are provoked?" By the use of this questionnaire he has measured driving aggressiveness and found an association between high scores on the questionnaire and actual motor accidents. Thus there are links on the one hand between anxiety and aggression and on the other between aggression and vehicle accidents.

Deaths from vehicle accidents can reasonably be regarded as a particular kind of accident-proneness. There are several studies indicating that the accident-prone individual is anxious. Heimstea et al. (1967) set up a simulated driving task in which they were able to measure driving errors and hence accident-proneness. They put 175 men and 175 women through the task and then asked them to check adjectives particularly applicable to themselves. Those who made most errors scored high on adjectives indicating anxiety and aggressiveness.

Alonso-Fernandez (1966) found similar results in Spain. He investigated a number of people who had been involved in car accidents and concluded that most of them were "alcoholics, and insecure and aggressive personalities". They tend to react to stress with a deterioration of motor co-ordination, and this in turn makes them accident-prone. The association between alcoholism and accident proneness is particularly interesting from our own point of view because it implies that countries with a high prevalence of alcoholism should have a high incidence of vehicle accidents, and this is exactly what we have found.

A study by Manheimer and Mellinger (1967) divided 684 children into three groups of high, medium and low accident proneness on the basis of their life histories of involvement in accidents. They found that the high accident-prone group had a number of symptoms of maladjustment, which can probably be regarded as associated with anxiety.

Litman and Tabachnick (1967) attempted a posthumous psychological assessment of fifteen men who had died in car accidents and concluded that they were "active, impulsive, quick, independent, adventurous and rebellious". These are signs of the highly aroused personality, with which anxiety is associated (Lynn, 1966; Claridge, 1967; Eysenck, 1967). Many of these men had been under pressure at the time of the accident and this may be interpreted as having increased their anxiety still further.

The same result has been found in an investigation of pilots involved in flying accidents, the psychology of which is probably reasonably similar to that of vehicle accidents. Biesheuval and White (1949) studied a group of these accident-prone pilots in South Africa and compared them with pilots who had not had accidents. They found that the pilots involved in accidents were more emotional and panicked more easily. There can be little doubt that these had the anxious personality. Another finding of this study was that the accident-prone pilots were more extraverted. This is quite a common result in the literature of accident-proneness, but since extraversion and anxiety are largely independent personality factors (the correlation between them being a low negative one) this association has little relevance for our present purposes.

Most studies of the relationship between anxiety and accident-proneness either take the form of examining the personality of people who have had accidents, or involve experiments in which people are made anxious and subsequently make more mistakes in some kind of task. Another possibility is to make people anxious when they are operating in real-life situations, such as pilots of aeroplanes, car drivers and so forth, and observe whether they have accidents as a consequence. Such experiments have rarely been carried out. However, there is one case which comes close to this situation. In South Africa there was considerable racial tension during 1956–7 in which the native population boycotted the buses. The effect of this boycott on the accident rate of bus drivers in South Africa was investigated by Shaw and Sichel (1961). They found that the number of accidents rose by around 50 per cent during the period of the boycott and afterwards declined rapidly to its previous level. They attributed this rise to the "considerable emotional disturbance" which prevailed at the time and by which the bus drivers would possibly be particularly affected, since they bore the brunt of the protest.

The conclusion from these studies would seem to be that there is a fairly well-established association between anxiety and proneness to vehicle accidents. Our own results extend this association from individuals to nations and show that where the national anxiety level is high, the vehicle accident rate is also high.

A somewhat similar explanation could be advanced for national differences in the murder rate. It is known that criminals as a class tend to be high on anxiety (Eysenck, 1959), although murderers are not necessarily typical of criminals. Nevertheless, while little is known of the personality of murderers, it seems reasonable to assume that they are inclined to be emotional, anxious and aggressive individuals. One indication of this is the tendency of murderers to commit suicide. Three American studies of suicides found that in 5, 4 and 0·8 per cent of cases the person concerned had previously committed a murder (Cavan, 1927; Dorpat, 1966; Schmid, 1933). Even the last percentage is some 160 times higher than the murder rate in the United States population as a whole. Another approach is to start with murderers and suspected murderers and see how many commit suicide. In the United States, the average from four studies is 5 per cent, the range falling between 2 and 9 (Durret and Stromquist, 1925; Wolfgang, 1958; Guttmacher, 1960; Dublin and Bunzel, 1933), and it may be interesting to note that more murderers in the United States die from suicide than from execution (Wolfgang, 1958). In England over the period 1900–59, Morris and Blom-Cooper (1967) have reported that as many as 30 per cent of murderers have subsequently committed suicide.

If these results may be interpreted as indicating that murderers tend to have a high anxiety level, we might expect that the high-anxiety countries would have a greater incidence of murder than the low-anxiety countries. This is indeed the case, as may be seen in Table 11. Murders are two or three times as prevalent in the high-anxiety countries (Austria, Japan, West Germany, France and Italy) as in most of the low-anxiety countries (Ireland, the U.K. and the Netherlands). The rank correlation is +0·33, which is too low for conventional levels of statistical significance with this number of countries. It is, however, significant at the 10 per cent level, which may be acceptable. The correlation is reduced by the extraordinarily high murder rate in the United States, for which special historical factors associated with the frontier tradition and the ease of obtaining firearms are probably responsible. In view of this it may be thought permissible to leave the United States out of the calculation, and when this is done the correlation rises to +0·42. This is statistically significant at the 5 per cent level on a one-tailed test, which seems legitimate as we are predicting the direction of the correlation. Thus in the murder rates we

TABLE 11. DEATHS PER 100,000 POPULATION, 1960

Country	Murders	Country	Murders
Australia	1·5	Italy	1·5
Austria	1·2	Japan	1·9
Belgium	0·7	Netherlands	0·3
Canada	1·4	New Zealand	1·1
Denmark	0·5	Norway	0·4
Finland	2·9	Sweden	0·6
France	1·7	Switzerland	0·6
West Germany	1·0	U.K.	0·6
Ireland	0·2	U.S.A.	4·7

SOURCE: *U.N. Demographic Yearbook 1966.*

have a further national characteristic which may be explicable in terms of our anxiety thesis.

Another manifestation of high anxiety seems to be a strong need for independence. It is probable that this is also related to aggression, since those who have little need for independence are presumably docile and willing to accept the domination of others. The relation between anxiety and the need for independence has been demonstrated directly by Barron (1963). In this experiment he devised the following technique for asserting the strength of the need for independence. His subject was put in a group of ten or so other people and shown three lines of different length. He was then shown a fourth line and asked which of the first it equalled in length. But before being asked for his judgement, he had to hear all the others in his group, who were accomplices of the experimenter, give a false judgement. Then when the subject's turn came he was in a dilemma over whether to conform or whether to assert his independence. On the basis of a dozen repetitions of this experiment Barron obtained two groups which he called *Yielders* and *Independents*. His next step was to ask the groups to tick such adjectives out of a list which particularly applied to themselves. The Independents tended to tick adjectives like "emotional", "excitable" and "moody", while the Yielders ticked "patient", "considerate" and "stable". This demonstrates directly the relationship between anxiety and independence.

This experiment is particularly interesting because almost exactly the same technique was used by Milgram (1961) in a study of national differences between the Norwegians and the French. The actual experiment involved matching acoustic tones instead of lines. The subjects had to listen to two tones and judge which lasted longer. Five accomplices of the experimenter first give false judgements, and the subject then has to give his own judgement. The Norwegians were male students from the University of Oslo and were carefully matched with French students in Paris. The result was that the Norwegians asserted their independence on 38 per cent of the trials, but the French did so on 50 per cent of the trials. Since in terms of our own thesis France is a higher-anxiety country than Norway, this is of course exactly the result we should have predicted.

In a further variation of the experiment the subjects who asserted their independence were insulted by such remarks as "Voulez-vous faire remarquer?" and "Skal du stikke deg ut?" (Are you trying to be funny?). In both groups these taunts increased the tendency to conform, and after being subjected to them only 25 per cent of Norwegians continued to assert their independence, although 41 per cent of French still did so. But in discussing this experiment Milgram makes an observation which is very interesting from our own point of view: "the reactions of students in the two countries was even more striking. In Norway subjects accepted the criticism impassively. In France, however, more than half the subjects made some retaliatory response of their own when the group criticised them. Two French students, one from the Vosges mountain district and the other from the Department of Eure-et-Loire, became so enraged that they directed a stream of abusive language at their taunters." We have already drawn attention to the close relationship between high anxiety and aggressiveness. To those who are familiar with the French reverence for *la gloire*, the militaristic traditions of the *grandes écoles*, the aggressive foreign policy of General de Gaulle, or even with French driving, this result will probably occasion little surprise. But in this experiment the aggressiveness of the French has been demonstrated by scientific methods. This finding of a high level of aggression and independence in France gives further confirmation to our thesis that the French have a high level of anxiety.

CHAPTER 8

ATHEROSCLEROSIS AND CORONARY HEART DISEASE

WE NOW turn to two medical conditions in which anxiety is sometimes regarded as a contributory cause: atherosclerosis (arteriosclerosis) and coronary heart disease. Atherosclerosis is a condition in which the smooth inner lining of the arteries becomes roughened and thickened leading to narrowing of the bore of the vessels and the possibility of obstruction. It is a chronic degenerative condition which progresses slowly over the years and is probably present in all adults in affluent countries to a greater or lesser degree. This arterial condition is responsible for a number of illnesses, the two commonest being coronary heart disease and stroke. Coronary heart disease can manifest itself as coronary thrombosis, cardiac infarction and angina pectoris. The condition seems to be exceptionally common in the low-anxiety countries, particularly Ireland and the U.K. National death rates from atherosclerosis and coronary heart disease are shown in Table 12.

To determine whether this can be interpreted as part of the anxiety syndrome the correlation has been computed between the atherosclerosis

TABLE 12. DEATHS FROM ATHEROSCLEROSIS AND CORONARY HEART DISEASE PER 100,000 POPULATION, 1960

Country	Deaths	Country	Deaths
Australia	256·2	Italy	188·4
Austria	242·8	Japan	50·1
Belgium	142·3	Netherlands	168·2
Canada	237·0	New Zealand	243·7
Denmark	246·6	Norway	210·0
Finland	221·5	Sweden	281·5
France	78·4	Switzerland	229·7
West Germany	199·2	U.K.	314·6
Ireland	313·5	U.S.A.	306·3

SOURCE: *U.N. Demographic Yearbook 1966.*

and coronary heart disease death rates and national anxiety levels. The correlation is -0.63, which is significant at the 1 per cent level and indicates a high prevalence of atherosclerosis and coronary heart disease in low-anxiety countries.

Such a result may occasion some surprise, since coronary heart disease is sometimes regarded as a function of anxiety. However, the part played by personality in these conditions has been a subject of considerable dispute. Forssman and Lindegard (1958) reported that coronary patients were subject to depression. Unfortunately, the term depression is one of the more ambiguous in psychiatry, but if this is psychotic depression and our previous argument of an inverse relation between psychotic depression and anxiety is accepted, then this result is clearly in line with our thesis; it is the depressed, unanxious people who are prone to coronaries. This would explain the high incidence of atherosclerosis in Ireland and in the U.K.

On the other hand, it should be admitted that some investigators have claimed that coronary patients tend to be anxious. For example, Friedman and Rosenman (1960) claimed that coronary patients were typically extremely competitive and restless, which they regarded (reasonably enough) as symptoms of anxiety. Finn et al. (1966) administered Cattell's 16 P.F. questionnaire to sixty-three male Irish coronary patients and found that they scored more highly than the American norms on the principal anxiety factors (C, O and Q4). One of the difficulties which beset this and many other investigations is that the patients were tested after they had had a coronary attack. It could easily be argued that this is what has been responsible for raising their anxiety level, since such patients are faced with the prospect of unemployment, reduced capacity and death itself. This possibility makes the assessment of the coronary personality a difficult problem.

In addition to the various claims that there are personality correlates of coronary heart disease and atherosclerosis, many investigators have concluded that there are no significant or established correlates. Finn et al. (1966) concluded their review of the literature with the statement that "the situation today would seem to be the same as that in 1959 when Ostfeld stated that, after 50 years of study, the relevance of psychological stress to vascular disease is still unclear". Kessel and Munro (1964) concluded their review with the opinion that there was little evidence to support the theory of a "coronary personality".

However, many studies have indicated a relation between atherosclerosis and coronary heart disease on the one hand and calorie intake and obesity on the other (e.g. Albrink, 1967, p. 1165; Friedberg, 1967, p. 543). An extensive study by Kannel *et al.* (1967) involved over 5000 subjects over a 12-year period and examined the relationship between weight changes and coronary heart disease. Gain in weight over the age of 25 was found to be strongly related to sudden death from coronary heart disease and angina pectoris. Huenemann (1968) has shown that those who were overweight in childhood are more prone to atherosclerotic heart disease, hypertensive vascular disease and cardiovascular renal disease. It is true that there have been some investigations which have not shown an abnormally high calorie intake in coronary patients. In Ireland, Finegan *et al.* (1968, 1969) found no significant differences in calorie intake between CHD patients and matched controls, either in men or women. It should, however, be noted that these results depend on patients' own accounts of what they eat, and it is not improbable that they may understate their calorie intake. To admit to a high calorie intake may seem tantamount to admitting personal responsibility for the illness, and this is something about which patients may well feel reluctance. It may be noted that where Mulcahy and his associates considered body weights, they found their CHD patients were heavier than the controls (112 against 107 in the units of the Metropolitan Life Insurance Tables, based on the American ideal weight of 100), though they claimed to eat the same amount. This result was obtained with both males and females and casts some doubt on the patients' veracity.

Our own finding of a high negative correlation between national atherosclerosis deaths and anxiety levels clearly tells against the theory that anxiety is a contributory factor to coronary heart disease. Indeed, it suggests that low anxiety may be a contributory cause. The most probable explanation of this relationship would seem to be that low anxiety is associated with a high calorie intake, as we have previously argued, and that the high calorie intake is a contributory factor in coronary heart disease. This would explain the exceptionally high incidence of atherosclerosis in the U.K. and Ireland as a secondary result of the exceptionally high calorie intake, which is itself partly a function of the low anxiety level. This high correlation between the incidence of atherosclerosis in different countries and the national calorie intake has previously been noted by Keys (1963).

CHAPTER 9

DUODENAL ULCERS AND ESSENTIAL HYPERTENSION

IN THIS chapter we consider the national incidence of two further conditions which are often ascribed to psychological stress and anxiety: duodenal and gastric ulcers, and essential hypertension. The incidence of these conditions in different countries as recorded in the national death rates statistics is shown in Table 13. It will be seen that the figures do not look particularly promising.

This pattern of results makes it improbable that either ulcers or hypertension can be part of the anxiety syndrome, as defined by our original

TABLE 13. DEATHS FROM HYPERTENSION WITHOUT HEART DISEASE AND FROM ULCERS PER 100,000 POPULATION, 1960

Country	Hypertension	Ulcers
Australia	10·2	6·6
Austria	6·1	9·4
Belgium	25·8	5·7
Canada	5·5	5·1
Denmark	2·5	6·7
Finland	2·9	5·6
France	4·8	3·2
Germany	4·0	6·1
Ireland	12·4	7·4
Italy	7·6	6·3
Japan	9·2	11·9
Netherlands	4·4	4·9
New Zealand	4·6	6·7
Norway	4·4	3·0
Sweden	3·7	7·6
Switzerland	4·1	5·7
U.K.	13·7	10·2
U.S.A.	7·0	6·3

SOURCE: *U.N. Demographic Yearbook 1966.*

76

four variables. On these criteria, Austria and Japan are high-anxiety countries and Ireland and the U.K. low, yet on ulcers and hypertension these four countries are grouped together towards the extreme on both measures. To determine whether ulcers and hypertension could be regarded as even slightly associated with the national anxiety levels the correlations have been computed. The rank correlation between anxiety and ulcers is $-0 \cdot 04$ and between anxiety and hypertension $-0 \cdot 18$. Neither of these correlations is of any appreciable size or statistically significant, so we may conclude that the national rates are not explicable in terms of national anxiety levels.

This conclusion suggests three possible lines of argument. The first is that ulcers or hypertension are the genuine indices of national anxiety levels and not the four conditions we have put forward. The second is that ulcers and hypertension are not functions of anxiety but of something else. And the third that the national data are unreliable statistics on which no weight can be placed. Of these alternatives, the second seems the most likely.

As far as ulcers are concerned, it must be admitted that there are some reports of stress being a causative factor, and this is *prima facie* evidence of anxiety being implicated. Sawrey and Weiss (1956) and Sawrey *et al.* (1956) have demonstrated the production of gastric ulcers in rats as a result of stress. The rats were kept for 30 days in a box in which they could only obtain food and water by crossing an electrically charged grill from which they received electric shocks. Seventy-six per cent of these rats developed gastric ulcers.

Similar results have been reported in monkeys by Porter *et al.* (1958). They strapped monkeys into seats and required them to press a lever every 20 seconds, to avoid an electric shock delivered to the feet. These sessions lasted 6 hours, alternating with 6-hour rest periods. In these experiments the monkeys have frequently died from ulcers, presumably as a result of anxiety.

While these results may suggest that stress induces ulcers, there is evidence that ulcers develop as a result of excessive parasympathetic rather than excessive sympathetic activity. Further work by the team who carried out the monkey experiment described above is in line with this interpretation (Brady *et al.*, 1958). The investigators put the monkeys on the task for 18 hours, rather than the 6-hour task alternating with 6-hour rest periods. These 18-hour monkeys never developed ulcers. They concluded that only intermittent stress induces ulcers. To test this conclusion they took measurements of the stomach acid production, which is the immediate factor causing ulcer formation, and found that acidity rose during the rest periods. This is presumably a rebound phenomenon following the stress of the task. This result supports the interpretation of ulcer formation as primarily an effect of excess parasympathetic activity, since it is known that a period of sympathetic activity sets in train an increase of parasympathetic activity (Gellhorn, 1956).

This conclusion is supported by further physiological evidence. While it should be stated that the physiology of ulcer formation is not fully understood, there is some measure of agreement that two mechanisms are involved in the control of hydrochloric acid secretion in the stomach which in excess leads to ulcer formation (Maclean, 1960; Magoun, 1963). One mechanism originates in the parasympathetic centre in the anterior hypothalamus, which transmits stimulation via the vagus to the stomach walls and releases the acid. The second mechanism is through the posterior hypothalamic release of adrenocorticotrophic hormones which stimulate the adrenal cortex; this releases cortisone, which in turn generates gastric acid secretion (Maclean, 1960; Magoun, 1963). In the first of these mechanisms the parasympathetic system plays an important part, so that it is possible that individuals who develop ulcers have excessive parasympathetic activity, not the excessive sympathetic activity which is the physiological basis of anxiety.

Hypertension has also sometimes been attributed to anxiety and claimed to be more prevalent among anxious people. Essential hypertension is a state of permanent high blood pressure for which the cause is unknown. But in spite of much research on the possibility that anxiety may play a part, the hypothesis remains unproven. At the end of an extensive review of the literature on whether personality factors cause hypertension, McGinn et al. (1964) conclude that "no direct evidence is available . . . and tangential studies offer conflicting results".

There is some evidence that stress induces a rise in blood pressure. For example, Alexander (1939) and Wolf et al. (1948) reported that the blood pressure of their patients undergoing psychoanalysis rose during particularly disturbing sessions involving the discussion of unpleasant experiences. Pfeiffer and Wolff (1950) confirmed this effect with normal subjects discussing "threatening" topics. On the other hand, Innes et al. (1959) were unable to confirm these results.

Objective threats have also been found to induce increased blood pressure. For example, Graham (1945) reported that 27 per cent of a sample of soldiers who had seen active service in the African desert campaign in World War II had elevated diastolic blood pressure some months later. Two weeks after a tremendous explosion in Texas City, 56 per cent of a sample of survivors had high diastolic blood pressure (Ruskin *et al.*, 1948). An ingenious investigation has been reported by Grimak (1959). He hypnotised parachutists and had them relive the jump under hypnosis. This seems as good an anxiety-provoking situation as could be devised. He found that blood pressure went up when the plane took off, remained high during the flight, *fell* when the subjects jumped, and fell again when the parachute opened. This result throws some doubt on the theory that increased blood pressure is a straightforward monotonic reaction to increased anxiety. Another curious result has been reported by Marcussen (1950), who gives several cases in which symptoms of high blood pressure disappeared when the subject was exposed to extreme environmental stress, such as being a prisoner of war in a Japanese camp, but reappeared upon return to normal life. Nevertheless, the weight of the evidence does seem to suggest that stress normally induces a rise in blood pressure.

Prima facie, this would suggest that anxious people would tend to have high blood pressure. However, attempts to demonstrate a relationship between anxiety as a personality characteristic and hypertension have had little success. Hamilton (1942) used self-ratings and assessment by two friends to evaluate the personality of young hypertensive subjects and concluded that they tended to be submissive, introverted, docile, unselfconfident, slow, lethargic and uninterested in the opposite sex, but not anxious. Harburg, *et al.* (1964) administered the Cattell 16 P.F. test to college men hypertensives and found that they were high on sensitivity and submissiveness, but not exceptional on anxiety. Cattell and Scheier (1959) have also found that there is no relation between hypertension and anxiety measured by the 16 P.F. Robinson (1959) has reported no relationship between blood pressure and Eysenck's neuroticism factor, which is largely a measure of anxiety. Thus although there is some evidence that stress raises blood pressure, the weight of the evidence is fairly strong against an association between hypertension and anxiety as a stable personality characteristic. This conclusion enables us to understand why neither hypertension nor ulcers are related to national anxiety levels.

While neither duodenal ulcers nor hypertension have any significant or sizeable correlation with the anxiety syndrome, it is interesting to note that they do tend to be associated with each other. Attention seems first to have been drawn to this association by Rudin (1968) in his study of epidemiological patterns in seventeen advanced countries for the year 1950, to which reference has already been made. In addition to suicide, liver cirrhosis and homicide, Rudin also considered ulcers and hypertension. Rudin took the view that the correlations fall into two clusters, the first consisting of homicide, suicide and alcoholism, which is our anxiety factor, and a second independent cluster of ulcers and hypertension.

Rudin's complete matrix of intercorrelations is shown in Table 14. The correlation between deaths from hypertension and ulcers in Rudin's year and sample of countries was $+0.54$, which is both large and statistically significant. For our own year and sample it is $+0.23$ which taken in conjunction with Rudin's result, still suggests that an association between ulcers and hypertension could exist. There is also some evidence for this association in individuals, i.e. there is some tendency for those suffering from hypertension to develop ulcers (Palmer, 1937).

Thus there seems to be a second factor running through nations, independent of the anxiety factor, and manifesting itself in a high prevalence of ulcers and hypertension. Is it possible that that factor could be the same as the second major factor which both Eysenck and Cattell have found in their work on individual personality: extraversion? The strongest evidence for this interpretation would seem to be the report of Cattell and Scheier (1959) for the existence of a significant correlation between extraversion and high systolic blood pressure. This study certainly lends

TABLE 14. CORRELATIONS ABOUT THE YEAR 1950

Cause of death	Suicide	Liver cirrhosis	Ulcers	Hypertension
Homicide	0·44	0·40	−0·10	−0·25
Suicide		0·49	0·19	−0·36
Liver cirrhosis			−0·30	−0·28
Ulcers				0·54

SOURCE: Rudin, 1968.

weight to the hypothesis. Unfortunately, it has not been replicated by Harburg *et al.* (1964) or Robinson (1959), so the issue must remain in some doubt.

Although these seem to be the only direct studies of the relation between extraversion and hypertension, some indirect evidence is available from the quite extensive work on hypertension and hostility. This bears on the thesis because of the association of extraversion with aggression and hostility. For example, extraverts tend to enjoy aggressive jokes and to approve of such things as flogging and hanging (Eysenck, 1947, 1953). Thus the demonstration of an association between hypertension and aggression and hostility would strengthen the extraversion interpretation of national differences in hypertension.

The hostility theory of hypertension seems to have been put forward first by Alexander (1939a). He suggested that the pre-hypertensive suppresses his feelings of hostility and this leads to tension manifesting itself somatically in elevated blood pressure. In time this involves the permanent vascular changes associated with hypertension. Following the formulation of this hypothesis, a number of workers have reported hostility or repressed hostility in hypertensives, including Saul (1939), Wolf *et al.* (1948), Gressel *et al.* (1949) and Saul *et al.* (1954). These results are all derived from clinical psychotherapy sessions, where it must be admitted that the assessment of hostility tends to be subjective. Studies using objective test measures of hostility have not always been so conclusive and Shapiro (1960) at the end of a review of studies on the relationship concludes that the existing data are still inconclusive.

Nevertheless, the possibility that the prevalence of hypertension and ulcers might reflect national levels of extraversion remains an attractive one. Unfortunately, other evidence must be brought to bear against it. Ulcers do not seem to be a function of the extraverted personality. Indeed, Kanter and Hazelton (1964) have reported a study of thirty young men with duodenal ulcers and found that they were significantly more introverted than normal. This result tells rather strongly against the thesis that hypertension and ulcers are positive functions of extraversion.

A further check on the thesis can be made by using the extraversion scores for male students which have been collected for eight of the eighteen countries by Cattell and his colleagues. These scores are shown in Table 15. Using these as an index of national extraversion levels, the correlation between extraversion and hypertension is $-0 \cdot 06$, and between extraversion and ulcers −0·69. The second fails to reach statistical significance at the 5 per cent level.

It seems impossible to draw any conclusion from this confused pattern of intercorrelations, except that both ulcers and hypertension do not seem to be related to national anxiety levels and that there is no overwhelming consensus of results indicating that they should be. Whether they really form an independent cluster, and if so what they represent, must remain for the present unclear.

TABLE 15. EXTRAVERSION SCORES OF MALE UNIVERSITY STUDENTS
DERIVED FROM CATTELL'S 16 P.F.

Country	Extraversion	Country	Extraversion
U.S.A.	5·50	U.K.	4·76
Ireland	5·04	Australia	4·72
New Zealand	5·00	Germany	4·37
Canada	4·93	Japan	3·08

CHAPTER 10

TOBACCO CONSUMPTION

THE smoking of tobacco is sometimes regarded as a manifestation of anxiety and, if this reasoning is correct, might be expected to be positively associated with national anxiety levels. In fact the association is the other way about. Figures for the consumption of tobacco as a whole, and of cigarettes separately, are given in Table 16. It will be seen that there is some tendency towards a negative association between tobacco consumption and the national anxiety levels. Both Ireland and the U.K., the two lowest anxiety countries, have a high *per capita* consumption of tobacco, while in Japan, France and Germany the consumption of tobacco is relatively low. The rank correlation of national anxiety level with total tobacco consumption and with cigarette consumption is -0.55 in both cases. This correlation is significant at the 5 per cent level.

This high and significant negative correlation indicates that in countries with a high level of anxiety the consumption of tobacco is relatively low. Although this result is possibly surprising, it is not altogether inconsistent with what is known about the correlates and effects of tobacco. Investigations of the personality correlates of smoking generally indicate that it is not positively associated with anxiety. For instance, in an extensive investigation of 2400 subjects, Eysenck (1965) found that there was no association between smoking and neuroticism, the Eysenck factor which most closely resembles anxiety. There was, however, a significant association between cigarette smoking and extraversion, a factor which has some small negative association with anxiety (Eysenck, 1957). Thus the Eysenck results suggest a negative association between cigarette smoking and anxiety, which is exactly what our result indicates at the international level.

While some investigators have claimed that there is a relationship between smoking and anxiety (e.g. Seltzer, 1967), several independent workers have supported Eysenck's view that extraversion is the chief

83

TABLE 16. NATIONAL TOBACCO CONSUMPTION FOR 1960

Country	Cigarettes per adult per annum	Tobacco (lb)
Australia	2440	7·9
Austria	1720	4·3
Belgium	1570	6·7
Canada	2910	9·4
Denmark	1470	8·1
Finland	2100	4·1
France	1320	4·8
West Germany	1630	5·6
Ireland	2560	6·5
Italy	1300	3·3
Japan	1880	4·3
Netherlands	1700	8·5
New Zealand	1930	7·8
Norway	550	4·4
Sweden	1160	4·5
Switzerland	2380	7·0
U.K.	2760	6·8
U.S.A.	3810	10·5

SOURCE: Tobacco Research Council, Research Paper No. 6.

personality correlate. Cattell and Krug (1967) confirmed the Eysenck result on student smokers in the United States. Schubert (1965) also obtained this result in a study of 1270 students in New England.

In view of this consensus of results it might be expected that the relationship between cigarette smoking and extraversion would hold between countries. A measure of extraversion can be obtained from the questionnaire results of male university students derived from Cattell's 16 P.F. test. These results are available for eight of the eighteen countries and have been shown in Table 15.

We can now calculate the correlation between these national extraversion scores and tobacco consumption. The correlation with total tobacco consumption is +0·83 (significant at the 1 per cent level) and with cigarette consumption +0·65. These results indicate that, internationally, tobacco consumption is a positive function of national levels of extraversion, just as it is with individuals. There is a certain discrepancy because in individuals (in the U.K.) the association between extraversion and tobacco consumption is strongest with cigarette smoking and is weakened if total smoking is taken as the index of tobacco consumption; whereas, in countries, the correlation of national extraversion and the total tobacco consumption is stronger than with cigarette consumption. However, the difference between the correlations of national extraversion with total tobacco consumption and with cigarette consumption is not statistically significant, so it is doubtful whether much should be made of this discrepancy.

Thus the extraversion results are broadly consistent between individuals and between nations: in both cases extraversion is associated with high tobacco consumption. On the other hand, the anxiety findings appear less consistent since there is a strong negative relationship between anxiety level and tobacco consumption in nations, but no relationship between tobacco consumption and Eysenck's neuroticism factor in individuals. This apparent contradiction is explained when it is recalled that Eysenck's neuroticism is not a pure anxiety factor, and that he also has extensive results showing a positive correlation between extraversion and smoking. Since extraversion is negatively associated with anxiety, this result is in line with our own international results.

The finding that cigarette smoking is negatively correlated with anxiety is consistent with the physiological properties of nicotine. It belongs to a class of drugs which are broadly known as stimulants (Eysenck, 1965) and have the effect of making those who take them slightly more efficient over a variety of perceptual and motor tasks. For example, an experiment by Warwick and Eysenck (1963) used the test of critical flicker fusion. The test consists of a light flashing on and off, and as the speed of the flashes is increased there comes a point at which it is seen as a steady light. This is the point at which the eye fails to discriminate the flashes. The administration of 0·1 mg of nicotine improved the perception and the subjects could distinguish the flashes in what they saw previously as a steady light.

There is a considerable literature showing the stimulant effects of nicotine among which the following two reports are representative. Frankenhaeuser et al. (1968) had subjects smoke cigarettes and recorded a subsequent increase in the secretion of adrenaline, and rises in skin temperature, heart rate and blood pressure. Ulett and Itil (1969) observed the effect of smoking on EEG rhythms and reported an increase in frequency as a result of smoking. All these results indicate that nicotine has a stimulant effect.

Apart from increasing the efficiency of the sense organs and of reactions, stimulants also increase anxiety (Lynn, 1966; Eysenck, 1967). For this reason we should expect that people who normally have a high level of anxiety would tend not to take stimulants, whose effect would be to raise their anxiety still further. It seems probable that people like best to be at some intermediate level of anxiety, neither excessively high nor excessively low. Evidence for this view has been marshalled by Berlyne (1960). If this is so, we should expect those who have exceptionally high anxiety levels to take depressants to bring their anxiety level down. This is apparently one of the reasons for the high prevalence of alcoholism in high-anxiety countries like France. Conversely, where the level of anxiety is low there should be a higher consumption of stimulant drugs, such as tobacco. This would account for the high consumption of tobacco in countries which have low anxiety levels, like Ireland and the U.K.

CHAPTER 11

SEX AND CELIBACY

CONSIDERABLE attention has been paid by psychologists to the relation between anxiety and sex. It is usually believed that the two are negatively related and that anxiety tends to inhibit sexual interest and activity. Such a view was advanced by Freud on numerous occasions (e.g. 1936) and there is some evidence in its favour. For instance, Cattell has devised a test to measure the strength of a person's sexual drive or, as he prefers to call it, sex "erg". Scores on this test correlate negatively with scores derived from anxiety questionnaires (Cattell and Scheier, 1961). Clearly this gives some support to the thesis that anxiety tends to inhibit sexual drives.

There are also sound physiological reasons for expecting an inverse relation between sexual activity and anxiety. Sexual activity is largely mediated by the parasympathetic system and anxiety by the sympathetic system, and these two systems have a tendency to suppress each other on a kind of see-saw principle: when one is up it tends to push the other down (e.g. Gellhorn, 1957). There is not much doubt that in cases of intense anxiety, sexual activity is often inhibited (in much the same way as we have seen eating is, another parasympathetically mediated activity). Wolpe (1958) and others have discussed a number of cases where intense anxiety seems to have inhibited sexual activity and where a reduction of anxiety through treatment has been followed by a release from the sexual inhibitions.

In view of this apparent association we might expect that there would be some tendency for sexual activities to be muted in our high-anxiety countries. A thorough investigation of this possibility would require detailed inquiries like those of Kinsey in all eighteeen countries, and unfortunately nothing like this amount of information exists. The data are at best fragmentary and we must make do with what are available. The most complete are derived from university students and we have collected evidence from various sources on the percentages of students in different countries who have had experience of premarital intercourse. Even here the information is not as full as one would have wished, but it is a case of making do with what there is or going without, and the former seems the better course. Table 17 shows the figures for eight countries. All the information was collected between the middle nineteen-fifties and the middle nineteen-sixties, which corresponds well with the period from which our other statistics have been taken. The results from the U.K., Norway, Canada, Germany, Italy and the United States are taken from a single investigation by Packard (1968); the results from Sweden are taken from Karlsson, *et al.* (1962) and those from Denmark from Christensen and Carpenter (1962). All the investigators put the question of whether their subjects had experience of premarital inter-course, which seems unambiguous enough. But it is additionally fortunate that six of the countries were covered by Packard with an identical questionnaire, using identical procedures involving anonymity and mailing the questionnaire direct to the investigator. The identity of procedure should ensure that the results are reasonably comparable from one country to another. Packard's investigation involved around 200 students from each country with the exceptions of Italy, where only forty women were tested, and the United States, where the number tested was over a thousand. In the United States the subjects were drawn from over twenty universities, which was wise because of the many different types of uni-versity in that country. In each European country the students were taken from one university. This seems reasonable enough. In the U.K. all uni-versities are now virtually indistinguishable one from another, with the possible exceptions of Oxford and Cambridge, and it is to a considerable degree a matter of luck at which one a student find himself. In Germany many students move from one university to another during the course of their undergraduate careers, so that a sample from any university should give a reasonable cross-section of German students. In Norway few universities exist. Thus Packard's sampling seems likely to give reasonably representative results. The response rate he obtained was over 50 per cent in every country, a figure which compares favourably with many other investigations.

If we now consider the results in Table 17, it will be noted that there is a certain tendency for a higher proportion of male students to have had experience of premarital intercourse in the countries where anxiety levels are low. The extreme cases are the U.K., the lowest-anxiety country with

TABLE 17. PERCENTAGES OF STUDENTS EXPERIENCING PREMARITAL
INTERCOURSE

Country	Men	Women
U.K.	75	63
Norway	67	54
Sweden	65	45
Denmark	64	60
U.S.A.	58	43
Canada	57	35
Germany	55	59
Italy	—	10

the highest proportion of experienced students, and Germany, the highest-anxiety country with the lowest proportion of experienced students. Unfortunately the data do not lend themselves to conventional statistical testing, since rank correlations are not normally regarded as reliable with less than ten cases. In any case, the relationship does not seem to hold so well with the women students. The question must await the collection of further data from other countries before it can be resolved.

Another possible way of assessing the effect of anxiety on sexual behaviour in different countries is to consider the proportion of people who are married, although it must be conceded that in the present age the proportion of people married can at best be only a very rough guide to the amount of sexual activity in a country. Nevertheless, it may be worth considering and the statistics are easily obtainable from the census returns. They are shown in Table 18. Broadly, the figures seem to be in line with expectation. There is some tendency for the high-anxiety countries (Austria, Japan, France, Germany) to have a higher proportion of single people than most of the low-anxiety countries (the U.K., New Zealand, Australia and Canada). This is in line with Freud's view of the inhibiting effect of anxiety on sexual behaviour, although possibly the better interpretation of this trend is that high anxiety tends to make people more cautious about shouldering the burdens of marriage, rather than inhibiting sexual appetites.

The correlation between anxiety rank and the proportion of single people is positive, but it is only $+0\cdot30$ in the case of men and $+0\cdot28$ in the case of women, neither of which is sufficiently high for statistical significance.

TABLE 18. PERCENTAGES OF SINGLE MEN AND WOMEN, AGED 15–49

Country	Year	Women	Men
Australia	1961	26·2	38·2
Austria	1961	33·8	42·9
Belgium	1961	26·8	34·4
Canada	1961	28·4	37·8
Denmark	1960	29·6	39·9
Finland	1960	35·3	42·8
France	1962	31·7	41·9
West Germany	1961	30·9	39·8
Ireland	1961	47·9	60·9
Italy	1951	—	49·9
Japan	1960	35·6	45·5
Netherlands	1960	33·7	40·9
New Zealand	1961	24·9	35·8
Norway	1960	30·4	41·2
Sweden	1960	32·3	42·9
Switzerland	1960	38·2	45·0
U.K.	1961	28·3	36·2
U.S.A.	1960	22·1	30·8

SOURCE: *U.N. Demographic Yearbook 1965*, table 7.

Examination of the figures for celibacy given in Table 18 will show that the correlation is spoiled by the case of Ireland. At least two explanations might be suggested for this discrepant country. The first is that it is not impossible that there is a curvilinear relationship between anxiety and sexual arousal, such that little sexual activity takes place with both low and high anxiety and most when anxiety is in the middle range. This would explain the gradual diminution of sexual activity with ageing which has been well documented by Kinsey *et al.* (1948). This could be due, at least in part, to a decrease in anxiety as people age, for which the evidence was reviewed in Chapter 4. Although the physiology of sexual arousal is still not completely understood, it is well established that the hypothalamus plays an important part (Morgan, 1965). The hypothalamus also has a role in the maintenance of anxiety, so that it is not impossible that excitation could pass from the anxiety centre to the centre for sexual arousal. On this theory, anxiety could be too low for maximum sexual arousal in Ireland and it would reach its optimum in the United States, where there are fewest single people, and then as anxiety gets higher it would begin to inhibit sexual arousal, producing low marriage rates in the high-anxiety countries such as Japan and Austria. Unfortunately there are not enough countries to subject the possibility of such a curvilinear relation to a statistical test.

Another explanation for the discrepant case of Ireland would be in the strength of the Roman Catholic church. This has probably exerted a certain influence for the dampening down of sexual activity in Ireland. The country has exercised a severe censorship on literature of a kind likely to arouse sexual appetites, including some of the works of Mr. Graham Greene and Miss Edna O'Brien. The sale of contraceptives is also illegal in Ireland, so that it is perhaps not surprising that sexual behaviour should be somewhat inhibited. If this admittedly *ad hoc* explanation can be accepted, the correlations provide some support for Freud's theory that anxiety has an inhibiting influence on sexual activity.

CHAPTER 12

ANXIETY AND ECONOMIC GROWTH

THERE is a high correlation between national anxiety levels and economic growth. A country's rate of economic growth is the rate at which its total national wealth increases, and among the countries we have been considering this rate has generally lain, in the post-1945 period, between 1 and 10 per cent per year. There is, however, considerable variability between countries. Some countries, particularly Japan and West Germany, have had outstandingly high growth rates, while in others, notably the U.K. and Ireland, the growth rates have been low.

While economic growth has normally been regarded as lying in the province of economics, many economists have accepted that psychological factors may well be important. This seems obvious enough. If we consider individuals, it is clear that the rate at which their income grows depends to a considerable degree on their qualities of intelligence, ambition, hard work, willingness to save and so forth. The same is true of the wealth of nations, which is no more than the aggregate of the individuals of which it is made up. This view has been taken by a number of leading economists. For example, Kaldor (1954) has written that "the most plausible answer to the question why some human societies progress so much faster than others is to be sought, in my view, not so much in fortuitous accidents . . . or in favourable natural environment . . . but in human attitudes". Similarly, Rostow (1960) regards "the propensity to seek material advance" as an important psychological factor for the achievement of economic growth.

National economic growth rates are subject to quite considerable year-to-year fluctuations according to whether a particular country is in a state of boom or recession. To get a reliable figure it is necessary to take the average of a number of years. To obtain as reliable an average as possible, while avoiding the years of immediate post-war reconstruction, we have taken the average of the period 1950–65. This is shown in relation to national anxiety levels in Fig. 6, where it will be seen that there is a fairly pronounced tendency for countries with high anxiety levels to have high economic growth rates. The rank correlation is $+0\cdot67$ and is significant at the $0\cdot01$ level.

The interpretation of this correlation is a matter of some complexity and it would take us too far away from the central theme of this monograph to consider it in detail. Nevertheless, some comment can be made. In the first place, it is doubtful whether the correlation simply arises from

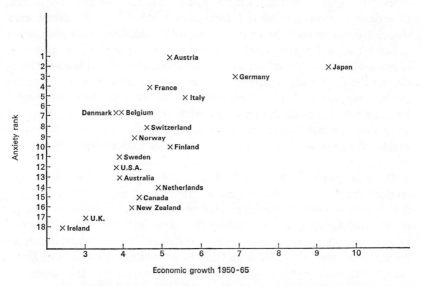

FIG. 6. Relationship between economic growth rates and anxiety ranks for eighteen countries (rho $= +0\cdot67$, sig. at 1 per cent).

the effects of the 1939–45 war. It is sometimes argued that the extensive war devastation in Germany and Japan has been responsible for the fast growth rates of these countries and it might be thought that it could also have raised the populations' anxiety level, thus giving rise to the correlation. Neither of these suppositions stands up to examination. Japan and Germany have continued to be exceptionally strong economies in the late nineteen-sixties and this can hardly be attributed to the effects of the war. And as far as anxiety levels are concerned, such evidence as we have suggests that these have remained much the same over the course of this century in all the countries we are considering. This conclusion will be argued in more detail later. It seems doubtful whether either the national growth rates or the anxiety levels can be attributed to the effects of the 1939–45 war.

A possible explanation of the relation between anxiety and economic growth could be that anxiety is associated with achievement motivation. This motivation is essentially Weber's Protestant work ethic, and evidence has been collected by McClelland (1961) to show that the level of achievement motivation in a country is in some circumstances related to the rate of economic growth. Now if achievement motivation and anxiety were associated, there would be a straightforward explanation of the association between national anxiety levels and growth rates. The evidence, however, is against the existence of any such association. Cattell and Scheier (1961) discuss the matter and conclude that anxiety and achievement motivation are independent, and achievement motivation measured by questionnaire has no appreciable correlation with anxiety (Lynn, 1969). Thus it does not seem that the association between anxiety and economic growth can be explained in terms of any correlation between anxiety and achievement motivation.

There are probably two principal reasons why a population with a high level of anxiety should achieve a fast rate of economic growth. The first is that people with high anxiety tend to work harder. This was demonstrated directly by Furneaux (1957) in an investigation of the tendency of university students who score highly on Eysenck's neuroticism factor to do well in examinations. He found that these students devoted more hours per week to work than the more emotionally stable students. It is important here to distinguish between the effects of anxiety in motivating work and its effects on learning efficiency. There is a good deal of evidence suggesting that anxiety impairs learning efficiency in tasks which have to be performed in a set time. Much less work has been carried out on its effect on performance, in real-life situations. Such evidence as there is supports Furneaux's finding that high anxiety can, at least in some circumstances, mobilise energies for greater effort. For example, Feldman (1964) tested two groups of youths with different anxiety levels on a laborious task involving holding a stylus on a small disk on a revolving turntable. The anxious youths were applicants for apprenticeships and were told that the task was a test whose results would affect whether or not they were accepted by the company. The unanxious had already been accepted as apprentices and were told that the task was simply a psychological experiment in which they were acting as subjects. It seems quite reasonable to accept Feldman's inference that the first group would have been made anxious by the situation. They did consistently better than the unanxious group and it seems reasonable to infer that their higher anxiety motivated their superior performance.

A somewhat similar experiment has been reported by Broadhurst (1964) on rats. The task consisted of swimming underwater through a 10-foot-long tank. The rat must hold his breath during the swimming and is able to breathe again when he gets to the end. Having established how long it takes rats to perform this task, Broadhurst then took a group and held them under water for 8 seconds before releasing them for the swim. The result was that they swam faster than rats released straight away. We may reasonably infer that being held under water raised the rats' anxiety level and motivated their better performance.

In a further series of experiments Broadhurst has bred two different genetic strains of rats, which he has called the "reactive" and the "non-reactive". These correspond to what we should call the anxious and the unanxious. These rats differ in their swimming speeds through the tank, the reactive (anxious) rats swimming faster than the non-reactive. Possibly it is not going too far to suggest that the same rule may apply to the superior economic growth rates of countries with anxious populations, like Germany and Japan, compared with those with unanxious populations, like the U.K. and Ireland. It is conceivable that the high general anxiety level motivates the population to work harder and that this manifests itself in a fast growth rate.

It should not be surprising that anxiety frequently motivates efficient performance, for this is the biological purpose for which the anxiety reaction has evolved. The physiological manifestations of anxiety, such as the accelerated heart rate and breathing and the increased sensitivity of the sense organs, mobilise the animal for energetic action. These reactions have developed during the course of evolution because they have constituted an invaluable aid to survival, mobilising the animal for fighting or escaping when situations of danger arise. Animals without anxiety reactions would have been rapidly extinguished. It is true that in conditions of civilised living there are certain situations in which anxiety can impair efficiency, especially those involving complex skills, such as driving cars (as we have seen). But it is doubtful whether this sort of skill has much effect on economic growth, which is probably more determined by the amount of effort which the population puts into work.

The idea that anxiety can motivate increased effort is somewhat unusual in psychology. There may be several reasons for this. One is the weight of experimental work on the performance of complex skilled tasks under laboratory conditions, where anxiety normally has a deleterious effect. A second reason may be that psychologists are sometimes inclined to equate high anxiety with anxiety neurosis, and anxiety neurotics are not good at sustained work effort. Anxiety neurotics, however, are a special kind of highly anxious persons, probably characterised by lack of self control or ego-strength. This was the view taken by Freud and corroborated by objective questionnaire tests by Cattell and Scheier (1961). It would be an error to infer that all moderately or even highly anxious people are like anxiety neurotics.

We have seen that laboratory experiments suggest that anxiety improves performance. Because of the artificiality of laboratory conditions, it is always wise to check the conclusions of laboratory experiments against real-life situations, even though these cannot be so rigorously controlled. To do this we can examine the effects of what must have been one of the most anxiety-provoking events of the century, the British bombing raids on Hamburg in the summer of 1943. Galbraith (1958) suggests that the ordeal was worse than anything the German people had experienced since the Thirty Years War. In three nights of terror a third of the city was devastated. The heat was so intense that the tarmac caught alight in many areas. Between 60,000 and 100,000 were killed, about as many as at Hiroshima. The bombing fell mainly on the residential areas, so that many lost their homes, possessions and members of their families. But this stress did not reduce the efficiency of the German workers. Production figures dropped for about a fortnight while the worst of the damage was being made good, but after that it returned to normal. Since there was a considerable loss of life, it seems that productivity per man must have increased following the bombing ordeal. Whatever the results of some laboratory experiments, it seems impossible to avoid the conclusion that in real life Western populations react positively to very considerable degrees of stress and anxiety.

The application of this conclusion to differences in anxiety levels between nations implies that the populations in the more anxious countries should work harder. Unfortunately there is little direct evidence that work effort in different countries is correlated with anxiety levels, as our thesis would predict. Work effort is not easy to measure. Among workers it is not necessarily reflected in the hours put in, since with greater application more can be accomplished in a shorter number of hours. Among executives the hours of work are probably a better indication of work effort, and here there is some evidence that Americans work harder than the British, as our thesis would predict from their higher anxiety level. Merrett (1968) reports two investigations of the working week of senior British executives which gave figures of 42 and 53 hours, compared with two investigations of American executives which gave working weeks of 57 and 60 hours. To this can be added a survey of British research students who were found to work an average week of 42 hours (arts and pure science) and 48 hours (medicine and applied science) (Bradley and Hindmarch, 1968). All the British results are fairly well below those from the United States. Our thesis predicts that further examination of the working week in other countries would confirm its association with national anxiety levels.

Thus one advantage of a high anxiety level in the population, from the point of view of fast economic growth, may be that the people work harder. The second principal advantage is probably that there is a greater proportion of creative people. The causal links suggested here are that there is an association between high anxiety and creativity, and between creativity and economic growth. As far as anxiety and creativity are concerned, their connection is almost certainly the basis of the traditional belief for an association between genius and neurotic instability, which was asserted by Pascal ("l'éxtrême esprit est voisin de l'éxtrême folie"), Lamartine ("le maladie mental qu'on appelle génie"), Dryden ("great wits are sure to madness near allied"), Aristotle ("mental instability has been noted in Socrates, Euripides, Plato and in many others, especially poets") and many other observers of human nature.

Some psychologists have taken the view that the association between anxiety (or some other form of mental instability) and creative genius does not exist and that the traditional view is wrong. This conclusion rests principally on the investigation by Terman (1925) of several hundred highly intelligent children, who were found to be somewhat more emotionally stable than average. Terman unwisely called his intelligent children "geniuses", which has misled some psychologists into thinking that he has proved that geniuses are emotionally stable and not neurotic, as foolish people like Aristotle, Dryden, Pascal and so on believed. Actually, of course, high intelligence is by no means synonymous with genius, if the integrity of language is to be respected. Genius was better described by Thomas Edison as "one per cent inspiration and ninety-nine per cent perspiration", that is to say, it requires creativity and effort in addition to high intelligence. It is in these qualities that anxiety enters into the personality of genius. We have already seen that anxiety motivates work. There is also evidence that it motivates creative achievement.

As far as historically established geniuses are concerned, one of the most thorough studies is that of Herzberg (1929). He investigated the lives of thirty eminent philosophers and concluded that almost half were cases of severe neurotic instability. The most common complaints were depression, including Descartes, Kant, Hume, Herbert, Schopenhauer and Spencer; and anxiety, including St. Augustine, Bruno, Rousseau and Kierkegaard. The same conclusion was reached by Brain (1948), who investigated the lives of the 150 poets who are represented in the *Oxford Book of English Verse* and born after 1700. He considered that twenty-two were either insane or severely neurotic. While this is a better record than the philosophers, Brain concluded that the percentage was higher than would be expected in a normal population and that his results supported the traditional belief in an association between genius and neurosis. Cattell and Butcher (1968) have also recognised the existence of this association, both among scientists, where they give as examples Priestley, Darwin and Kepler, and among creative writers, musicians and painters, including Beethoven, Ravel, Bartok, Flaubert, Ruskin, Nietzsche, Strindberg, Proust, Dylan Thomas, Van Gogh, Utrillo and Modigliani.

Among living creative people, who can be given psychological tests, the most extensive investigation has been made by Barron (1963). He tested fifty-six established American creative writers and found that they scored higher on questionnaires of neuroticism and anxiety than the normal population. We may perhaps add to this the findings of Furneaux (1957), Kelvin *et al.* (1965) and myself (Lynn, 1959) that students and sixth-formers who score highly on neuroticism questionnaires do well in examinations. Since good examination performance depends partly on creativity (though admittedly also on intelligence and effort), these results could be interpreted as supporting the association between anxiety and creativity.

But what has such an association to do with economic growth? It is suggested that the answer to this is that entrepreneurship is a creative activity and that a country with good proportion of creative men will have some who will channel their creative energies into entrepreneurial enterprise. This in turn will give rise to economic growth. Creativity is not commonly thought of in association with entrepreneurship. However, the qualities involved in entrepreneurship and more conventional creative activities seem closely similar. The entrepreneur must first create a new product or service in his imagination. Thus Henry Ford could imagine a future in which ordinary people drove cars and Sir Billy Butlin must have had a vision of the English enjoying themselves in regimented holiday camps. Next the entrepreneur must mobilise the qualities of energy and self-discipline necessary for translating the vision into actuality—he must display Edison's "ninety-nine per cent of perspiration" necessary for creative achievement. This constellation of abilities required for successful entrepreneurship is surely similar to that of the creative artist, who creates a new imaginative vision and also needs the self-discipline and energy to translate it into reality.

Unfortunately psychologists have had little success in devising tests of creativity so that it is difficult to demonstrate directly that entrepreneurs are creative. There is, however, evidence that entrepreneurs tend to be high on anxiety, like other creative men. The most extensive demonstration of this has been made by Collins *et al.* (1964) in an investigation of over 100 entrepreneurs in Chicago. On the basis of the Thematic Apperception Test they concluded that these entrepreneurs had had severely neurotic temperaments since childhood. This aspect of their results is particularly interesting because it shows that the high level of anxiety in entrepreneurs is not simply a reaction to entrepreneurial life, which is admittedly stressful and anxiety arousing. In a study of forty English entrepreneurs I have confirmed that entrepreneurs score higher on Eysenck's neuroticism questionnaire than salaried executives or professional men (Lynn, 1969).

Taken together these results suggest that the anxious personality tends to be creative, and one way in which creative energy can manifest itself is in entrepreneurship. This is possibly why societies which in history have displayed great creative achievement in the sciences and arts have generally been economically prosperous at the same time. Classical Greece, Renaissance Italy and seventeenth-century Holland are examples. This is probably to be explained by a rise in the creative energy of the population, manifesting itself in both entrepreneurial and cultural achievement.

The final link in the chain here suggested is between a high level of entrepreneurship in a country and a fast economic growth rate. Such an association seems probable though difficult to prove statistically. Entrepreneurship is the capacity for creative innovation in business, and without this few businesses can hope to remain profitable for long. Market conditions are continually changing and competitors constantly introducing improved products which drive the sluggish out of business. One example may be given. In the nineteen-fifties there was a thriving British motor-cycle industry making the heavy and powerful machines that were in favour at that time. In the early nineteen-sixties the directors of the Japanese firm of Honda guessed that the British market was ripe for a lighter machine. They designed a light Honda and introduced it into the British market. The British manufacturers went on placidly producing the type of machine which they had sold successfully for so long. Within five years the market had been virtually captured by Honda and sales of British machines were reduced to a fraction of their former volume. This episode illustrates a weakness in the innovational and creative entrepreneurial outlook among the British manufacturers which can be responsible for a low rate of economic growth if it is widespread throughout a nation.

Thus it is suggested that a high level of anxiety in a nation tends to motivate the population to work both hard and creatively. This leads to efficiency in business enterprise and manifests itself in a high rate of economic growth. Hence the high correlation between national anxiety levels and economic growth rates which was noted at the beginning of this chapter.

CHAPTER 13

A FACTOR-ANALYTIC TREATMENT OF THE PROBLEM

THE theme of this monograph is that a number of epidemiological variables are associated together in such a way that some countries (Austria, Japan, etc.) show a distinctive pattern of high rates of suicide, alcoholism, vehicle accidents and tobacco consumption in conjunction with low rates of mental illness, calorie intake, coronary heart disease and so forth; while in other countries (Ireland, the U.K., etc.) the pattern is reversed. That such a tendency exists is a fact. There are, however, a variety of statistical methods by which the presence of this pattern can be demonstrated. There is much to be said for the view that several of these alternatives are equally reasonable, so that it does not matter greatly which is used. To some psychologists the most obvious method would be to subject all the variables to factor analysis and then interpret the factor which emerged. This approach, however, suffers from the disadvantage that factor analysis is not familiar to many anthropologists, sociologists, geneticists, economists and others who may be interested in the thesis of the differences in national character advanced in this monograph. Even among psychologists the methodology of factor analysis is by no means universally understood. Thus I have felt that to have written the whole of this monograph around an initial factor analysis would have prejudiced its acceptance among those who are unsympathetic to or unfamiliar with the technique, and might have savoured of blinding the reader with science. Accordingly, I have preferred to use the simplest possible statistical method for demonstrating that a particular pattern of epidemiological variables runs consistently through a number of countries. However, there will doubtless be many who would like to see a factor analysis of the data and accordingly such an analysis is presented in this chapter.

The factor analysis is based on the following variables: suicide, mental illness, calorie intake, alcoholism, coronary heart disease and athero-

TABLE 19. THE CORRELATION MATRIX

For eighteen subjects, correlations above 0·47 are statistically significant at the 5 per cent level.

	Rate*	1	2	3	4	5	6	7	8	9	10	11
1. Mental illness	Low	(1·0)	·72	·57	·58	·50	·49	·46	00	·06—	·29—	·21
2. Coronary deaths	Low		(1·0)	·64	·61	·30	·49	·47	—·10	00	·02	—·07
3. Vehicle deaths	High			(1·0)	·79	·44	·14	·20	·51	·08	·31	—·02
4. Calorie intake	Low				(1·0)	·26	·17	·26	·30	·20	·05	—·03
5. Suicides	High					(1·0)	·37	·18	·34	·14—	·15	·19
6. Alcoholism deaths	High						(1·0)	·21	—·20	·19	·01	·12
7. Cigarette consumption	Low							(1·0)	—·26	·02	·22	·15
8. Ulcer deaths	High								(1·0)	—·54	—·13	—·23
9. Murders	High									(1·0)	—·36	·12
10. Celibacy	High										(1·0)	—·08
11. Hypertension	Low											(1·0)

* Variables which loaded negatively on the first factor have been reversed in order that the existence of a general factor might be shown clearly in the correlation matrix by the absence of any large negative correlations. These variables are marked as having a low rate.

sclerosis, vehicle accident deaths, cigarette consumption, ulcers, hypertension, celibacy and murder. The questionnaire results are omitted because they are only available for a limited number of countries. The correlation matrix is shown in Table 19. The matrix was factor analysed by principal component analysis with unities in the main diagonal. There were four factors with latent roots greater than unity and these are given in Table 20. Only the first factor will be discussed, since the proportion of the variance contributed by the others is small.

This first factor seems to be our anxiety factor, since the first seven variables which we have already argued are functions of anxiety are all well loaded on it. In fact, the factor analysis gives substantially the same results as the simpler form of analysis used hitherto. The first seven variables are well loaded on the factor but the other four variables (ulcers, hypertension, celibacy and murder) do not load appreciably on the factor. Thus, the result of the factor analysis is much the same as that reached in the previous chapters.

The factorial analysis also provides an alternative method for ranking the nations for their anxiety level. This involves the calculation of the factor scores of the nations on the basis of the seven variables appreciably loaded on the first factor, instead of only on four of them (suicide, mental illness, alcoholism and calorie intake) as used previously. The calculation of the factor scores has been carried out in the following steps. The

TABLE 20. FACTOR LOADINGS OF INTERNATIONAL DATA

Variables	Rate	Unrotated factor loadings			
		I	II	III	IV
Mental illness	Low	·87	−·12	·28	·06
Coronary deaths	Low	·84	−·20	·02	·32
Vehicle deaths	High	·82	·32	−·38	−·07
Calorie intake	Low	·79	·26	−·17	·15
Suicides	High	·60	·22	·18	−·39
Alcoholism deaths	High	·52	−·24	·43	−·03
Cigarette consumption	Low	·49	−·72	−·23	00
Ulcer deaths	High	·19	·72	−·48	−·18
Murders	High	·07	·59	·63	−·04
Celibacy	High	·03	−·23	−·71	−·37
Hypertension deaths	Low	·11	−·27	·33	−·80
Eigenvalues		3·69	1·86	1·76	1·10
Variance (%)		33·5	16·9	16·0	10·1

TABLE 20a. RANK ORDERS OF NATIONS ON ANXIETY ON THE
BASIS OF TWO DIFFERENT RANKING METHODS

Rank order based on four original variables	Rank order based on factor scores
1. Austria	1. Japan
2. Japan	2. Germany
3. Germany	3. Austria
4. France	4. Italy
5. Italy	5. France
6.5 Belgium	6. Belgium
6.5 Denmark	7. Netherlands
8. Switzerland	8. Norway
9. Norway	9. Finland
10. Finland	10. Denmark
11. Sweden	11. Switzerland
12. U.S.A.	12. Sweden
13. Australia	13. Australia
14. Netherlands	14. Canada
15. Canada	15. U.S.A.
16. New Zealand	16. New Zealand
17. U.K.	17. U.K.
18. Ireland	18. Ireland

nations were ranked on each of the seven variables; the rankings were multiplied by the factor loadings; the products were summed for each nation; and the nations were finally re-ranked on the basis of the summed products. This procedure gives the rank order shown in Table 20a; and for purposes of comparison, the previous rank order is also given in this table. The factor scores method gives a broadly similar rank order, with only the Netherlands moving more than four places from one ranking to the other.

The argument that national anxiety levels assessed on the basis of epidemiological measues are significantly correlated with national anxiety levels derived from questionnaire results, taken from university students, can be checked with the new ranking. The nations' ranks on the basis of the factor scores gives a correlation of $+0 \cdot 73$ ($P < 0 \cdot 02$) with the questionnaire results. The alternative ranking also correlates significantly with rates of economic growth: the correlation is $+0 \cdot 82$ ($P < 0 \cdot 001$). Both correlations are substantially the same as those given by the former ranking method.

It is difficult to tell which of the two rank orders is the better, i.e. closer to the true rank order, and to preserve consistency we shall continue to use the original order in subsequent chapters. It is doubtful whether it would make any material difference which of the two rank orders is used.

CHAPTER 14

FURTHER INSTANCES OF THE
ANXIETY FACTOR

Up to this point we have been concerned with only one set of countries. The reader may wonder whether the correlations could not have arisen as a result of some extraordinary sort of fluke and if we could not check the existence of the national anxiety factor by taking other groups of countries. Surely it is the hallmark of science that observations should be repeatable?

Such a view is frequently held but is not necessarily correct. The possibility that our anxiety factor might occur elsewhere needs consideration from both a technical and a theoretical point of view. Theoretically, our thesis does not require that the factor should emerge in other groups of countries, or of areas within countries, or of the same countries at a different period of time. This should become clear enough if we consider some examples. Suppose that all the data existed for the various republics which make up the Soviet Union. Suppose further that in this sample we found a positive correlation between calorie intake and alcoholism, instead of our own negative correlation, such that people in the republics in the far north consumed both more calories and more alcohol than those in the south. Such a correlation could in this instance be plausibly interpreted as a result of the extreme cold of the north motivating the inhabitants of those desolate parts to take in more calories both in the form of solid food and alcohol. None of this would invalidate our own interpretation of anxiety as the factor underlying our own set of intercorrelations. It would simply mean that where other conditions, such as extreme variations in temperature, are operating, anxiety became relatively unimportant as a determinant of our variables. It may be only where these other conditions are held fairly constant, as in our own set of advanced countries lying in the temperate zone, that anxiety becomes a significant determinant of our epidemiological variables.

This point may be a difficult one to some readers and bears some discussion. Our eighteen countries comprise a particular group on which our measures yield a general factor. The contribution of the general factor to the variance naturally depends on the particular set of cases. Our model here is similar to that of the contribution of heredity to intelligence test results. It is now generally appreciated that this depends upon the characteristics of the sample of subjects and will vary to some degree from one group of subjects to another. It is agreed by those who have paid attention to the matter that in advanced Western societies individual differences in intelligence are largely determined by inheritance. In this sense inheritance is the principal cause of differences in intelligence in advanced society. (Just as anxiety, according to the arguments we have deployed, is an important cause in advanced societies of national differences in suicides, calorie intake and so forth.) But this does not mean that heredity will always be found the most important determinant of differences in intelligence in all societies or at all periods of history. On the contrary, where environmental conditions are more varied within a society (e.g. only some people are taught to read and so on), heredity becomes less important and certain environmental conditions can become the principal cause of differences in intelligence. But such a demonstration for, say, classical Athens would not in the least invalidate the view that among advanced Western countries it is heredity that is the principal cause of differences between people in intelligence. Thus we see here that the importance of heredity as a cause of the differences between people in intelligence varies with the circumstances.

This point is now generally appreciated, at least by psychologists. The same principle applies to our factor and its interpretation in terms of anxiety. Thus our contention has been that at the present time national anxiety levels are an important cause of the differences between the advanced nations in their incidence of suicide, alcoholism, etc., but this does not imply that anxiety need be an important determinant of these things in all circumstances, nor even that these national characteristics should be always expected to intercorrelate. The crucial point here is that we do not know all the conditions affecting our variables. This makes it impossible to predict precisely what pattern would be present in other circumstances. Thus our thesis is not vulnerable to any failure to find that the anxiety factor is less significant (i.e. accounted for much less of the variance) in other sets of data. The anxiety factor could be absent; or it could account for such a low percentage of the variance as to be either barely discernible or even, because of the unreliability of the data, completely indiscernible.

It may be thought that our theory is somewhat elusive, capable of explaining significant correlations where they appear but unembarrassed when they do not. But such a view would only be taken by those who think that theories in the social sciences should consist of laws of the same simple kind as occur in the physical sciences, that is universal associations between a small number of known variables. Admittedly, a good number of social scientists do seem to believe this, but it is doubtful whether this is the right view of theory in social science. The type of theory presented in this monograph is more akin in its logical properties to Darwin's theory of evolution than to the classical theories of physics. It shares with evolutionary theory the two important characteristics that it cannot yield precise predictions and that the observations which follow from the theory are difficult, if not impossible, to repeat.

For a theory which can offer neither predictions nor repeatability to claim to be within the realm of science may seem preposterous to those who have accepted the criteria of a scientific theory frequently laid down by philosophers. However, consideration of Darwin's theory will confirm that it cannot claim either of these properties. We cannot predict from evolutionary theory what forms of life will exist a million years hence. Or granted that man and the apes are structurally similar, we cannot predict that detailed investigation will reveal that man evolved from the apes, or that the two have a common ancestor. There could equally well be convergent strands of ancestors which once differed much more considerably from each other (as occurred with the apparently similar marsupial and placental carnivores). Thus the theory can explain a number of possibilities, whatever they should turn out to be. The reason for this is that, although the principles of the theory are simple enough, in their application they interact with a number of variables some of which are unknown and some of which have modes of operation not fully understood. This makes precise prediction impossible. All that we can say from such a theory is that some events are possible and likely while others are unlikely or even impossible. This makes theories of the Darwinian type weaker than the theories of physics, but it does not mean that they are without explanatory value.

Not only is Darwin's theory without precise predictive value. It is also practically impossible to repeat. Theoeretically, it could be repeated by putting some amoeba on a planet resembling the Earth and in some thousand millions of years time some more complex forms of life should have evolved. Darwin's theory yields a clear prediction here, but only of a rather vague kind, and one that is technically somewhat difficult to demonstrate. It has been cogently argued by Hayek (1964) that all theories in the social sciences are of this kind and our own theory certainly conforms to some degree to this model.

Actually although our own theory belongs to the same genre as Darwin's, it does have more predictive power. For instance, our theory certainly predicts that among the eighteen nations the prevalence of anxiety neurosis should be well correlated with the national anxiety levels. This prediction cannot be tested at the present time because there are not enough reliable statistics for the prevalence of anxiety neurosis in different countries. However, this is merely a technical difficulty and a precise prediction is there. This is probably more than can be derived from evolutionary theory.

There is a further respect in which our own theory belongs to the genre of evolutionary theory and this is that it can predict what will not happen more precisely than what will happen. Darwin's theory is particularly strong in predicting that a large number of things cannot happen, e.g. the birth of unicorns, gryphons, pigs with wings, etc., though it is much weaker in predicting what will happen. On the positive side it can only predict a range of possibilities. Our own theory is similar. We can predict that our indices of anxiety will not be found systematically correlated in the opposite directions from those presented earlier in this monograph. However, even this negative prediction is subject to some reservations. It would depend upon the group of countries or areas being relatively homogeneous: it would no doubt be possible to obtain a group of countries showing a positive correlation between, say, suicide and psychosis rates if some of the countries were advanced and others so poor that they had no records of either. It should perhaps also be noted that there could well be particular instances of societies where our associations do not hold. For example, it is by no means impossible that some community may encourage suicide as a way of expiating failure and at the same time maintain an absolute taboo on alcoholic inebriation. This would be a particular exceptional instance but not a systematic correlation against our thesis.

*   *   *   *   *

Thus the characteristics of the Darwinian type of theory are that it cannot yield precise predictions of what will happen, although it is somewhat stronger in predicting what will not happen. Further, it is technically very difficult to repeat the observations which the theory attempts to explain, although this is in a certain sense only a technical difficulty and in principle the operation of the theory of evolution is predictable elsewhere than on Earth.

Our own theory presented in this monograph shares these two features. For instance, we can certainly predict that our indices of anxiety would not be systematically correlated in the opposite direction among the various provinces which comprised the ancient Roman Empire. We can even predict that the same anxiety factor might well emerge. While these predictions would be extraordinarily difficult to test, it may seem that there should be other samples of countries where these technical difficulties would be much less extreme. In point of fact the difficulties of showing the factor elsewhere are formidable but such evidence as it has proved possible to collect is presented in the remainder of this chapter. It may seem that the communist block or the South American republics would be possibilities, but in both cases the number of countries is small and the data are fragmentary and suspect. Another possibility is to use the Western nations at a different historical period. A certain amount of data was collected for the latter part of the nineteenth century by Durkheim, although it is not by

TABLE 21. RELATION BETWEEN SUICIDE AND INSANITY IN DIFFERENT EUROPEAN
COUNTRIES (1866–76) (rho = −0·40)

	Insanity per 100,000	Suicides per 1,000,000
Wurtemburg	215	180
Scotland	202	35
Norway	185	85
Ireland	180	14
Sweden	177	85
U.K.	175	70
France	146	150
Denmark	137	277
Belgium	134	66
Bavaria	98	86
Cisalpine Austria	95	122
Prussia	86	133
Saxony	84	272

any means complete. Nevertheless, some of it does bear on our thesis. For instance, he presented the statistics for the suicide and psychosis rates for a number of countries for the years 1866–75. The full data are shown in Table 21. It will be seen that there is some tendency for the two to be negatively associated, as in our own sample. A century ago, as today, the U.K., Ireland, Norway and Sweden had the low-anxiety pattern of high psychosis and low suicide, while Germany and Austria had the reverse pattern indicating high anxiety. The correlation is -0.40, which is not statistically significant, although it is much the same as the correlation (-0.50) between the same two measures among our eighteen countries for 1960. This makes it look as if the same factor might well emerge in Europe in the second half of the last century, if only the rest of the data were available to make up the correlation matrix.

Another possibility for finding the factor elsewhere is to consider regions within countries. Does not our theory demand that the rates of suicide, psychosis, etc., should be correlated within countries as well as among countries? The answer to this must be "not necessarily", at least not to any significant extent, for the existence of the expected correlations would depend upon the variation in anxiety level among the regions within a country. If the variations in anxiety are slight, as would be expected in a country which is culturally, climatically and racially homogeneous, then the correlations would only be low or even, due to the unreliability of the statistics, non-existent. We are thus in the position that finding such correlations within countries would strengthen our theory, but the failure to find them would not weaken it.

In any case the data for regional variations within countries are hard to come by, especially for calorie intake. However, some evidence does exist. Data for suicide and alcohol consumption in the different departments in France were assembled by Durkheim for the eighteen-seventies. His results are shown in Fig. 7. Durkheim asserted that it was obvious from inspection that the two were unrelated, which may seem curious in view of the heavy concentration of suicide and alcoholic intake in Normandy and the Île de France and the low incidence of both in the Massif Centrale. Since what may seem obvious to one observer is less clear to another, the correlation has been calculated and comes out at $+0.41$, which is significant at the 1 per cent level. This result is, of course, in accord with our theory.

These results are fragmentary and necessarily so because it has proved

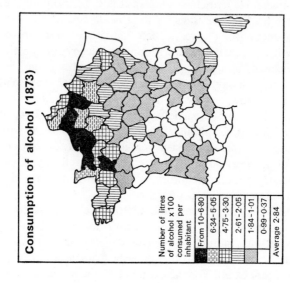

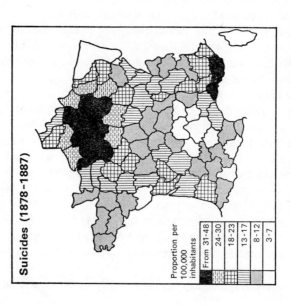

Fig. 7. Distribution of suicides and alcohol consumption in France in latter half of nineteenth century (from Durkheim, 1897).

extraordinarily difficult to find any other set of cases on which data for anything like the full complement of our variables exist. The closest approximation to a full set of data seems to be the different states which comprise the United States of America. Even here the data are not complete, since no figures apparently exist for the calorie intake or the tobacco consumption in the individual states, nor are there any questionnaire results from representative samples of the population. Nevertheless, there are data for a sufficient number of the variables to make an examination of their intercorrelations worthwhile.

The states have been treated in exactly the same way as the countries. The "subjects" comprise the forty-nine mainland states in the year 1956 and the variables were first calculated as rates per 100,000 population. The variables were then intercorrelated and the resulting matrix is shown in Table 22. The correlation matrix was then factored by the maximum likelihood method described by Hemmerle (1965).

Five factors were extracted and the loadings of the variables on these are shown in Table 23. The first factor seems best interpreted as a factor of age, the proportion of old people in some states being higher than in others. It will be noted that many of the variables are highly associated with age. Seven of the nine are deaths of one kind or another. When there is a higher proportion of old people in a state, there naturally tends to be a higher proportion of deaths from alcoholism, coronary heart disease, duodenal ulcers, and hypertension. There are also more suicides, since these are most frequent among old people (Stengel, 1964). Celibacy has a small positive loading, since this term in this set of data includes all those who are not married, including the widowed and divorced, and there are more of these among old people. There is a high negative loading with deaths from vehicle accidents, which is explicable because it is well established that older people have less car accidents (e.g. Eysenck, 1965). Finally, there is a negative loading with murder and this is also explicable because murder, like other crimes, tends not to be committed so frequently by old people. Thus all the variables seem to fit an age interpretation. In order to check this, the percentage of the population aged over 65 was calculated for each state, and these percentages correlated with the scores on the factor. The correlation is +0·50 (significant at the 1 per cent level), which confirms the age interpretation.

It may be wondered why age appears here as the first factor but did not appear among the group of eighteen nations. The chief reason is probably

TABLE 22. CORRELATION MATRIX FROM U.S. DATA

	1	2	3	4	5	6	7	8	9
1. Celibacy		−0·11	−0·06	0·01	0·04	0·25	−0·22	−0·12	0·02
2. Car deaths			−0·06	−0·31	−0·71	−0·42	0·67	0·20	−0·61
3. Suicides				0·31	0·15	−0·06	−0·35	−0·24	0·29
4. Alcoholism					0·44	0·68	−0·12	0·10	0·61
5. C.H.D.						0·59	−0·59	0·18	0·69
6. Psychosis							−0·14	0·40	0·57
7. Murder								0·45	−0·54
8. Hypertension									−0·04
9. Ulcers									

that the variables in the matrix are not the same. The variables in the group of nations include some which are not related strongly to age, such as calorie intake and tobacco consumption, whereas these are absent in the American data. The greater proportion of variables associated with age would naturally make age a factor of greater significance in the American results.

Turning now to the second factor, two interpretations may be suggested. One is that this is a factor of the proportion of Negroes in each state, and the other that it represents extraversion. These two interpretations are not of course incompatible and would amount to the same thing if Negroes tend, on average, to be more extraverted than Caucasians.

Taking first the percentage of Negroes in the population it should be noted that there are considerable differences in this percentage from one state to another. The extremes range from 0·04 per cent in North Dakota to 82·7 per cent in Mississippi. With such a wide variation one would expect this to be an important factor if Negroes differ from Caucasians in their propensity to die from several of the conditions represented in the matrix. This seems to be the case.

The data to support this conclusion are shown in Table 24. The variable with the highest (negative) loading is hypertension deaths, and the incidence of these is more than twice as common among Negroes as Caucasians. This is a frequent finding. For instance, in South Africa deaths from hypertension in 1960 were 19·5 per 100,000 among Negroes and 12·3 per 100,000 among Caucasians (*U.N. Demographic Yearbook 1966*). The

TABLE 23. THE FACTOR LOADINGS OF THE U.S. VARIABLES

Variables	Factors				
	1	2	3	4	5
Alcoholism and cirrhosis deaths	0·71	−0·20	0·55	−0·20	−0·01
Car deaths	−0·72	−0·35	0·19	−0·14	0·30
Celibacy	0·18	0·12	0·01	0·50	0·42
C.H.D. deaths	0·85	0·04	−0·32	−0·12	−0·14
Hypertension deaths	0·11	−0·89	−0·34	−0·12	−0·05
Murders	−0·58	−0·69	0·28	0·04	−0·14
Psychosis rate	0·81	−0·43	0·13	0·25	0·06
Suicides	0·21	0·31	0·21	−0·56	0·31
Ulcer deaths	0·81	0·13	0·07	−0·16	−0·07

TABLE 24. RACIAL DIFFERENCES IN EPIDEMIOLOGICAL VARIABLES

	Rates per 100,000 pop. (1956)	
	White	Non-white
Hypertension deaths	5·8	12·4
Homicides	2·3	23·3
Motor accident deaths	23·3	26·8
Cirrhosis deaths	11·0	8·5
Suicides	10·8	3·8
C.H.D. deaths	269·1	144·4
Hospitalised psychosis*	412·5	742·5

SOURCES: *Vital and Health Statistics*, Series 20, no. 2.
Mortality Trends in the U.S. 1954–63.
Characteristics of Patients in Mental Hospitals (1965).
National Center for Health Statistics Washington 1966. Series 12, no. 3.
*The hospitalised psychosis figures are approximate.

same difference has been found by investigators in the United States (Schulze and Schwab, 1936; Kroeber, 1948; Lennard and Glock, 1957).

The next highest loading, also negative, is the deaths from murder. Here again death from this cause is considerably more frequent among Negroes. As may be seen in the table, in 1956 the death rate was slightly over 1000 per cent higher among Negroes than among Caucasians. With such a large difference, it naturally follows that, as Radzinski (1959) has observed, "there is a rather striking direct relationship between homicide and the concentration of Negroes in a community". A similar pattern occurs in South Africa, where the murder rate among Negroes is typically around six times that among Caucasians (*U.N. Demographic Yearbooks*). Thus the high loading of murder on the factor accords well with the interpretation that it reflects the percentage of Negroes.

The variable with the third highest loading is the hospitalised psychosis rate. This again is negative, and once more the rate among Negroes is around double that in Caucasians. The next variable is deaths from vehicle accidents. This is also negative and again higher among Negroes. The fifth variable is the suicide rate. This is the first positive loading, and the first variable for which Negroes have a lower incidence than Caucasians. As can be seen in Table 24, the proportion of Negro suicides is about a third of that of Caucasians. The sixth highest variable is deaths from liver cirrhosis. This is a negative loading and is the first which is not consistent with the interpretation, since deaths from liver cirrhosis are lower among Negroes than Caucasians. However, the loadings are now becoming low and there may be some contaminating influence accounting for this discrepancy. Finally, the positive loading of deaths from atherosclerosis, though very low, is in the direction demanded by the interpretation, since deaths from this cause are less common among Negroes.

While the evidence for an interpretation of the factor as the percentage of Negroes seems strong, it has been checked by calculating the percentage of Negroes in each state and correlating these percentages with the state's scores on the factor. The correlation is -0.78 and is statistically significant at the 0.1 per cent level. This result confirms our interpretation of the factor.

The other possible interpretation of factor two is that it is a factor of introversion. There is a negative loading with deaths from vehicle accidents, and there is fairly strong evidence for an association between introversion and careful driving (Drew *et al.*, 1958; Eysenck, 1965). There is a negative loading with deaths from hypertension, and Cattell and Scheier (1959) have reported a relationship between extraversion and high blood pressure (although, as noted in Chapter 9, two studies fail to confirm this result). Thirdly, there is the high negative loading of murder. The literature on the personality of murderers is limited, but it would not seem surprising if, in common with other criminals, they tended to be extraverted. Some confirmatory evidence is available from a study of Kahn (1965), who factor analysed thirty-nine ratings of various kinds on forty-three murderers pleading insanity. This is admittedly not a random sample of murderers. However, the factor analysis yielded a factor which the author labelled "hostile-aggressive", which is probably a facet of extraversion. Another study of a random sample of 241 murderers diagnosed a propensity "to externalise their aggression" (Pittman and Handy, 1964). Such a result may seem little short of tautology, but once again the description resembles extraversion.

There is a paucity of evidence on the relation of extraversion to the two other factors which load strongly on the factor, namely chronic hospitalised psychosis and suicide. The negative loading of deaths from liver cirrhosis seems contrary to an introversion–extraversion interpretation, since alcoholics appear to be more introverted than the normal population (Eysenck and Eysenck, 1964, p. 16). However, the introversion–extraversion interpretation of factor two seems a good deal less strong than an interpretation in terms of the percentage of Negroes. It is offered more in the spirit of a possibility for further investigation. Obviously a direct study of the average extraversion scores among Negroes would be one of the first steps in such an investigation.

We now come to the third factor, and this is the one which seems to have the appearance of anxiety. All the variables have loadings compatible with this interpretation, with the exception of the psychosis rate. The loadings of the rates of vehicle deaths, suicides, alcoholism and murder are positive and the deaths from atherosclerosis negative. The only anomaly is the positive loading of the psychosis rate. However, the loading is small and can be attributed to the swamping of the anxiety factor, among this set of variables and states, by the more powerful factors of age and the percentage of Negroes, which lead to positive correlations between the psychosis rate and several of the other indices of anxiety. The rather high negative loading of hypertension deaths on the factor does not seem of great significance one way or the other as far as the interpretation in terms of anxiety is concerned, since the relationship between hypertension and anxiety is itself unclear.

Thus it seems reasonable to conclude that the anxiety factor has been replicated among the states of the United States of America. It must be admitted that the factor emerges less strongly among this group of states. However, this is to be expected where other powerful influences on the variables are present, as has been argued earlier in this chapter. All our thesis demands is that some trace of the anxiety factor should be present in other samples of states, and this prediction has been confirmed among the American states.

CHAPTER 15

SOME DETERMINANTS OF NATIONAL
ANXIETY LEVELS

THE influences responsible for national differences in anxiety present an intriguing problem. No doubt each nation has its own particular pattern of historical experiences which may have raised or lowered the anxiety level of its population. Because of their unique nature, such influences are difficult, if not impossible, to attack by the canons of scientific method. Nevertheless, some attempt must surely be made to come to grips with the problem of the causes of national anxiety levels. The influences affecting personality characteristics are commonly differentiated into environmental and hereditary and we shall follow this distinction, considering environmental determinants of national anxiety levels in this and the subsequent chapter and turning finally to the possibility of an inherited factor.

We have already considered two conditions which might reasonably be supposed to affect national anxiety levels, namely the level of affluence and the amount of urbanisation. These were considered in Chapter 2 in our initial discussion of the interpretation of the factor. It will be recalled that there was no significant association between national anxiety levels and *per capita* incomes; the two least affluent countries of our group, Ireland and Japan, are at opposite extremes in anxiety, while the most affluent country, the United States, falls in the middle range.

Nor was there any significant relation between national anxiety level and the degree of urbanisation. The two countries with the lowest anxiety levels, Ireland and the U.K., are at opposite extremes of urbanisation; while at the same time there are both comparatively urbanised (Germany) and comparatively agricultural (Italy) countries in the high anxiety group. Thus we must conclude that neither the degree of affluence nor the extent of industrialisation or urbanisation are significant factors affecting national anxiety levels.

119

The only other writers to have considered the existence of national differences in anxiety seem to be Cattell and Scheier (1961), who collected anxiety questionnaire scores from university students in seven countries in the late nineteen-fifties and found the following rank order of countries, from high anxiety to low: Poland, France, Japan, Italy, Norway, the U.K. and the United States. They suggested that the anxiety level could be explained in terms of the political stability or instability of the countries. A high degree of political instability in the recent past, characteristic of Poland, France and Japan, might tend to make the population anxious, while the greater stability of the U.K. and the United States might give the population a greater sense of security, and hence reduces the anxiety level.

Our own estimates of the anxiety levels of all the advanced Western countries seem to go some way to substantiate the view Cattell and Scheier put forward. In particular, Ireland, New Zealand, Canada and Australia now emerge as low-anxiety countries and Germany as a high-anxiety country. These results seem to fit this thesis reasonably well. The high-anxiety countries (Austria, Japan, Germany, France and Italy) have suffered major military defeats and occupation by foreign powers, drastic changes of constitution, execution and imprisonment of political leaders, and serious debasement of the currency. The French franc has been devalued eighteen times since 1918. The prospect of one's savings vanishing overnight may well be conducive to the elevation of anxiety.

In contrast, the low-anxiety countries (Ireland, the U.K., New Zealand, Canada) do not seem to have undergone the same traumas. None of them has suffered military defeat or such severe debasement of the currency. It is true that Ireland had a civil war in the early nineteen-twenties, but this was almost forty years before the date of collection of our data and it seems doubtful whether its traumatic effect would have been comparable to the destruction suffered by the high-anxiety countries in the 1939–45 war.

Thus Cattell and Scheier seem to have a good point in noting the association between national anxiety levels and political instability. On the other hand, we may question whether there is a simple one-way causation, with political instability simply increasing anxiety, as these authors suggest. Such a thesis raises the problem of the causes of the political instability in certain countries and prompts the question of whether there may not be personality and temperamental national differences which themselves make some countries more politically unstable than others.

Such an interpretation gains further force when we recall the association between anxiety and aggression reviewed in Chapter 7 on accident proneness. Anxiety can motivate aggression, and it does not seem impossible that political instability could result from a high level of aggression in a country. Thus, it could be reasonably maintained that Germany, Japan and Italy have only themselves to thank for their political instability, since if they had not embarked on aggressive programmes of military conquest they would not have suffered the subsequent political, social and constitutional disruptions and instability. The same may be said of the frequent changes of constitution in France. Is it not likely that these are partly caused by the volatile temperament of the people? Military aggression and social chaos are surely not events which just happen to certain unfortunate countries, as the Cattell and Scheier view implies, but things which the people have themselves brought about because of their own qualities of personality and temperament. If this argument is correct, political instability comes to look less convincing as a cause of national anxiety levels and begins to look more like a consequence of high anxiety in a population. Such a view does not of course imply that there may not be a two-way causal interaction between national personality and political stability. Indeed, it seems possible that an anxious population would tend to produce conditions of political instability, and these in turn serve to maintain national anxiety levels or raise them still further.

It would strengthen the case for political instability as a generator of high national anxiety levels if it could be shown that anxiety in a country rises following traumatic political events. Unfortunately, the only component of national anxiety levels for which statistics go back for any length of time is the suicide rates. Examination of these shows that they remain relatively constant over long periods. The rates for the eighteen countries since the 1870's are shown in Table 25. A high degree of constancy over the years is apparent. Possibly the most profound political trauma of this century, which might have been expected to raise national anxiety levels, was the First World War. In the Edwardian world there was a widespread and apparently justifiable belief in human progress and perfectability. Major wars seemed to belong to the past and Western civilisation to be secure and unchallenged, either from within or without. This stable world has been shattered by the First World War, the Russian Revolution, the depression, the rise of socialism, communism and fascism, the Second World War, the atom bomb and the cold war. Yet these do not seem to have had any appreciable effect on national anxiety levels, as assessed by the suicide rates, which in most countries have remained at much the same level since 1910. It is true that there was some general rise from 1871 to 1910, but this is largely due to the increasing expectation of life in this period (as Swinscow, 1951, has shown). Since the majority of suicides are committed by old people, an increasing expectation of life automatically gives rise to a higher incidence of suicide.

TABLE 25. INTERNATIONAL SUICIDE RATES OVER THE LAST CENTURY
(per 100,000 population)

Country	1871–5	1910–14	1926–30	1960
Australia	—	12·8	12·2	10·6
Austria	9·4	25·7	35·3	23·1
Belgium	6·9	14·0	15·8	14·6
Canada	—	—	—	7·5
Denmark	25·8	18·6	16·8	20·3
Finland	3·1	9·6	16·8	20·5
France	15·0	22·2	19·1	15·8
Germany	13·4*	21·9	25·9	19·5
Ireland	1·4	3·2	3·3	3·0
Italy	3·5	8·5	9·6	6·3
Japan	—	19·0	20·6	21·6
Netherlands	3·6	6·2	7·1	6·6
New Zealand	—	12·1	13·9	9·7
Norway	7·3	6·0	6·5	6·5
Sweden	8·1	17·6	14·5	17·4
Switzerland	21·6	23·7	25·3	19·0
U.K.—England and Wales	6·6	9·9	12·3	11·2
Scotland	3·5	5·7	9·8	7·8
U.S.A.	8·0	15·4	15·0	10·6

*Prussia only.

We are therefore inclined to doubt whether political upheaval is likely to be a major factor in determining national anxiety levels. There is a good deal it does not appear to account for. It does not seem especially convincing as an explanation of the low anxiety in Ireland, whose rebellion and civil war would seem to have entailed more instability than has been experienced in the course of this century in the U.K., New Zealand, Australia, Canada and possibly some other countries which have higher anxiety levels. Nor does it seem able to explain why the anxiety levels in

1910 should have been so much higher in Austria, Switzerland, Germany and France than in the U.K., Ireland, Australia and New Zealand. It therefore seems necessary to look elsewhere for the factors determining national anxiety levels.

It might be argued that strong Roman Catholicism has tended to lower anxiety in some countries. It was suggested by Freud (1919) that religion reduces people's anxieties, since it gives them comfort and a secure frame of reference for behaviour and belief, and thereby reduces uncertainties and anxieties. Weber (1904) suggested that Catholicism reduced anxiety more effectively than Protestantism because Protestantism thrusts more personal responsibility on the individual and this increases anxiety. These seem plausible possibilities. To test them the proportion of Roman Catholics in the population of the eighteen countries have been taken from the Catholic Directories. These have been assembled in Table 3. It will be noted that the figures do not seem to give much support to the thesis that anxiety is low in strongly Roman Catholic countries. While the thesis may seem plausible for Ireland, several predominantly Roman Catholic countries have high anxiety levels, notably Austria, France and Italy. The rank correlation between the proportion of Roman Catholics and the anxiety ranking is $+0 \cdot 15$, which is, of course, both low and totally insignificant. The conclusion seems to be that Roman Catholicism is not an important factor in reducing anxiety levels among this group of countries and at the present time.

Another possibility is that high anxiety levels could be the result of a fast rate of economic growth. We saw in Chapter 12 that there is a close association between national anxiety levels and economic growth rates and argued that the anxiety was responsible for a fast growth rate. But could there not also be a reverse relationship, high growth rates giving rise to anxiety?

This possibility is difficult either to prove or disprove, but there are some considerations which can be set against it. In the first place, we can account for the association between high anxiety levels and high economic growth quite well in terms of anxiety providing the right motivation for growth, as we argued in Chapter 12, so there is no problem needing to be explained. The establishment of this causal relationship does not, of course, preclude the possibility that growth could raise anxiety, but as we have a perfectly sound explanation we are not forced to make this inference.

Secondly, a high growth rate means that the standard of living of the people is rising rapidly. Why should this make people anxious? It seems more probable that those who are being left behind in the economic growth race, such as the British and the Irish, should be the people who would become anxious. It is known that children who are at the bottom of the class tend to feel anxious. It has been found in the U.K. that children at the bottom of a grammar school are more anxious than those at the top of a secondary modern (Callard and Goodfellow, 1962), so that this does not seem to be simply a negative relation between anxiety and intelligence, but an anxiety reaction to failure. Is this not likely to occur on a more extensive scale in the populations of nations? It certainly seems probable that failure is an important cause of anxiety in adults. Of our epidemiological variables, probably the one which has been most investigated in relation to success and failure is suicide. It has several times been shown that the suicide rate goes up in times of economic depression, such as the 1929–30 slump, and goes down in times of boom. Indeed, Swinscow (1951) has estimated that in the U.K. there is a correlation of $+0 \cdot 93$ between the male suicide rate and the numbers of unemployed over the years 1923–47. On this basis we might expect that the comparatively low growth (i.e. depressed) economies of the U.K., Ireland and New Zealand would have the high anxiety levels. Yet the contrary is the case. It is the people in the successful and strong economies of Japan and Germany who have the high anxiety levels, while those in the weak and sluggish economies of the U.K. and Ireland are unanxious.

Furthermore, we have seen from the suicide figures that national anxiety levels have been remarkably constant since 1910. Yet economic growth has everywhere improved greatly in the post-1945 period, largely as a result of the Keynesian revolution in the management of the capitalist economy. By comparison with the post-1945 decades, 1919–39 was a period of economic stagnation in which little economic growth occurred. Yet the universal rise in economic growth rates has not been followed by a rise in anxiety levels. This seems to show as conclusively as can be expected that anxiety does not rise as a result of fast economic growth.

Yet another argument can be drawn from the case of the U.K., which experienced a high rate of economic growth during the industrial revolution and into the second half of the nineteenth century. If this high growth rate had engendered high anxiety, we should expect to find an exceptionally high suicide rate in the U.K. in the eighteen-seventies. Yet the contrary is the case, as may be seen in Table 25. The British suicide rate at that time was less than half that in France and Prussia, and less than a third of that in Switzerland and Denmark.

Our conclusion is that it seems doubtful whether the national anxiety differences can be explained as a result of differences in affluence, degree of urbanisation, political instability, the strength of religious conviction, or the speed of economic growth. It is necessary to look elsewhere for the causes of the national differences in anxiety. In the next two chapters we consider what appear to be stronger possibilities, namely climate and race.

CHAPTER 16

CLIMATIC EFFECTS ON ANXIETY

THE possibility that climate could have an effect on personality takes us into one of the more curious and recondite backwaters of psychology. It is an area where one must expect to encounter cranks and enthusiasts for theories of a bizarre nature. Nevertheless, I hope to establish in this chapter that the theory that climate could affect personality should not be too hastily ruled out of court. There are, of course, a number of possible climatic variables, of which the three most plausible appear to be summer heat, solar radiation and storm frequency (together with the number of electromagnetic long waves). It is not always easy to distinguish these from each other since, for example, populations exposed to hot summers are also exposed to high doses of solar radiation. But for simplicity of exposition we will take them in this order.

1. *Summer Heat*

There seems to be some tendency for the high-anxiety countries to have somewhat warmer climates: this is particularly true of Japan, Italy and France, at one extreme, compared with the U.K. and Ireland at the other. Could there be a tendency for high temperatures to raise anxiety levels?

In the smaller countries, such as Belgium and Denmark, the population is concentrated in a sufficiently small area for it to be possible to measure the temperature to which people are exposed at different months with a considerable degree of accuracy. In the case of the larger countries, such as Canada and the United States, there is much greater variation within the country, so that the problem of measurement becomes more difficult. In spite of this difficulty, a reasonably accurate method of assessing national differences in temperature has been devised by Markham (1942). He took the temperatures for all the principal centres of population in a country and then calculated the overall mean, weighting the population centres according to the actual numbers involved. Thus for Australia he took the temperatures in Sydney, Melbourne, Adelaide, Brisbane, Perth and Hobart. Since there were 1,200,000 people in Sydney in the year Markham made his calculations (1931) and 60,000 in Hobart, Sydney was weighted 20 times Hobart in arriving at the overall temperatures in Australia. Although Markham's year, 1931, is some thirty years before our own year, it seems doubtful whether population shifts have been sufficiently appreciable to invalidate his figures to a very significant degree, and I have therefore used his results as they stand. He used his technique to calculate the mean annual temperature, the temperature of the coldest and hottest months, and the relative humidity of the coldest and hottest months. The results of these calculations are shown in Table 26.

We can now examine the relation between these temperature figures and the national anxiety levels. Correlations have been calculated between the national anxiety levels and the temperature figures and also with the range of temperature between the hottest and the coldest month. These correlations are shown in Table 27. It will be seen that the largest correlation is

TABLE 26. CLIMATIC CONDITIONS
(From Markham, 1942)

	Coldest month		Warmest month		Mean annual temp. °F
	Temp. °F	Relative humidity per cent	Temp. °F	Relative humidity per cent	
Australia	52·0	78	71·0	62	61·8
Austria	30·0	83	67·5	67	49·0
Belgium	35·0	86	63·0	76	48·5
Canada	18·0	82	68·0	72	44·0
Denmark	31·5	88	62·0	75	46·0
Finland	20·0	88	63·0	73	40·4
France	39·0	85	68·0	69	53·0
Germany	32·0	85	65·0	71	48·0
Ireland	43·0	86	60·0	81	50·0
Italy	42·0	75	76·0	59	59·0
Japan	38·0	69	79·0	79	57·8
Netherlands	37·0	89	64·0	76	50·0
New Zealand	48·0	81	63·0	74	55·5
Norway	27·0	84	62·0	70	43·0
Sweden	28·0	86	62·0	68	43·0
Switzerland	32·0	85	65·7	72	48·5
U.K.	40·0	86	61·0	74	49·0
U.S.A.	31·0	77	73·0	69	52·0

with high summer temperatures, i.e. the high-anxiety countries have hotter summers. The second highest correlation is with the range between the hottest and coldest months, i.e. there is a greater range in the more anxious countries. The negative correlation with the coldest month shows a tendency for the more anxious countries to have colder winters.

TABLE 27. CORRELATIONS BETWEEN NATIONAL ANXIETY LEVELS AND
VARIOUS CLIMATIC FACTORS

Temperature variable	Value of rho
Temperature in hottest month	+0·46*
Humidity in hottest month	−0·29
Range of temperature (hottest to coldest)	+0·40*
Temperature in coldest month	−0·23
Humidity in coldest month	−0·23
Mean annual temperature	+0·02

*Significant at 10 per cent level.

The correlations with the hottest month and the range of temperatures do not reach the 5 per cent level of statistical significance (for which the required value of P is 0·47). They are, however, significant at the 10 per cent level and it is suggested that this is sufficient for us to give serious consideration to the possibility that these climatic factors may be involved in the determination of national anxiety levels.*

The thesis that hot summers might raise national anxiety levels is in some ways attractive. It is becoming proverbial that race riots tend to break out in the United States when the temperature rises in the summer and, as we have seen, aggression is one of the reactions to high anxiety. The tendency of hot summers to exacerbate violent inclinations was apparently well known to Shakespeare, since he observed in *Romeo and Juliet* that the Montagus and Capulets were particularly prone to disputes on hot days:

> I pray thee, good Mercutio, let's retire.
> The day is hot, the Capulets abroad,
> And if we meet we shall not scape a brawl;
> For now, these hot days, is the mad blood stirring.

* It is arguable that the nations are not a sample but the complete universe of advanced Western nations and therefore considerations of statistical significance do not apply.

Let us therefore adopt provisionally the thesis that the national anxiety differences are partly caused by the hot summers in the more anxious countries. Such a thesis has several implications, of which three are particularly important. The first is that it should be possible to demonstrate in the laboratory that excessive heat has the effect of raising anxiety. We will consider the evidence for this later in the chapter. A second implication is that the population should become more anxious in the summer months. And thirdly, this seasonal rise in anxiety should be greater in the countries with hotter summers; the reason for this being that the people in the hotter countries would be particularly exposed to the effects of high temperatures during the summer.

Taking first the proposition that the rise in temperature in the spring and summer tends to increase anxiety, it would seem to follow that all our indices of anxiety should be subject to seasonal fluctuations, rising in spring and summer and falling in autumn and winter. Unfortunately, there are certain difficulties with some of our variables. Nevertheless, there are some cases in which the seasonal trends fit the theory reasonably well.

Taking the matter of suicide first, there is a well-known and apparently universal tendency for suicides to increase in the spring and summer. Much evidence was amassed by Durkheim (1897), and subsequent investigations have amply confirmed his conclusions. The seasonal tendency works in reverse in Australia, suicides rising in that country from September to December (Swinscow, 1951). Durkheim estimated that if the year is split into the six coldest and the six warmest months, suicides occurred in a ratio of about two (cold) to three (warm) and asserted that of the many countries and cities he examined there were no exceptions to this rule. The year can be further split into the four seasons, counting winter as December to February; spring as March to May; summer as June to August; and autumn as September to November. On this division, the summer months almost invariably produce the most suicides. One of Durkheim's tables supporting this conclusion is shown in Table 28.

If we grant the previous arguments that suicide is partly determined by anxiety, it seems clear that these figures give some support to the thesis that increasing temperatures raise anxiety levels. It may be of interest to note that such a thesis was put forward towards the end of the last century by Morselli (1879) and Ferri (1887), who explained the rise of both suicide and violence in the summer months in terms of an increase in the excitability of the nervous system, a notion which evidently resembles the

TABLE 28. SEASONAL VARIATIONS IN SUICIDES IN NINETEENTH-CENTURY EUROPE

	Winter	Spring	Summer	Autumn
Denmark (1858–65)	177	284	312	227
Belgium (1841–9)	195	275	301	229
France (1835–43)	201	283	306	210
Saxony (1847–58)	195	281	307	217
Bavaria (1858–65)	192	282	308	218
Austria (1858–9)	185	281	315	219
Prussia (1869–72)	199	284	290	227

SOURCE: Durkheim, 1897.

contemporary concept of anxiety. Durkheim disliked the theory and argued against it on the following grounds. In the first place, he says it must be admitted that some suicides are committed by people in states of nervous excitement, but as many more are committed by people in depressed states. If heat stimulates the overexcited types, it should relieve the depressed types. These two effects should cancel each other out and so there should be no overall tendency for high temperatures to increase suicide rates. However, Durkheim's objection here assumes that there is an equal split between high-anxiety and low-anxiety suicides, and this is a difficult position to sustain. If suicide is mainly a function of high anxiety, as we have argued in Chapter 5, then its tendency to increase in the summer months would fall naturally into place (assuming also that a rise in temperature raises anxiety levels).

Durkheim's next argument is that there are more suicides in the spring than in the autumn, as can be seen from his table, although the temperatures are pretty well the same. We can, however, counter this objection by introducing the well-known satiation effect, according to which any stimulus has a reduced impact after it has been applied for some time. Thus those who live in the vicinity of glue factories, gas works and so forth eventually cease to notice the noxious smells which are so striking to newcomers. Applying this law, people would be well satiated to heat by the time of the autumn, so that in fact a rise in suicides in the spring, a further rise in mid-summer, and a fall to below spring level in the autumn is pretty well exactly what would be expected if the satiation effect is borne in mind.

A third argument marshalled by Durkheim is that there is not a perfect correlation between suicide and temperature. For instance, he observes that in a typical May Prussia, Italy and France have virtually identical suicide rates, but the temperatures range from 50 degrees in Prussia, to 57 degrees in France, to 64 degrees in Italy. In deploying this argument Durkheim is using a favourite strategy of controversialists, consisting of the argument that because one variable is not the sole cause of another it can have no effect on it at all. Naturally, few would be unwise enough to espouse the position that high temperatures are the sole cause of suicide, since on this theory it would be difficult to explain the suicides that occur in mid-winter. Indeed, one wonders why Durkheim did not pursue his own logic to its conclusion and argue that high temperature cannot be a cause of suicide because some suicides do occur in the winter. Such an argument is revealed in its true fatuity when taken to this length. It is now generally recognised that phenomena like suicide have a number of causes (i.e. their incidence is affected by a number of conditions) and that the identification of a particular factor as a cause is inferred from correlational study. Exceptions to a correlation, such as those cited by Durkheim, are due to the effect of some other factors. Thus it seems doubtful whether Durkheim's objections have any substance and we should rather conclude that the suicide data seem to give quite good support to the rising temperature thesis of suicide.

It may be objected that suicides normally begin to rise in the spring, generally reach a maximum in April, May or June, and then decline slightly in July and August. This trend can be seen in Fig. 8. On the other hand, the temperature continues to rise in July and August. Thus temperature and suicide cannot be cause and effect. There are, however, three arguments which could be deployed against this objection. One is the satiation factor, which has just been discussed. It is plausible to suppose that people are fairly well satiated to increasing warmth by June, so that they respond less to the higher temperatures of July and August. A second consideration is that suicide is a once-for-all action and not the kind of thing one can go on doing again and again as the temperature continues to rise. If we suppose that a person is made anxious during the course of the autumn or winter (say by bereavement or bankruptcy) we can assume that he may become predisposed to suicide. The rise in temperature in March and April could then constitute the last straw, raising the anxiety level to the point at which he commits suicide. He cannot then commit suicide again in August. By the time the end of June has been

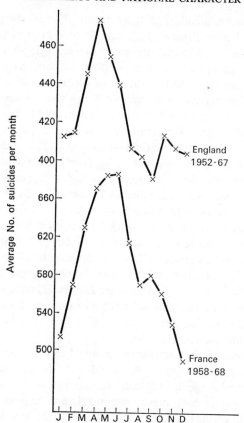

FIG. 8. Seasonal variations in suicides.

reached a good number of those who were predisposed to commit suicide that year would have already done so. On this argument a fall in the July and August suicides would be expected.

Yet a third argument is that although summer temperatures correlate with national anxiety levels, it may not be temperature as such which raises anxiety. There could be some correlate of temperature which is the crucial factor. There are a number of such possibilities. Two of the more obvious are sunlight and radiation. Both of these generally reach their maximum in June in countries in the temperate zone and tend to decline by August. The effect of this is that there is generally a higher correlation between suicide and monthly variations in radiation or sunlight than between suicide and temperature. For example, I have calculated these correlations for England and Wales taking the monthly radiation figures in London given by Brooks (1950) and the total number of suicides over the period 1930–48. The correlations of suicide with radiation are $+0\cdot68$ for males and $+0\cdot63$ for females, whereas those for temperature are only $+0\cdot25$ and $+0\cdot26$. This makes it look as if radiation is the important factor. However, it would seem unwise to regard this as strong evidence for radiation rather than temperature, because of the satiation factor and the once-for-all nature of suicide. Indeed, it may be that epidemiological data are too coarse for it to be possible to isolate what factor associated with rising temperature is the crucial one for raising anxiety. This may well be a problem whose solution requires experimental manipulation of all the possible variables.

Indeed, the problem of determining whether the climatic factor which seems to affect suicide rates is temperature itself, or some correlate of temperature, is extraordinarily complex. Several of those who have considered the question in detail have stressed the importance of different aspects of weather changes. For instance, de Rudder (1952) investigated 200 cases of suicide occurring in 1939 in Frankfurt. He found no relationship with temperature, hours of sunshine, precipitation or atmospheric pressure, but there was a significant tendency for suicides to occur in conjunction with both warm- and cold-weather fronts. The same finding has been reported by Tholuck (1942). A weather front occurs at the boundary of two air masses, and when one air mass replaces another there are changes in temperature, humidity, ozone content, acidity and other chemical and electrical properties of the atmosphere. Any one of these could be the crucial variable affecting people's anxiety level and predisposition to suicide, or it could be the change itself, the particular variable which changes being comparatively unimportant. This would be a plausible view, since the organism tends to be activated by any change in the stimuli impinging on it, and this activation might be expected to increase the level of anxiety. On the other hand, there are weather changes in the autumn as the temperature decreases which do not seem to be accompanied by rises in suicide or other manifestations of anxiety. This seems to suggest that the crucial conditions are connected with a change from cold to warm rather than vice versa.

A further study relating suicide to climatic change has been reported by Rohden (1933) in Switzerland. He noted a significant increase in suicide (and also in crime) at periods when the foehn prevails. The foehn is a warm dry wind which blows in the mountain valleys of Switzerland and the Tyrol. It is said to make people feel irritable, and there is a tradition that juries take a more lenient view of *crime passionelle* committed when the foehn blows. This again would seem to support the theory that it may be the change from cold to warm which raises anxiety, though it would be rash to suggest that the crucial variable is by any means clear.

It seems reasonable to conclude that the rise of suicide rates in the spring and summer may well be the result of increasing temperatures or some related climatic change having the effect of generating anxiety. Now we must ask whether the other indices of anxiety also fluctuate seasonally in the same way? To turn next to the consumption of alcohol, there are some tendencies in this direction. It is useful to consider beer and spirits separately (and wine too in countries where a significant amount of alcohol is drunk in this medium). The association between beer consumption and temperature is remarkably high. Popham (1969) has investigated this association in seven provinces of Canada. If December is omitted because of the distorting effects of purchases for Christmas, the correlations in all seven provinces are above 0·9, indicating an almost perfect association between temperature and beer consumption. The same association exists in England and in California, as may be seen in Fig. 9.

There seems little doubt from these figures that beer drinking does fluctuate seasonally in the way our anxiety theory demands. The fluctuation is sometimes attributed to an increase in thirst with higher temperatures, but this does not seem altogether convincing for the rise in consumption in the spring. The temperature in Ontario in March is only 32·4°F which hardly seems the kind of temperature in which the population are likely to become desperate for a cool beer. Yet the March beer figures are higher than those of January and February. Similarly in the U.K., the March temperature is only 44·2°F. But even if thirst is accepted as a factor, this would not, of course, rule out the possibility that anxiety is also operating to increase beer consumption. However, thirst does not seem convincing as the total explanation and it seems reasonable to conclude that the beer-consumption data give some support to a temperature theory of anxiety.

Turning now to the consumption of spirits, the seasonal fluctuations are less clear. Data for England, Ontario and California are shown in Fig. 10. In all three localities there is heavy buying in October, November and December. Perhaps this may be attributed to accumulating stocks for Christmas revelries, in which the consumption of spirits traditionally takes its place. If these three months are ignored, there is some tendency for consumption to rise with increasing temperatures in the first half of the year. The peak month is March in California and England but does not occur until August in Ontario. This is not inconsistent with our thesis.

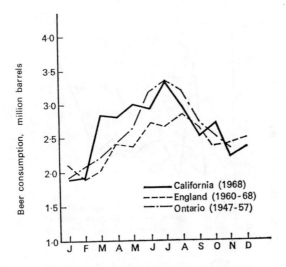

Fig. 9. Seasonal distribution of beer consumption.

March temperatures are higher in California and England than they are in Ontario, so that the peak would be expected to come earlier in the year. Taken as a whole, it would probably be claiming too much to maintain that the spirit figures give any strong support to a seasonal theory of anxiety. On the other hand, it could certainly be worse for the theory if, for instance, they were constant all the year round. Thus at least it seems reasonable to conclude that spirit consumption does not tell crucially against the theory.

The seasonal trends in psychosis are generally expressed as psychiatric admissions. Typically these show the same rise in the spring and summer that occurs with suicide and alcohol consumption, as may be seen from some representative results shown in Fig. 11. Prima facie, these seem evidence against our thesis, since we have taken the position that psychosis is principally a manifestation of low anxiety. But on closer examination it will be seen that the figures are not crucially damaging to our thesis. Our index of national anxiety levels has been largely chronic hospitalised psychosis, not psychiatric admissions. It is the acute psychotics who can frequently be given drug treatments and discharged after a few weeks who

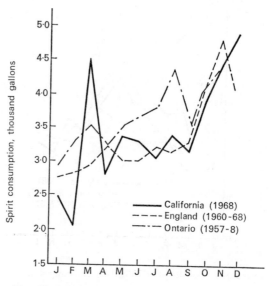

Fɪɢ. 10. Seasonal distribution of spirit consumption.

are often characterised by high anxiety. Thus the tendency for psychiatric admissions to rise in the spring and summer could reflect the increase in anxiety among acute patients and is not inconsistent with a temperature theory of anxiety. What our thesis would seem to predict is that only the low anxiety psychoses would decline in the spring and summer. Unfortunately it is difficult to test this implication because psychotics are not normally differentiated into high- and low-anxiety cases. Furthermore, the low-anxiety cases often develop slowly over a period of years, and it is to a considerable degree a matter of chance when they are finally diagnosed as

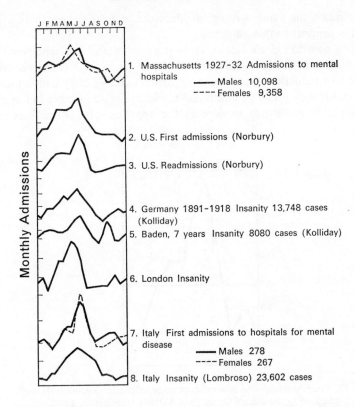

FIG. 11. Seasonal incidence of mental disorders (from Huntington, 1938).

psychotic and admitted to hospital. Perhaps the nearest approximation to high-anxiety psychoses for which it has been possible to find seasonal fluctuations are the mania cases. The central feature of mania is the very high level of excitability which is probably associated with high anxiety. In support of this interpretation, Ström-Olsen and Weil-Malherbe (1958) have reported that patients excrete much larger quantities of adrenaline and noradrenaline during their manic phases, and there is reasonably good evidence that this is a symptom of anxiety. The same result has been reported by Gellhorn and Loofbourrow (1963), who have also found other signs of increased sympathetic reactivity in patients during their manic episodes. Hence manic excitability should increase in the spring and early summer much the same way as suicide. Some results shown in Fig. 12 give some support to this inference.

Turning now to calorie intake, there is a well-established tendency for calorie intake to fall as temperatures rise. This is of course generally ascribed to a reduction in the necessity for maintaining body temperature. However, there could be an additional tendency for an increase in anxiety with higher temperatures to depress the appetite. The two effects are

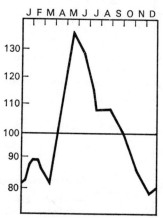

FIG. 12. Four hundred and seventy-two cases of manic-depressive insanity admitted in the excited stage, 1924–8 (from Huntington, 1938).

difficult to distinguish, but at least the evidence is not inconsistent with a causal relationship between high temperature and high anxiety. We are confronted with similar difficulties with vehicle accidents. They too ought to rise in the spring and summer if our theory is correct. However, accidents are so much affected by other seasonal factors such as the number of hours of darkness, the amount of rain, and the increased alcohol consumption over Christmas, that it is virtually impossible to isolate temperature conditions as a factor.

We turn finally to the question of sexual activity. It will be recalled that we suggested in Chapter 11 that there may be a curvilinear relation between anxiety and sexual activity, both very low and very high levels of anxiety tending to reduce the amount of sexual behaviour. If this is so, we might expect an increase in sexual activity accompanying the rise in anxiety in spring and early summer. The occurrence of such an increase is, of course, a well-entrenched popular belief. For instance, the Greek poet Hesiod wrote that "in the active season when summer begins, goats are fattest, wine is at its best, men are weakest, and women most wanton". There is some evidence that this popular belief is well founded. Thus Burt (1944, p. 170) found some very high correlations between the numbers of juvenile sexual offences in London and the mean monthly temperature (0·68), hours of daylight (0·85) and hours of sunshine (0·87). The most extensive investigations of this question are probably those of Huntington (1938), some of whose results are shown in Fig. 13. It will be noted that the number of conceptions rises quite sharply between March and July. The peak month seems to depend on the temperature or some correlate of temperature such as hours of sunshine or daylight, since the peak comes earlier in southern latitudes. The peak occurs in Norway in July, Sweden in June, Belgium in May, Switzerland in May, Northern Spain in April and Southern Spain in February. Similarly, in North America the peak month for conceptions gets progressively earlier as the latitude drops from Ottawa to Florida.

The rise in conceptions in spring and early summer need not necessarily be due to a rise in anxiety or in temperature. Huntington discusses the problem in detail and controls some of the more obvious possibilities, such as a greater number of marriages occurring in the spring. The same seasonal tendency occurs with illegitimate births and also in rats (as may be seen in the figure), which seems to rule out the operation of some form of family planning. Another indication that there is a genuine rise in sexual drive in the spring and summer is the increase in sexual assaults which takes place at this time, as is also apparent in Fig. 13b.

Huntington's conclusion was that conceptions in late spring and early summer entailed births in early spring and that this had adaptive advantages because young babies have less chance of survival in both midsummer (owing to their vulnerability to disease) and mid-winter. Hence human beings have a residual instinctive tendency to mate in late spring, in the same way as many animals do. It is not impossible that this tendency could be mediated by a rise in general nervous excitation, i.e. in anxiety. If this is so, the seasonal variations in conception would also fall into place as part of the rise in anxiety in spring and early summer.

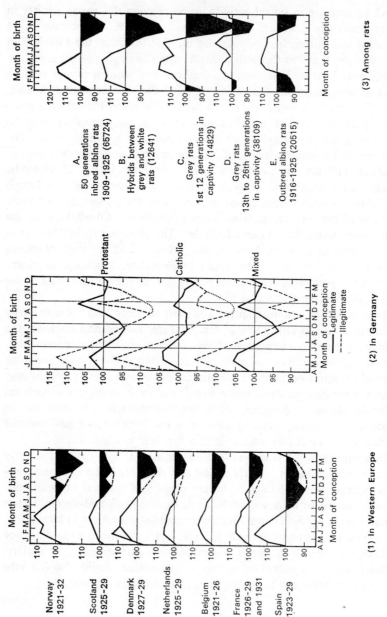

FIG. 13a. Seasonal variation in conceptions (from Huntington, 1938).

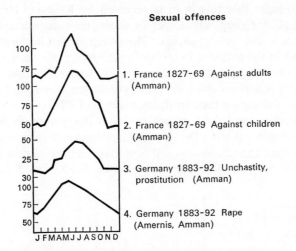

Sexual offences

1. France 1827–69 Against adults
   (Amman)

2. France 1827–69 Against children
   (Amman)

3. Germany 1883–92 Unchastity,
   prostitution (Amman)

4. Germany 1883–92 Rape
   (Amernis, Amman)

Fig. 13b. Seasonal variation in sexual offences (from Huntington, 1938).

*   *   *   *   *

We have seen that several of our epidemiological variables wax and wane in such a way as to suggest that anxiety may rise in the spring and summer and fall in the autumn and winter. We now consider whether there is any evidence on seasonal fluctuations in the anxiety level of individuals which would be consistent with this thesis. The following phenomena will be considered.

1. *Sleep*. It might be expected from our theory that people would sleep more deeply or longer in the autumn and winter than in the spring and summer. If we take the view that the anxiety personality dimension corresponds to the continuum of arousal or activation, as argued in Chapter 3, then we should expect sleep to be deeper where the level of anxiety is low. During sleep all the physiological concomitants of anxiety are reduced, e.g. the respiration rate, palmar conductance, EEG frequency and so forth. The reason for this is that deep sleep is a manifestation of a low level of arousal or activation (e.g. Magoun, 1963; Lindsley, 1951). Furthermore, it is well known that sleep difficulties and disorders are prominent symptoms of anxiety. There are thus fairly good theoretical reasons for expecting that if the general anxiety level rises in the spring and summer, people would sleep more lightly at these times.

Some evidence that this is so is reviewed by Kleitman (1963). Haas (1923) found that sleep was deeper in winter than in summer. Hayashi (1925) has reported that Japanese children sleep longest in the winter, and next longest in the autumn; in the spring their sleep shortens, and in the summer it shortens still further. Erwin (1934) found the same result in a study of 409 American children. Laird (1934) has also found that sleep is poorer in the spring than in the autumn, and Kleitman (1963) found that the inhabitants of the northern part of Norway sleep about an hour less in the summer than in the winter. These seasonal variations in sleep are not confined to man. Slonim and Scherbakova (1954) studied a herd of hamadril monkeys and found that they slept a mean of 14·5 hours in the

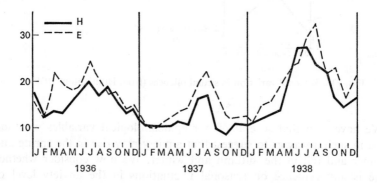

Fig. 14. Seasonal variation in motility during sleep in two girls. Ordinate gives seconds spent in movement per hour, (from Kleitman, 1963).

December to February quarter, but this was reduced to 8·5 hours in May to July.

Kleitman (1963) carried out an extensive study on the seasonal variations in depth of sleep on his two daughters, Hortense and Esther, during 1936–8. He set recording devices under their beds to measure the amount of movement during sleep and used this as an index of the lightness of sleep. On this criterion there is a clear rise from winter and spring, a further rise in summer, and a fall in the autumn. Kleitman's results are shown in Fig. 14. As may be seen, they bear a general resemblance to the seasonal curves for suicide, beer consumption and some of our other epidemiological phenomena. It should be admitted that one might explain these results as a direct effect of cold, since during the winter the outlying parts of the bed are colder and could discourage movement. This interpretation, however, would not seem to explain the longer duration of sleep in the winter, which several investigators have reported. It seems reasonable to conclude that the seasonal variations in depth of sleep fit in quite well with the thesis that anxiety levels rise in the spring and summer.

2. *Body temperature and other physiological indices.* There are several sources of evidence to suggest that body temperature can be used as an index of anxiety. Emotional excitement is frequently accompanied by a rise in body temperature. For instance, Brock (1945) and Kleitman (1945) have both found that subjects' body temperatures rise when they are watching exciting films. Renbourn (1960) found that body temperature (and also pulse rate) rose in boys and young men before taking part in competitive sporting events, when it seems reasonable to assume they were feeling anxious. Another approach can be derived from factor analysis. High body temperature has been found by Cattell and Scheier (1961, p. 208) as part of their anxiety factor, together with higher heart rate, respiration rate, psychogalvanic reactions and other well-established indices of anxiety. It is also well known that body temperature drops in sleep when, as we have just argued, anxiety is reduced. Hence we might expect that there would be a rise in body temperature in the spring and summer.

This matter has been investigated by Kleitman (1963, p. 191), who took no less than 18,000 temperature readings from two subjects. He found that night and early morning temperatures showed no seasonal variation. However, during the day the subjects' temperature rose higher during the summer and "there were many more temperature readings above 99°F . . . for both subjects". A somewhat similar study has been reported by Adam and Ferres (1954) who compared the body temperatures of groups of subjects in Oxford (mean dry bulb temperature 64·1°F) and in Singapore (mean dry bulb temperature 79·9°F). The Singapore subjects had significantly higher body temperatures (0·43°F higher for rectal temperatures, 0·35°F for oral ones) than those at Oxford.

An ingenious study showing the dependence of body temperature and other physiological indices of anxiety on atmospheric temperature has been reported by Damarin (1959). This investigation took the rather unusual form of recording both a variety of physiological measures from a single cancer patient, and climatic variables, three times a week for a period of 20 months. The measures were then factor analysed. One of the factors included atmospheric temperature and several of the other variables loaded on the factor have the appearance of anxiety, particularly the greater excretion of corticosteroids and 17-OH ketosteroids, faster respiration rate and pulse rate, and higher body temperature. The import of these variables being loaded on a single factor is, of course, that on warm days all these indices of anxiety tend to increase. The most straightforward interpretation of the factor seems to be that warm days have the effect of raising the indices of anxiety. The full factor is shown below:

	Loading
Higher corticosteroids in urine	43
Lower glucuronic acid in serum	−40
Higher respiration rate, p.m.	34
Higher pulse rate, p.m.	33
Higher sodium excretion in urine	28
Lower 17-OH ketosteroids	−22
Lower alkaline phosphatase	−20
Higher body temperature, p.m.	15
Higher atmospheric temperature	15
Low humidity (at nearby airport)	−12
Higher total protein measurement	12
Record of more concern and attention by nurse	09

3. *Heat effects on the individual.* We come now to consider more closely the way in which anxiety levels might be raised during spring and summer. One possibility is that heat acts as a stress and thereby has the effect, like other stressful stimuli, of inducing anxiety. It is known that animals, including man, have what Morgan (1965, p. 393) calls a "temperature drive", i.e. "a drive to maintain environmental temperature within certain limits". The centre for temperature regulation is located in the anterior hypothalamus (Hardy *et al.*, 1962). When the temperature rises or falls outside comfortable limits, the hypothalamic temperature centre is activated and the animal is stimulated to reduce or increase its own temperature and bring it back to the comfortable zone. In other words, high and low temperatures constitute a stress from which the animal seeks to escape.

The question of where the comfortable zone is for man has been discussed by Markham (1942). His conclusion was based largely on the work of heating engineers and was that the ideal temperature lies between 60°

the national anxiety levels should subside to the same base. However, this is not necessarily so. It is quite possible that the anxiety-inducing effects of heat stimulation last for some considerable time, perhaps as long as a year. If this is so, the effect of the hot summers of, say, Japan would be to raise the population's anxiety level to a peak, from which it would drop only gradually during the autumn and winter. The Japanese would then be recharged, as it were, when the temperature rises again in the next spring. It is not at all improbable that anxiety behaves in this way since this is probably the principle operating in shock treatment given to psychotics. Many of these patients, as we have seen, have fallen into a state of low anxiety, which they can be shaken out of by shock treatments, such as insulin or electro-convulsive therapy. This is the view of the mode of operation of shock treatment taken by Gellhorn (1957), who presents considerable evidence for a rise in sympathetic tone (increased pulse rate and so forth) following the use of shock therapy. Presumably, the low aroused psychotic has fallen into a low-anxiety rut in which the excessively low anxiety leads to an all pervading apathy and ennui, which itself serves to keep the patient in an unstimulated and low-anxiety condition. This is a kind of vicious circle phenomenon which can be broken by shock treatment. Once the neural structures in the brain stem and thalamic reticular formation are reactivated, the patient's anxiety level is raised to normal levels and thereafter becomes self-sustaining. A detailed substantiation of this interpretation will be found in Gellhorn (1957).

A somewhat similar thesis from a psychological point of view has been advanced by Mednick (1957) to account for the excessively high anxiety levels of anxiety neurotics. Mednick argues that the anxiety neurotic also falls victim of a vicious circle or positive feedback process, in which an excessively high anxiety level tends to be self-sustaining. This is the reverse of the low-anxiety vicious circle which characterises the chronic psychotic. Mednick suggests that when a person gets into a highly anxious state he becomes sensitive to all sorts of minor stimuli which would normally be below threshold. These serve to maintain his high anxiety level. This vicious circle can be broken by the tranquilliser drugs in much the same way as the opposite kind of vicious circle of some psychotic states can be broken by shock therapy.

If this theory is accepted, it would seem that the Japanese, Italians and others exposed to high summer temperatures may in effect be given annual shock treatments which serve to keep their anxiety at a high level for the remainder of the year. The Irish and British are comparatively protected from these annual shock treatments and so their anxiety is maintained throughout the year at a lower level.

Our thesis does not, of course, depend upon Gellhorn's theory of shock treatment being correct and our purpose is only to show that the view that a stress or shock can raise anxiety for a considerable period of time is consistent with contemporary physiological and psychiatric knowledge. On this view we should not expect the anxiety level of the high-anxiety countries to fall back immediately in the autumn to the same level as that of the low-anxiety countries. The anxiety level should subside gradually during the autumn and winter.

Another objection to the heat-stress theory of national anxiety differences could be that the epidemiological data suggest that anxiety levels begin to rise around March, which is the time when suicide, alcohol consumption and so forth begin to increase. It can hardly be plausibly maintained that the populations of temperate zones are subjected to heat stress in the month of March. This objection might conceivably be countered by the assumption that people develop conditioned anxiety reactions to heat and these could be activated by the spring sun. People develop conditioned reactions to all sorts of remarkable stimuli and it does not seem impossible that sunshine could be among them. But if this solution is thought implausible, it would not follow that the summer heat has no anxiety-inducing effect. The correct inference would be that we should look for another factor to explain the rise of anxiety in the spring.

It may be thought that the thesis of high temperature as a stress inducing an increase in anxiety involves a paradox. Stress is generally regarded as unpleasant and people will seek to avoid it. Yet every summer many thousands of people in the northern regions leave their grey and overcast skies for a holiday in the southern sun. Is this great exodus seeking stress and desirous of having its anxiety level elevated? How can we explain this apparently masochistic urge?

The solution may lie in an application of Berlyne's (1960) theory of the arousal jag. Until this theory appeared, it had been commonly assumed that animals and men strive to reduce their anxiety levels to as low a level as possible and would avoid any situation which increased anxiety. Berlyne then pointed out that human beings spend a considerable amount of their time giving themselves moderate increases in arousal, for which he coined the term "arousal jags". The concept of arousal has much in common with our own concept of anxiety, as was argued in Chapter 3, both being personality dimensions which seem to rest upon the level of neural activity in the reticular formation. As Berlyne himself says "what are usually called emotional states are, it seems, states of high arousal" (p. 48). Thus Berlyne's theory that people like to give themselves arousal jags is tantamount to saying that people enjoy moderate increases of anxiety.

Berlyne makes a good case that people do indeed enjoy arousal jags. Many human pleasures involve risk and consequently an element of anxiety that the potential danger may actually occur. Such activities include driving cars fast, mountaineering and gambling. Arousal jags are also obtained vicariously from violent dramas on television, in the cinema or theatre, in fiction, and from watching competitive sport. The popular press constantly administers arousal jags to its readers by suggesting that imminent dangers lie in wait—"NEW WAR THREAT", "MISSISSIPPI RAPIST STRIKES AGAIN", etc. Evidently the populace enjoys these frissons, since newspaper circulations flourish on them. Berlyne's theory enables us to understand why people seek out holidays in the sun. This may be another source of arousal jags.

2. Solar radiation

Most of our discussion of the possibility that anxiety could rise in the spring and summer has been considered under the rubric of heat. However, it is not improbable that some correlate of heat could be more important and of these possibly the most likely is solar radiation, especially ultra-violet radiation. This increases sharply during the first 6 months of the year, so that it might account for the rise of some of the indices of anxiety which occurs in the spring (e.g. suicide and alcohol consumption). Radiation also reaches a peak in June, which gives it a closer fit than temperature with some of the epidemiological seasonal variations, particularly suicide.

There has been some experimental work suggesting that ultraviolet radiation may increase anxiety. For example, Myerson and Naustadt (1939) exposed subjects to a short period of ultraviolet radiation and found that the excretion of 17-ketosteroids almost doubled. Ultraviolet radiation appears to increase the circulation of histamine or histamine-like substances, which have a generally stimulating effect on gastric secretion, the adrenal cortex and the thyroid, and increase the number of erythrocytes (Ellinger, 1963). The number of erythrocytes has been identified by Cattell and Scheier (1961, p. 193) as part of their anxiety factor. It has also been found that there is a rise in erythrocytes between winter and summer (Watanabe, 1958). Hence it is not impossible that ultraviolet radiation could stimulate anxiety and be a factor accounting for a rise in axiety in the spring. Could differences in ultraviolet radiation explain the different anxiety levels in our eighteen countries? World maps for solar radiation have been assembled by Black (1956) and an index of the radiation to which the population is exposed was obtained by taking the capital city as representative of the population as a whole. A correlation can then be computed between the amount of solar radiation and national anxiety level. This correlation is $+0 \cdot 29$, i.e. the greater the solar radiation, the higher the anxiety. Once again we have a somewhat tantalising correlation, not sufficiently high for statistical significance, yet at the same time in the predicted direction and not so low as to provide virtual certainty that no significant relationship exists. The thesis that solar or ultraviolet radiation could be a significant factor remains a possibility.

3. *Storms and Electromagnetic Long Waves*

There is a school of biometeorologists who maintain that storms have a psychologically stimulating effect on people. Possibly this, if true, is associated with a rise in anxiety. Why storms should have such an effect is a matter for some speculation. The two commonest theories seem to be that storms increase the number of electromagnetic long waves and also the amount of ozone in the atmosphere (Huntington, 1945). Of these, more attention has been paid to the electromagnetic wave theory. These waves are relatively few in winter, increase sharply around May and June, and reach a maximum in August (Tromp, 1963). Hence they provide a possible source of seasonal variations in anxiety. One of the most remarkable studies to lend support to this theory is Reiter's (1952) extensive investigation of vehicle accidents in Germany. He found a significant increase on days when there were considerable disturbances of the electromagnetic long waves. In a further study, Reiter (1956) carried out an analysis of 362,000 industrial accidents in Germany over the years 1950–2 and again found that there was a significant increase of the order of 20–25 per cent on days or periods of electromagnetic disturbance. These are particularly interesting results in view of our use of accidents as an index of national anxiety levels.

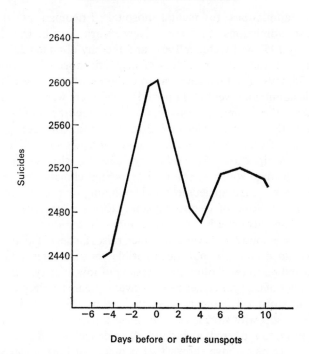

FIG. 15. Rise of suicides in conjunction with sunspot activity (from Düll and Düll, 1938).

The number of electromagnetic long waves increases when there are sunspots (Huntington, 1945). Hence it is possible that the rise in suicides which Düll and Düll (1938) found during sunspots could be due to the increase in electromagnetic long waves leading to a rise in anxiety levels. The Dülls' results were based on a study of 735 days when sunspots were particularly active. They examined the numbers of suicides in Germany for the 6 days before the day of greatest sunspot activity, and the 10 days afterwards. The result showed that suicides rose by about 8 per cent with the increase in sunspot activity. The Dülls' results are shown in Fig. 15.

This result has received some confirmation from a study by Reiter (1953), who has reported a significant rise in suicide rates in Germany on days of strong disturbance of electromagnetic long waves.

It has also been reported that electromagnetic storms have an effect on psychiatric admissions to mental hospital. Friedman *et al.* (1963) took daily admissions to seven New York psychiatric hospitals between July 1957 and October 1961, and thereby obtained 28,642 cases. They then took the number of days of magnetic storms in periods of 28 days and 35 days. The final step was to examine whether the numbers of psychiatric admissions went up in periods when there were a large number of storms and they found that this was so. They report a number of significant correlations of the order of $0 \cdot 2$ to $0 \cdot 3$; and, considering the very large number of subjects, there can be no doubt that some kind of significant relationship exists. The difficulty here, as with all the climatic results, is to isolate which of several interrelated climatic factors are the crucial ones for human anxiety levels. The finding that psychiatric admissions rise at the time of electromagnetic storms is consistent with the results that they also rise in the spring, in so far as both storms and the spring seem to embody some variable which raises anxiety. This conclusion, as was explained above, is not incompatible with the interpretation that chronic hospitalised psychotics are in a state of low anxiety.

The number of electromagnetic long waves increases in deep depressions and cyclonic storms. The theory was advanced by Huntington (1945) that this is the reason why storms seem to have a psychological energising effect. Huntington offered a variety of evidence for this theory. For example, he seems to have shown that people visit libraries more at the time of a storm. One of his most striking results is the effect of a storm on the I.Q. results of 355 freshmen at Amherst College in 1938. On the first day of the tests the weather was normal and the test results showed that this year's class scored 4 per cent above the average of sixteen preceding classes, a small variation of little significance. The next day a hurricane arose and as the class took the test the wind blew at 80 miles an hour and trees crashed to the ground outside the room. Normally Amherst College ranks at the 75th percentile among all the colleges which take the test. But when the test taken during the storm was marked, the college rose to the 95th percentile, with a mean score well above that ever achieved by Amherst students either before or since. Two days after the storm, the students took a third I.Q. test, and their scores on this had fallen back to the normal level for Amherst freshmen.

The interest of this study is that there is some evidence that anxiety in university students facilitates success in examinations. It is known that university students in the U.K. are somewhat more anxious than other young people of the same age (Lynn, 1959) and since one must pass examinations to become a student, this is prima facie evidence that anxiety is a factor in examination success. This inference is supported by a study by Kelvin *et al.* (1965) of the relation between anxiety and marks in the final examinations at the University of London. They found that the students who got "firsts" were quite substantially the most anxious, followed by those who got seconds; those getting thirds were less anxious still, while those securing bare passes were the least anxious of all. If we now put all this evidence together, it is not impossible that storms could increase the numbers of electromagnetic long waves, these could raise the anxiety level, and this could manifest itself in better examination performance.

The greater part of Huntington's theory, however, is concerned with historical evidence for the stimulating effect of stormy climates. He argued that civilisation is most advanced in those countries subject to the greatest number of storms. These countries are precisely the same as the eighteen with which we have been concerned and which were selected as a homogeneous group of the most affluent countries. Huntington maintained that the relative deline of such countries as Greece and Ireland over the last one or two millennia is partly accounted for by the decrease in the number of invigorating storms over these countries. For instance, in the great age of Irish culture around A.D. 500–800 the climate seems to have been warmer than at present, since wheat was grown on a widespread scale whereas today it is too damp for efficient wheat production. Huntington argued that in these conditions storms would have produced more atmospheric electricity and hence have been more stimulating than they are today. It will be apparent that Huntington's theory has some resemblance to our own anxiety theory of economic growth presented in Chapter 12. Huntington was concerned to show the gross differences in achievement and nervous energy levels between the Western nations and the rest of the world. Stormy climatic conditions increase the people's energy level and this in turn motivates their high standards of civilisation. Our thesis presented in Chapter 12 also maintains that nervous energy (anxiety) is a factor in cultural achievement, as assessed by economic growth rates. We also find among the advanced nations some evidence that climatic conditions could be an influence determining national anxiety levels. An anxiety theory of achievement would, of course, need considerably more working out in detail than would be appropriate here, since we are not primarily concerned with the subject in this monograph. Nevertheless, it seems of interest to draw attention to the similarity between Huntington's conclusions and our own.

The crucial question now is whether the national anxiety levels of our eighteen countries have any relationship with the number of storms. This question can be examined by consulting the world distribution of thunderstorms tables published by the World Meteorological Organisation (1953). This publication gives figures of the annual number of thunderstorm days recorded at numerous weather stations in different parts of the world. The figures represent averages collected over a number of years, the exact length of the records varying from one weather station to another. Many countries have a large number of weather stations, and the simplest method of obtaining a simple overall thunderstorm "score" for a country seemed to be to take the average of all the stations in a country. A more refined method would, of course, have been to weight each station by the number of people living in its vicinity, but considering that there are 264

TABLE 29. DISTRIBUTION OF THUNDERSTORM DAYS

Country	Weather stations (N.)	Thunderstorm days (average per year)
Australia	145	15·0
Austria	116	23·2
Belgium	23	17·6
Canada	200	10·6
Denmark	43	10·6
Finland	65	10·1
France	161	17·0
Germany	241	22·6
Ireland	4	6·8
Italy	92	16·5
Japan	57	20·0
Netherlands	31	27·4
New Zealand	65	7·6
Norway	99	6·2
Sweden	181	10·7
Switzerland	81	12·8
U.K.	16	8·8
U.S.A.	264	37·8

SOURCE: *World Distribution of Thunderstorm Days*, Pt. 1. World Meteorological Organisation: Geneva, 1953.

weather stations with thunderstorm records in the U.S.A., this would clearly be an onerous undertaking. A thunderstorm day is a day on which thunder is recorded, and any such day scores one mark, irrespective of the actual number of thunderstorms which occur on that day.

The data obtained from these calculations are shown in Table 29. From this we may calculate the rank correlation between the number of thunderstorm days per year and the national anxiety level. The correlation is $+0.53$ (i.e. the greater the number of storms the higher the anxiety) and is statistically significant at the 5 per cent level. If we take this result in conjunction with the other evidence suggesting that the presence of electromagnetic long waves, ozone or some other correlate of storms raises the anxiety levels of individuals (leading to increased suicide and accidents), then it does not seem impossible that the degree of storminess could be a factor determining our national anxiety levels.

4. *Conclusion*

It cannot be claimed that the territory surveyed in this chapter provides a conclusive answer to the possibility that some climatic factor is involved in national anxiety differences. Nevertheless, there does seem quite a considerable amount of evidence to suggest that some climatic influence may be present. Such an influence could account for both the national differences in anxiety and also for the seasonal variations, which are difficult to explain by anything other than some climatic factor. Heat, solar radiation and storminess are among the promising possibilities, and of these storminess is perhaps the most promising, since this is the climatic variable with the highest correlation with national anxiety levels. Even if storminess is the crucial factor, what element in storminess is important—the increase of electromagnetic long waves, or of ozone, or of some more esoteric factor—cannot for the moment be determined. Indeed, possibly the present discussion has taken the problem as far as a psychologist can be expected to push it and a more detailed consideration must be left to the meteorologist.

CHAPTER 17

ANXIETY AND RACE

WHATEVER judgement the reader may have formed about the plausibility of some climatic factor affecting national anxiety levels, it certainly seems doubtful whether this can be the only influence at work. The correlations between the climate variables and the national anxiety levels are modest. We should therefore pursue further the question of what other factors might affect national anxiety levels. In this chapter we consider the possibility of race.

The very raising of such a possibility is today unfashionable. But it is regrettable that what should be regarded as a scientific problem, possibly resolvable by scientific inquiry or else properly left in abeyance as an open question until techniques for answering it can be found, should have assumed the character of an ideological dogma. In this respect the insistence of some contemporary writers that there are no genetically determined psychological differences between different races is quite as objectionable as the racist theories of their opponents. For instance, M. Banton, a professor of Sociology at the University of Bristol, has defined racism as "the doctrine that a man's behaviour is determined by stable inherited characters, deriving from separate racial stocks which have distinctive attributes". He then goes on to state bluntly that "racism was a scientific error" (Banton, 1969). In reply to Banton and the substantial body of opinion he represents, the following points can be put. In the first place, there has been virtually no systematic work establishing the existence of national differences in psychological traits until the appearance of this monograph. Temperamental differences between the peoples of different countries have, of course, been long suspected, but it is only after these have been measured that it becomes fruitful to inquire into the causes of the differences. Until this time it seems better to suspend judgement on whether the causes of national temperament (if they can be established) are primarily environmental or genetic. To rule out the possibility of genetic determinants of national psychological differences before these have been established is surely to take a dogmatic stance quite incompatible with proper scientific objectivity.

It is sometimes imagined that the idea of race has ceased to be respectable among physical anthropologists. Such an impression could easily be gained from a book like Ashley Montagu's (1945) *Man's Most Dangerous Myth: The Fallacy of Race*. But notwithstanding the title, perusal of the text shows that Ashley Montagu fully admits the existence of several human races. This can be made clear by quoting his own words:

> In biological usage a race is conceived to be a subdivision of a species which inherits the *physical* characteristics serving to distinguish it from other populations of the species. In the genetic sense a race may be defined as a population which differs in the incidence of certain genes from other populations, with one or more of which it is exchanging or potentially capable of exchanging genes across whatever boundaries (usually geographical) may separate them. If we are asked whether in this sense there exist a fair number of races in the human species, the answer is very definitely that there do [p.6].

Thus we can see that race is apparently neither a "myth" nor a "fallacy", and it may be felt that Ashley Montagu's dramatic title is rather misleading.

The objections of Ashley Montagu and others to the concept of race seem to be twofold. In the first place, they maintain that there are no pure races, but that there has been considerable interbreeding and hence overlapping. This objection does not, of course, mean that there may not be different mixes of the originally pure races in different countries. For instance, we can maintain that Swedes tend to be tall, blond and blue-eyed and north Italians small, dark and black-eyed without being held to the belief that this rule applies to every single member of these two communities.

But the chief objection of Ashley Montagu and others to the concept of race seems to be that the doctrine was espoused by fascists and imperialists and used by such people to justify their political and military ambitions. This may be so. But it must surely be doubted whether even a successful debunking of race would do much to deter future Hitlers. Imperialist designs of one nation on another have been a constant feature of human history, although for the most part aggressors have not held doctrines of racial superiority. Possibly the most energetic imperialist power of the post-1945 period has been Soviet Russia, in whose constitution racial equality is officially embodied and whose anthropologists frequently denounce theories of racial differences as "the misanthropic ideology of imperialism" (Nesturkh, 1963, p. 108). But these official views have not prevented Russia from adding some nine formerly independent states of eastern Europe to her empire, or from a degree of anti-Semitism which outclasses anything current in the West. It is therefore surely being very hopeful to imagine that drawing a veil over racial differences will do anything to stop man's aggression to man—even if the suppression of truth were justifiable for political ends.

Now that national differences in anxiety have been established let us consider calmly the possibility that a genetic racial factor could be involved.

Perhaps we should note first that for some of our indices of national anxiety level a genetic explanation would probably seem *prima facie* plausible to much responsible opinion in psychology and psychiatry. This is perhaps particularly true of the national differences in psychosis rates. There is a substantial body of evidence from twin studies (to which reference was made in Chapter 4) showing that inheritance is an important, and very likely predominant, cause of psychosis. How therefore do we explain the fact that the incidence of psychosis in Ireland is more than four times higher than that in West Germany? Is it not likely that there is some genetic difference between the populations of the two countries?

The same argument may be applied to anxiety itself. Again, there is evidence that among the ordinary population differences in anxiety are to a considerable extent determined by inheritance. For instance, Shields (1962) investigated forty-two pairs of identical twins separated soon after birth and brought up in different families. The correlation between their scores on Eysenck's neuroticism factor was $+0.53$, which indicates a substantial genetic influence. A similar conclusion was reached by Eysenck and Prell (1951). Cattell (1957) also reports evidence for a substantial genetic basis for his anxiety factor. Thus, since we have fairly solid evidence that anxiety levels in individuals within Western countries are substantially determined by inheritance, it would not seem impossible that there could also be a genetic basis determining anxiety differences between countries.

The countries with which we have been concerned are all European, or, with the exception of Japan, their populations have been principally derived from European racial stock (i.e. Canada, United States, New Zealand and Australia). It is well established that there are a number of races in Europe which are represented in differing proportions in different

countries. There are two principal racial classifications. One is based on
W. Z. Ripley's *The Races of Europe* (1899), in which Europeans were
divided into three sub-races: Nordic, Alpine and Mediterranean. These
races are found principally in three horizontal bands across Europe.
The Nordics are chiefly in the U.K., Scandinavia, Holland and northern
Germany, the Alpines in central France, central and southern Germany
and north Italy, and the Mediterraneans are concentrated around the
shores of the Mediterranean. From Nordic through Alpine to Mediterranean the races become darker-skinned, darker-eyed, darker-haired, and
shorter in stature. There are also differences in head sizes, both Nordics
and Mediterraneans tending to dolichocephaly (narrow headed), while
the Alpines are more brachycephalic (round headed). According to
Kroeber (1948, p. 135), all physical anthropologists "admit at least these
three" races in Europe, and the same view is taken in the most recent
book of Coon (1966, pp. 62–63).

The second classification is based on J. Deniker's *The Races of Man*
(1900) and is an elaboration of Ripley's scheme. Deniker's Nordic race is
the same as Ripley's, but he subdivided the Alpine into Western European,
Eastern European, and Dinaric, and the Mediterranean into Atlanto-
Mediterranean and Ibero-Insular. There is general agreement that some
further breakdown of Ripley's three races is justified, and most subsequent
work follows Deniker or modifies his scheme in only comparatively minor
ways.

One of the principal criteria for classifying the European races is the
cephalic index, i.e. the ratio of the length of the skull to its breadth. The
index gives the breadth on the basis of a length of 100 millimetres. This
gives rise to two extreme types, namely dolichocephalics, whose heads are
comparatively narrow with a cephalic index around 76–79; and brachycephalics, whose heads are comparatively round with a cephalic index
between 83–86. There are, of course, intermediate types. The inhabitants
of the U.K., Ireland and Sweden are preponderantly dolichocephalic,
while the peoples of France, Switzerland, Germany, north Italy and
Austria are predominantly brachycephalic (Pittard, 1926). Finland,
Norway, Holland and Belgium have populations with intermediate
cephalic indices.

Some of the national differences are rather striking. For instance, only
13 per cent of Swedes are brachycephalic, as against 83 per cent of the
inhabitants of Bavaria (Kroeber, 1948, p. 128). Curiously enough, the

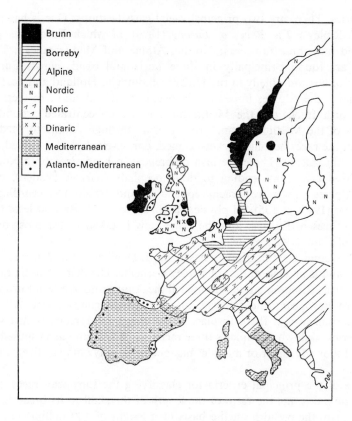

FIG. 16. Distribution of races in Europe (from Coon, 1939).

cephalic index seems to correspond quite closely to the anxiety level. The low-anxiety countries, the U.K., Ireland and to a lesser degree Sweden, are predominantly dolichocephalic; the high-anxiety countries, France, Austria, Italy and some of Germany, are predominantly brachycephalic. Could there be a genetic difference in anxiety between dolichocephalic and brachycephalic stocks? Since the two are genetically different it is by no means impossible that they should differ in the reactivity of the sympathetic system, or whatever the physiological basis of anxiety eventually turns out to be.

Possibly the most authoritative student of the physical anthropology of race in Europe is Carleton Coon, whose classification is extensively documented in his *Races of Europe* (1939). This is the classification which is relied on in the ensuing discussion. Coon divides Europe into eight races and several sub-races which are best illustrated in the map shown in Fig. 16. Fortunately not all of these are represented in the Western European countries with which we are concerned. Our attention will be confined to the six principal races: Nordic, Brünn, Noric, Borreby, Alpine and Dinaric.

We may now ask whether the distribution of racial groups in Europe is such as to be consistent with a genetic hypothesis of the national differences in anxiety with which we have been concerned. There are certain distributions which would clearly be incompatible with such an hypothesis. For instance, Ireland is the country with the lowest anxiety level and Austria the country with the highest. If it turned out that the same race is predominant in both Ireland and Austria, the thesis would obviously be ruled out of court immediately. The hypothesis would also collapse if the U.K., the second lowest anxiety country, were to have the same racial groups as Germany and France, the second and third highest European countries on anxiety. There are therefore several ways in which a genetic interpretation of the national differences could be ruled out by the anthropological evidence.

Let us for the moment confine our attention to European countries, leaving aside the United States, the countries of the old Commonwealth and Japan. This gives the following rank order in anxiety levels:

High anxiety	Medium anxiety	Low anxiety
1. Austria	6. Denmark	10. Sweden
2. Germany	7. Switzerland	11. Netherlands
3. France	8. Norway	12. United Kingdom
4. Italy	9. Finland	13. Ireland
5. Belgium		

The hypothesis of genetic racial differences underlying anxiety differences could be ruled out if any of the four high-anxiety countries had substantially the same racial basis as any of the four low-anxiety countries. On the other hand, the hypothesis would be mildly strengthened if any of the countries within the same group had racially similar populations.

Let us now consider the anthropological evidence, which is shown in

Coon's map, although the following discussion is based on Coon's more detailed text. Taking the high-anxiety countries first, it will be noted that Austria is principally populated by the Noric race, who are blond brachycephalics. The second commonest racial group in Austria is probably the Dinaric, a tall brachycephalic type of intermediate pigmentation. Neither of these races is represented in any of the four low-anxiety countries, Sweden, Holland, the U.K. or Ireland. This suggests the hypothesis that the Noric and Dinaric races could have high anxiety levels, and this is advanced as our first postulate.

In Germany, the north-west is populated principally by the Borreby race. They are large-headed brachycephalics. The Brünn and Dinaric races are also present, but in lesser numbers. The inhabitants of central Germany belong principally to the Dinaric, Alpine and Noric races. In the south the Dinarics preponderate, and there are also substantial minority groups of Norics, Borrebys and Brünns. The Bavarians are mainly Alpines and Dinarics. It is popularly imagined that the Germans and the English are racially similar and distinct from the Latins. Since the Germans are high on anxiety and the English low, this would of course be fatal for any thesis attributing national anxiety differences to race. It is therefore worth noting that Coon explicitly corrects this popular misunderstanding: "to summarise the data on the physical anthropology of Germany it seems necessary to stress the relative absence of conventional Nordics comparable to those found in Eastern Norway, in Sweden and in England" (1939, p. 546).

The principal racial groups in Germany are thus Borreby, Noric, Dinaric and Alpine. We have already postulated that the Noric and Dinaric races have high innate anxiety levels in order to account for the exceptionally high anxiety in Austria. Since Germany is also a high-anxiety country, we are now obliged to assume that the Borreby and Alpine races are also high on anxiety. Either both or one of them, however, could well be somewhat lower than the Norics and Dinarics, to account for the lower level of anxiety in Germany than in Austria.

With these provisional assumptions we can now turn to France. A standard work of French racial types is Montandon's (1935) *L'Ethnie Française*, in which he proposes the following racial proportions: Nordic, 1 per cent; Sub-Nordic, 30 per cent; Dinaric-like, 15 per cent; relatively pure Alpine, 30 per cent; Small Mediterranean (Ibero-Insular), 10 per cent; Atlanto-Mediterranean (Litoral) 10 per cent; Basque, 1 per cent;

others, 3 per cent. Coon points out that the Alpine race is preponderant, since there is a strong Alpine element in both the sub-Nordic group and in the Atlanto-Mediterraneans. Coon's conclusion is as follows: "In France, the Alpine race, a smaller-sized and less blond replica of the northern Borreby race, has re-emerged as the principal racial element and can be seen in a relatively pure form. France is essentially an Alpine nation" (p. 522). Since we have already inferred that the Alpine race is high on anxiety from its presence in both Austria and Germany, the racial composition of France adds strength to our hypothesis.

The fourth high-anxiety nation is Italy. The most extensive work on Italian physical anthropology is still that of Livi, who assessed no less that 300,000 recruits over the years 1859–63 and published the results in his *Antropometria Militare* in 1896. His research indicated that northern Italians are principally Alpines and Dinarics, while the southern Italians are for the most part a blend of Alpines and Mediterraneans. In the words of Coon: "the binding element which is common to all sections is the Alpine, which has re-emerged from obscure beginnings through a super-structure composed of Dinarics, Nordics and various kinds of Mediterranean accretions" (p. 559).

We have already inferred that the Alpine race has a high anxiety level from its presence in Austria, Germany and France, so that its preponderance in Italy confirms this interpretation. This concludes our consideration of the high-anxiety countries. The inferences can be summarised as follows. The four principal races in the four high-anxiety countries are the Noric, Dinaric, Borreby and Alpine, so that we infer that these are all high-anxiety races. We may also infer that the Norics and Dinarics are somewhat more anxious than the Alpines. This inference rests on the higher anxiety levels in Austria (Noric and Dinaric) than in France and Italy (Alpine), with Germany (all four races) in an intermediate position.

Let us now leave aside the group of medium-anxiety countries and turn to the low-anxiety group, consisting of Sweden, the Netherlands, the U.K. and Ireland. Of these, the country with the lowest anxiety level is Ireland. There are two principal races, of which one is the Brünn, principally concentrated in the west. These are remarkable for their exceptionally pale skins, which freckle easily on exposure to sunlight. In Kerry, 60 per cent of the population are freckled, which is apparently a world record. The rufous hair colour also reaches a world maximum in this group. The other principal race is the Nordic, who are found more in the east. In view of the very low anxiety level in Ireland it seems necessary to infer that both races are low on anxiety.

Turning now to the U.K., the predominant race is Nordic. There are some pockets of Atlanto-Mediterranean, particularly in Wales and along the west coast of Scotland, and also of Brünn, but neither of these form more than a small fraction of the total population. Coon's summary can be given: "in both Great Britain and Ireland, the invasion of the Keltic Iron Age Nordics was the event which brought in the largest single body of people, and the British today, by and large, owe more in a physical sense to these Kelts than to any other group of invaders" (p. 399). Hence the British and Irish have a good deal in common racially, which is consistent with their being the two countries with the lowest anxiety levels. The principal difference is the much greater preponderance of the Brünn race in Ireland. It is tempting to infer that Brünns are less anxious than Nordics, but some caution is necessary here because Iceland has a predominantly Brünn population and its overall anxiety level does not appear (from a consideration of its rate of suicides, psychosis and so forth) to be as low as that of Ireland. Consequently the most reasonable inference seems to be that the Brünns have an anxiety level about equal to that of the Nordics.

The third lowest-anxiety country is the Netherlands, and here again we find a predominance of Nordics: "the living Netherlanders . . . belong more to a Nordic type than any other" (Coon, p. 532). There is also a minority group of Frisians in which the Brünn and Borreby races are substantially represented. We have already inferred that the Brünn are a low-anxiety race from their presence in Ireland, while the Borreby race has been assumed to be anxious from their presence in Germany. It seems reasonable to infer that the existence of a Borreby element in the Netherlands has done something to raise the anxiety level of the population as a whole a little above that of the U.K. and Ireland, but the preponderance of Nordics puts the Netherlands into the low-anxiety group of nations.

The last low-anxiety country is Sweden, and once more the preponderant racial group is Nordic. We shall once more rely on Coon's summary: "abundant anthropometric data from Sweden makes it clear that the basic, and by far the most numerous element in the population is . . . Iron Age Nordic" (p. 331). As in the Netherlands, there are minority strains of Borreby and Brünn, so that the racial composition of Sweden and the Netherlands is closely similar, which is in line with their adjacent positions on the anxiety ranking. As with the Netherlands, it seems reasonable to assume that the presence of the anxious Borrebys has done something to raise the average anxiety level a little higher than that found in the U.K. and Ireland.

Thus a consideration of the racial strains in the low-anxiety countries does nothing to weaken the hypothesis that racial differences could underlie the differences in anxiety level. On the contrary, the prediction that the high-anxiety countries would differ racially from the low-anxiety countries has been borne out. There is very little overlap between the racial composition of the low-anxiety countries (Brünn and Nordic) and the high-anxiety countries (Noric, Dinaric, Alpine and Borreby).

We now turn to the group of countries in the middle anxiety range, consisting of Belgium, Denmark, Switzerland, Norway and Finland. The predictions about this middle group are that they should contain a mixture of the high- and low-anxiety races, with a preponderance of high-anxiety races in Belgium and Denmark and of low-anxiety races in Norway and Finland.

In Belgium there are two principal groups, the Flemings who are mainly Nordic and the Walloons who are largely Alpine and Borreby. The largest single race is Borreby (Coon, p. 291). Hence the races which we have inferred have high anxiety levels (Alpine and Borreby) preponderate over a fairly substantial group of unanxious Nordics, producing a population with an overall anxiety level in the high middle range.

The physical anthropology of Denmark has been comparatively poorly investigated, but what studies have been made suggest that the modern Danes are chiefly a mixture of Nordic and Borreby, i.e. of one race which we have inferred is anxious (Borreby) and one unanxious (Nordic). This mixture would put the anxiety level of the population of the country as a whole into the middle range.

The Swiss have sometimes been assumed to be largely Alpine, but a survey in 1927–32 revealed a mean cephalic index of 81·3, which is too low for pure Alpines. Coon's conclusion is that the Swiss are partly Alpine and Dinaric, and also that "a large Nordic element has survived here" (p. 550). Once again, therefore, we have in Switzerland a mixture of both high- and low-anxiety races.

Norway is principally Nordic, with a minority of Borreby and a still smaller percentage of Brünn. On the basis of our working assumptions, this would produce an overall average in the low middle anxiety range, which corresponds to the position which Norway actually occupies.

The last of the medium-anxiety countries is Finland. The Finns have a considerable Nordic element, together with East Baltic and Neo-Danubian races. We have no other evidence about the anxiety levels of the two latter groups, but on the basis of the substantial Nordic element we should expect the Finns to appear in the lower range of anxiety. The position of Finland as the least anxious of the medium-anxiety group seems consistent with this expectation.

This concludes our consideration of the thirteen European countries. It would appear that thus far the hypothesis that the differences in anxiety level between the countries have an innate racial origin has stood up well to a detailed survey of the racial composition of the individual countries. Formally, perhaps the best way of expressing this is as follows. We have made six assumptions, namely that there are four high-anxiety races (Noric, Dinaric, Alpine, Borreby) and two low-anxiety races (Nordic, Brünn). On the basis of these assumptions the position of all thirteen countries into high-, medium- or low-anxiety groups can be explained. This would seem to give the racial hypothesis quite considerable explanatory power.

It is now possible to check the hypothesis further against four of the remaining countries of our total of eighteen, namely the U.S.A., Australia, Canada and New Zealand. It will be recalled that these were all in the lower half in the original ranking of all eighteen nations; the order of this half is shown again below:

10. Finland	13. Australia	16. New Zealand
11. Sweden	14. Netherlands	17. United Kingdom
12. United States	15. Canada	18. Ireland

The racial hypothesis clearly implies that on examination of the four new countries we should find a predominance of the Nordic and Brünn races, while any predominance of Alpines, Norics, Dinarics or Borrebys would be a serious embarrassment to the theory.

New Zealand is a straightforward case. In the early nineteen-sixties, $91 \cdot 8$ per cent of the population were European and 98 per cent of these were of British origin, making around 90 per cent of the population British (Coon, 1966). It follows naturally that New Zealand should appear in the anxiety ranking next to the U.K. The other $8 \cdot 2$ per cent of the population in New Zealand are Maoris, mixed Maoris and Polynesians, about whose anxiety levels we have no conjectures to offer.

The racial composition of Australia is largely similar. Around 90 per cent of the population are of British or Irish origin, so that they are overwhelmingly Nordic and Brünn and consequently should fall, as they do, into the low-anxiety group of nations. Since 1945 there has been a certain influx of Italians, Dutch, Poles and other Continentals, who comprised 10 per cent of the population in the early nineteen-sixties (Coon, 1966). This should have had the effect of raising the average level of anxiety slightly which would account for Australia's position a little above the U.K. and Ireland.

The United States presents a particularly difficult problem because of the heterogeneity of its racial composition and the size of the population. In the 1960 census, 87·5 per cent of the population were recorded as white and 10·4 per cent Negro, the remaining 2·1 per cent being principally Japanese and Chinese. The first settlers in the United States were mainly English and Scots. The wave of immigration between 1790 and 1860 was largely German, Scandinavian, Irish and English. From 1860 to 1924 there were large numbers of Slavs, Italians, Greeks and Russian and Polish Jews. In spite of these later immigrants, it seems generally agreed that those of British descent remain the largest single group. The quota system allowed in more than twice as many Britons as any other nationals. The American anthropologist Kroeber has written that "Americans are descended in the main from Britons" (1948, p. 588).

The position taken by Coon et al. (1950) is that the great majority of white Americans belong to a composite which they designated the "northwest European race". These are the peoples who predominate in Scandinavia, the U.K., Northern France, Belgium, Holland and north-west Germany. The predominant race here is Nordic. Thus in the United States there would seem to be a substantial proportion of Nordics of English, Scots, Irish and Scandinavian origin, and a somewhat lower proportion of the higher-anxiety stocks from Germany, France and Italy. This mixture should account for the position of the United States in the low–middle anxiety range.

Finally, we come to Canada. The 1961 census broke the population down into ethnic groups. The largest single group was the British, which numbered, in round figures, 8 million. The next group was French, with $5\frac{1}{2}$ million, followed by the Germans with 1 million. In addition there are about half a million each of Russians, Italians, Dutch, Scandinavians and Poles. The large numbers of British should put Canada among the lower anxiety group of nations, while the substantial minorities of French and Germans should raise the anxiety level somewhat above that of the U.K. and Ireland. Possibly our theory would have predicted a slightly higher ranking for Canada than that she actually occupies, but a difference of one or two places in the rank order may not be of too great a significance and there is little doubt that Canada falls broadly into the anxiety range that would be expected on the basis of the racial composition of her population.

Thus the inferences which were made about the anxiety levels of the six principal west European races have been confirmed by consideration of the racial composition and anxiety levels of the United States and the white commonwealth. The only country we have not considered is Japan, which is so racially different from the others that no useful inferences can be made from it. The thesis which has been set up is of course open to testing in many other ways. It could be tested directly by examining differences in the indices of anxiety among people of different races within particular countries. The thesis would predict, for example, that in the United States suicide should be commoner among people of Austrian, German, Italian and French descent than among the Nordic peoples. There are a number of countries with several races where such tests could be carried out. For instance, in Belgium there are the Flemings who are principally Nordic and the Walloons who are principally Alpine and Borreby. Our hypothesis would predict that the Flemings should have lower suicide and alcoholism rates, together with higher mental illness and calorie intake. Similar predictions could be made in other countries where different races are represented in discrete areas, such as Switzerland and Canada. To chase these implications through would necessitate a detailed knowledge of each country's own medical literature and statistical records, which puts it beyond the scope of a single investigator.

Some physical anthropologists have reservations about Coon's detailed classification and prefer the broader groupings of Ripley into Nordic, Alpine and Mediterranean. The adoption of this simpler system would make little difference to the thesis that national anxiety levels are partly determined by the racial composition of the nations. The thesis would now set up the postulates that Nordics are a low-anxiety race, while Alpines and Mediterraneans are high. These assumptions would explain the low anxiety levels of the predominantly Nordic countries—the U.K., Ireland, Scandinavia, the Netherlands and the white commonwealth; and the high anxiety levels of the predominantly Alpine and Mediterranean countries—Austria, Germany, France and Italy; while the intermediate countries (Belgium and Switzerland) are racially mixed.

We must now consider whether the thesis of racial differences in anxiety can derive any support from laboratory investigations. Few studies have been made, but such as exist lend some support to the theory. For instance, Zborowski (1952) carried out a study of the attitudes to pain among Italians, Jews, Irish and Old Americans living in New York. He sampled medical opinion and reported that "Italians and Jews were described as tending to exaggerate their pain, while the Irish were often depicted as stoical individuals who are able to take a great deal of pain . . ."; some of the doctors stated that in their opinion the Jews and Italians have a lower threshold of pain than members of other ethnic groups, especially "members of the so-called Nordic group". No doubt the term "threshold" is being used a little loosely here and the medical men had in mind the reactivity to pain as well as the threshold as such. Zborowski's survey of hospital patients in New York confirmed these impressions and he concludes that the Old Americans have a "phlegmatic" reaction to pain in contrast to the Italians who are quick to "express a desire for pain relief".

A more objective study has been reported by Sternbach and Tursky (1965), who compared groups of Irish, Yankee (i.e. Americans of British descent), Italian and Jewish women on pain thresholds and psychogalvanic reactions to pain stimulation. On pain thresholds the order of the four groups from high thresholds to low was Irish, Yankee, Jewish and Italian, i.e. the Irish were the least sensitive to pain. The Irish and the Yankees also habituated their psychogalvanic reactions to pain more rapidly after a series of trials. These results are clearly in line with a racial theory of anxiety differences. Since all the groups were living in the same part of the United States, the differences cannot be ascribed to climatic conditions. It might, however, be possible to argue that there are environmentally induced cultural differences in reactivity to pain associated with the different ethnic groups.

In a further experiment, Tursky and Sternbach (1967) measured ethnic differences in heart-rate changes in addition to psychogalvanic reactions. They used the same groups of Old Americans of British descent, Irish, Italians and Jews and subjected them to electric shocks. The same group differences emerged. The Italians and Jews showed consistently greater psychogalvanic reactions and accelerated heart rate than the Old Americans and Irish. The Jews do not, of course, figure among our group of eighteen advanced nations, but they are predominantly of Mediterranean racial stock (Coon, 1939). Hence their apparently high anxiety level is consistent with the theory that Mediterraneans are more anxious than Nordics. Tursky and Sternbach also found that the Irish had consistently lower psychogalvanic reactions than the Old Americans, which is in line with our national differences. However, no such differences were apparent on the heart-rate measure. This could suggest a specific anxiety in the Irish, manifesting itself in low psychogalvanic reactions. Such a thesis might follow the lines of Malmo and Shagass' (1949) "weak link" theory of reactions to anxiety, according to which anxiety manifests itself in different symptoms in different people, depending upon the weak link in their physiology: thus in one individual, anxiety can be responsible for an elevated heart rate, while in another it can show itself in hostility associated with high forearm muscle tension, etc. A similar notion is enshrined in Lacey's (1950) theory of autonomic specificity, and indeed in view of the low intercorrelations between the autonomic reactions to stress it is difficult to avoid the conclusion that there are strong specific anxiety factors. The Tursky and Sternbach results are an indication that these specific factors could differ in different racial groups. However, there is not enough evidence to pursue such a possibility at the present and we must confine our considerations to the general anxiety factor.

Of course a genetic ethnic difference in anxiety is not necessarily the only possible explanation for Tursky and Sternbach's results. All the subjects in the experiment were native born Americans, which seems to rule out any climatic effect on the national differences. The authors themselves favour an environmental interpretation of their results, as might be expected from the environmentalist assumptions prevailing among many psychologists. They seem to believe that children in Old American and Irish families are brought up to display a stoical and stiff-upper-lip attitude towards pain, whereas the Jewish and Italian parents are more indulgent towards fussing and self-pity. However, Tursky and Sternbach offer no evidence for this interpretation. Even if these differences in the style of upbringing exist, it is by no means certain that they would affect such psychological reactions as the psychogalvanic response and heart rate. These reactions to pain are to a considerable extent determined by the underlying trait of anxiety or neuroticism (Lynn and Eysenck, 1961; Petrie, 1960), and there is fairly strong evidence that personality differences in anxiety have a substantial innate basis (e.g. Cattell, 1957; Shields, 1962; Eysenck, 1967). This would seem to make it not at all improbable that a genetic factor might underlie the different ethnic reactions to pain which Tursky and Sternbach have discovered. The authors themselves admit this possibility: "We cannot rule out possible genetic differences in autonomic responsivity. Our selection procedure virtually insured [sic] our drawing from four discrete genetic pools." Thus the Tursky and Sternbach results would follow from a theory that the Nordic peoples are innately less anxious than the Mediterranean.

Now that we have touched on the question of racial differences in physiological reactivity it seems worth noting that there is one study in this area on Japanese–Caucasian differences. Lazarus et al. (1966) compared Japanese and American students on psychogalvanic reaction while they were watching a pleasant film about the rice-picking in paddy fields, and a rather less pleasant one in which young boys had their genitals mutilated during a puberty ceremony. The Japanese students had much higher conductance levels than the Americans, suggesting a higher level of anxiety, and this was confirmed by a questionnaire measure which also indicated higher anxiety among the Japanese. The questionnaire (the Nowlis Adjective Check List of Mood Scales) also enabled the investigators to measure the degree to which the subjects were made anxious by the film and this showed that the Japanese were more affected than the Americans. These studies are the only ones it has proved possible to find which are relevant to the national differences with which we are concerned in this monograph. Limited though they are, they clearly give some additional support to our thesis of national anxiety differences.

Thus it may be concluded that there is a certain amount of evidence in favour of a racial factor in national differences in anxiety. While such a supposition is somewhat unfashionable among social scientists today, it may be interesting to note that virtually the same conclusion was reached by Sir Cyril Burt in 1912. He described the Mediterranean peoples as "vivacious, impulsive, fickle, choleric, alternatively melancholy and gay, light-headed and hot blooded". In contrast, the Nordics are "reserved, sanguine . . . and cold blooded". These differences look like the anxiety differences with which we have been concerned. Burt then went on to discuss whether these differences have arisen from the environment or heredity and concluded that, although environmental factors may well exert some influence, we have to recognise "the presence of hereditary mental differences even among the races of civilised Europe" (Burt, 1912, p. 199). The evidence reviewed in this chapter does something to substantiate Burt's conclusion.

If we are prepared to accept provisionally the hypothesis that the Nordic race is less anxious than the Alpine and Mediterranean (to use Ripley's simpler classification for the moment) the problem arises of why this should be. Two answers are generally possible to a problem of racial differences. Sometimes they arise because a particular racial characteristic has adaptive advantages in the climate of the territory which the race has inhabited. For instance, Negroes have probably developed brown eyes because these are more efficient than blue in hard and dazzling sunlight, and they have dark skins as a protection against the sun's rays. But racial characteristics can also develop as a result of genetic drift, i.e. any group of people interbreeding over the generations tends to develop certain characteristics (e.g. shape of nose) which do not serve any adaptive purpose. This seems to be the case with the fair hair, pale skins and blue eyes of the Nordics. Or at least, if these do have adaptive advantages in a north European climate, no one seems to have discovered yet what they are.*

Of these two possibilities, it seems doubtful whether there is any adaptive advantage to the Alpine and Mediterranean peoples in having higher anxiety levels. The chief feature distinguishing their environment from that of Nordics would seem to be their hotter and more stormy summers. Now we have seen that these hot and stormy summers may well tend to raise anxiety levels, so that both climatic and racial characteristics act in the same direction on the Mediterranean and Alpine peoples. This makes it improbable that their higher anxiety level has arisen through adaptive mechanisms. The reason for this is that there is almost certainly an optimum level of anxiety which lies somewhere in the middle range, neither too great nor too little. This is the position stated in the Yerkes-Dodson law, for which there is considerable evidence (e.g. Eysenck, 1967). Granted this law, it would seem that a people who are exposed to an environmental anxiety inducer, such as hot and stormy summers, ought to become over the generations slightly less reactive physiologically. The net effect would then be that their final anxiety level would be the same as that of people in cooler and less stormy climates. Yet what has

---

* Since writing this, I have seen Col. Gayre's theory that pale skins facilitate the absorption of vitamin C from sunlight.

occurred seems to be the opposite of this. It is the Alpine and Mediterranean people who are exposed to the hot and stormy summers and yet seem also to have a higher degree of physiological reactivity. The most likely inference would seem to be that, within the range of anxiety levels found in advanced societies, there is little adaptive advantage in being at one extreme or the other. If this is so, the differences seem more likely to have arisen as a result of genetic drift.

However, there is a further possibility which might have operated. It is well established that people with a thick body build, the eurymorphs, tend to be less anxious than people who are leaner, the leptomorphs (e.g. Eysenck, 1947; Rees, 1950). Now the Nordic race tends towards eurymorphy and the Mediterranean towards leptomorphy (Coon, 1939). There are adaptive advantages to being thick set for those living in cold climates, since heat is retained better in a thick body than in a thin one. Conversely, there are adaptive advantages for thinness in a hot climate because heat loss is facilitated. Thus it is not improbable that the Nordic peoples have become slightly eurymorph as a result of its adaptive advantage in the colder climates they have inhabited. It may also be that the eurymorphic body build entails some physiological factor which tends to lower the anxiety level. This would seem the most probable explanation of the body build–anxiety relationship, even though the mechanism of the effect is not understood. If this is so, then a Nordic–Mediterranean racial difference in anxiety could be the result of the differences in body build, which have themselves evolved because of their adaptive advantages. This explanation, however, would not fit the Alpines, who are the most eurymorphic of the three principal Caucasian subraces.

* * * * *

At the present stage, it would seem probable that both a racial and a climatic factor are required to explain the national differences in anxiety. The various seasonal effects discussed in Chapter 16 seem to demand some climatic influence. But the racial thesis advanced in the present chapter also fits a number of the facts.

We now present a further argument that both factors are involved. In Chapter 16 we cited the well-known fact that suicide increases in the spring. This cannot be explained by race and is presumably due to some climatic factor. In some countries this spring increase in suicides is considerably sharper than in other countries. It has been possible to collect data from

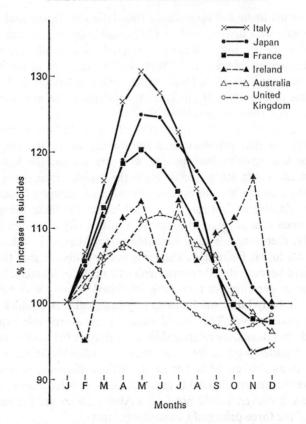

FIG. 17. The spring rises in suicide in three high-anxiety and three low-anxiety countries. Increases are expressed as a percentage of the January figure. To obtain smooth curves the data are expressed as Vincent curves (i.e. five-month averages). The countries and the years for which suicides are given are those from which it is possible to obtain data. In many cases these data are not easy to come by. For instance, in Ireland they are destroyed after three years, so only the three most recent years could be used.

six countries, three high anxiety (Italy, Japan and France) and three low anxiety (Ireland, the U.K. and Australia), and these are shown in Fig. 17. It will be noted that the spring rise in suicides in the three high-anxiety countries is considerably steeper than in the three low-anxiety countries. Why should this be? Can it be explained in terms of a climatic factor? It might be that the increase in heat, solar radiation or storms was greater in the three high-anxiety countries, thereby elevating the population's anxiety level and producing a steeper rise in the suicide rate. But this explanation will not work. As can be seen from Fig. 17 the month in which suicides attain their peak is May. There seems to be no climatic factor in May which differentiates the high-anxiety countries from the low. The two most significant climatic variables, namely the temperatures and the storminess, are shown in Table 30 for the largest cities of the six countries. The largest cities are taken as an approximate index of the weather to which substantial numbers of the populations are exposed.

It will be noted that the temperature in Australia (actually the November temperature in this case) is the highest of all six countries. The storm data are equally unsatisfactory, since although France has the most storms, the next two countries are the U.K. and Australia. It would seem, therefore, that the sharper spring rise in suicide rate in the three high-anxiety countries cannot be explained by a climatic factor.

TABLE 30. MAY TEMPERATURES AND STORMS IN THREE HIGH-
AND THREE LOW-ANXIETY COUNTRIES

Country	May temperatures	May storms
Japan	17·9	2
Italy	17·4	not available
France	14·5	4
Australia	19·6	3
United Kingdom	12·7	3
Ireland	10·8	1

How, then, are these different rises to be explained? They fall into place if we are prepared to accept a racial factor. From our assumption that the predominantly Nordic populations of the U.K., Ireland and Australia have a low anxiety level, it would follow that they would not be unduly disturbed by the climatic changes which occur in the spring. Hence the comparatively small spring rise in suicide among the Nordic peoples. In contrast, the peoples of Italy, France and Japan, being innately more excitable, would react more strongly to the climatic changes of the spring and this would yield the sharper rise in the suicide rate. Thus the spring rise in suicides only seems explicable if both climatic and racial factors are postulated as determinants of anxiety.

I have suggested a racial hypothesis to explain the national differences in anxiety because it seems to fit a number of facts reasonably well and it has the merit of further implications which can be tested. Since the question of the possibility of racial differences evokes strong emotions in some quarters, which makes rational consideration of the hypothesis more difficult, two points seem worth making. One is that the suggestion that one race could have a higher anxiety level than another does not imply either superiority or inferiority. As has become apparent during the course of this book, there is a price to be paid for both high and low anxiety; in a high-anxiety society there tend to be more casualties from suicide, liver cirrhosis and accidents, while in a low-anxiety society there are more mentally ill and more deaths from coronary heart disease. This seems to be a case of gaining on the roundabouts only to lose on the swings.

It is true that among advanced nations at the present time high anxiety seems to favour economic growth, so that in this respect it may be a disadvantage for a country to be populated predominantly by Nordics and Brünns. However, even here it is probable that the degree to which anxiety is beneficial depends on the political and social circumstances at a particular time and it is possible that a low anxiety level was a factor in the early establishment of constitutional government in the U.K. and the Netherlands. This is roughly the thesis advanced by Hagen (1962). He suggests that the English achieved constitutional government comparatively early because the different social classes were more easy-going and prepared to co-operate in a spirit of give and take than some of the more abrasive peoples on the continent of Europe. It is easy to see the similarity between Hagen's thesis and our own. The argument will not be pursued here, since the psychology of economic growth is only a minor theme in this monograph. Suffice it to say that the roughly equal achievements of all Western European nations over the last millenium suggest that neither high nor low anxiety can have given any nation a decisive advantage. It is much more probable that in some conditions and at certain stages of historical evolution a marginal advantage is gained by high anxiety, and at other stages by lower anxiety. At our particular stage of advanced capitalism it seems that high anxiety is more advantageous for economic growth, but these conditions could well change in the future. Furthermore, if high anxiety facilitates economic growth, the low-anxiety nations have been rather better at winning wars than those where the anxiety levels are high. So the advantages and disadvantages of different anxiety levels are probably finely balanced. Thus although I have proposed a hypothesis of racial differences in anxiety, it is not a thesis of racial superiority or inferiority.

Another point is perhaps more serious. There is a remarkably widely held view that the thesis that one variable is important in a particular set of circumstances implies that it is equally important in all other circumstances: e.g. that the thesis that racial differences are a significant factor in the anxiety levels of our eighteen countries in the years 1960/61 implies that the racial factor is always significant in the determination of anxiety. Those who subscribe to this incorrect logic then proceed to cite an instance where the variable in question appears to have little significance, and argue from this that the variable can have no influence in any other set of circumstances. All the steps in such an argument are of course fallacious, but it is remarkable how frequently this chain of false inferences is encountered. For instance, Durkheim considered a racial hypothesis to account for the low incidence of suicide among a group he called the Celts. He pointed out that among the ancient Celts suicide was quite common and concluded that "therefore, if it is rare today in populations of supposedly Celtic origin, it cannot be due to a congenital characteristic of the race but to changed external circumstances" (1897, p. 91).

Durkheim's argument is wrong. The contribution of any particular causal agent depends upon what other causal agents are operating in any particular set of circumstances. Consider the case of a pair of identical twins, both of whom have red hair. We may say with good sense that their similarity is due to heredity. But it would be possible to dye the hair of one of them black, and we could then say that in this instance the difference was due to a different environmental experience. Such a chain of reasoning would not, however, invalidate the conclusion that normally identical twins have identical hair colour because they have the same inheritance.

The principle is, of course, the well-known one that where environmental conditions are relatively uniform, differences between individuals tend to be determined to a considerable degree by heredity. This principle may well apply to our eighteen nations, which all broadly share a common culture, political system and high standard of living. This homogeneity has probably enhanced the significance of the genetic factor in comparisons between these countries at the present time. This hypothesis would not be disposed of by the demonstration that in certain conditions Nordics have a high rate of suicide. No doubt this might occur under the impact of certain environmental pressures or social customs.

For instance, there may well be a group of Nordics somewhere who have a high consumption of alcohol, whether because of environmental stress or social custom. Such a discovery would not impair our present thesis that among our group of advanced nations the racial factor is a significant cause of the differences in anxiety level.

We have now concluded our discussion of the possibility of a racial factor in national anxiety levels. As with climate it cannot be claimed that a racial influence has by any means been decisively established. On the other hand, there are a number of discrete pieces of evidence which all fall into place on the assumption that a racial factor is operating. If it is accepted that a good theory in science is one which accords with a number of facts and has no evidence against it, then a racial theory of national anxiety differences has some merit. But the chief claim of this monograph to the advancement of knowledge lies in its thesis of the existence of a national personality characteristic of anxiety which manifests itself in a variety of epidemiological indices. The factors responsible for these national anxiety differences are a further problem, and one which this monograph may encourage others to take up.

Finally, it may appear that at some points in this monograph certain of the hypotheses have been somewhat sketchily worked out. This has been inevitable with a central thesis which started in psychology, but has ramifications in psychiatry, physiology, anthropology, sociology, economics and meteorology. Where so many disciplines are involved, it is virtually impossible for any one writer to work out and test in detail the implications of the thesis in every field of its application. The best that can be done is to explore the thesis in some detail in those limited areas where one has competence, and to sketch its apparent implications in other fields rather more lightly for those who have more expertise to work out in detail. It is surely only in this way that integration of the numerous disciplines in the social sciences can be achieved.

CHAPTER 18

A SUMMARY OF THE ARGUMENT

THE idea of national character implies that there are some personality traits which distinguish the peoples of some nations from those of others. To establish the existence of such personality traits in individuals the psychologist finds a number of measures and must demonstrate that they intercorrelate with one another. These intercorrelating measures taken together define the trait.

In this monograph the logic of this procedure is applied to nations. The countries selected were chosen to form as homogeneous a group as possible and consist of the advanced Western nations of northern Europe, the old British commonwealth, Italy, the United States and Japan. In the first stage of the argument four measures of national character are taken, namely calorie intake and the rates of suicide, hospitalised psychosis and alcoholism. It is demonstrated that these intercorrelate together among nations in the same way as tests measuring a personality trait among individuals. The pattern of the intercorrelations is that some countries are characterised by low calorie intake and low psychosis in conjunction with high suicide and alcoholism; such countries include Austria, Italy, Japan, France and Germany. In other countries the pattern is reversed, notably Ireland, the U.K. and New Zealand.

The existence of a set of intercorrelating measures suggests the operation of a single underlying factor, and the next problem is to consider what this might be. Various possibilities are discussed, and it is suggested that the factor is anxiety. This is, of course, a major psychological concept and enables a link to be made between the factor underlying national differences and a substantial body of psychological knowledge. The interpretation of the factor as anxiety is strengthened by the discovery that the scores on anxiety questionnaires of male university students from a number of the countries correlate well with the factor.

We proceed next to consider whether the factor may manifest itself in other characteristics in addition to the four original ones. In successive chapters it is shown that what we now call the high-anxiety countries (Austria, Japan, France, Italy and Germany) have a high proportion of vehicle accidents but a low incidence of deaths from coronary heart disease and a low consumption of tobacco. Theoretical explanations for these relationships are advanced.

Further inquiry shows that the incidence of duodenal ulcers and essential hypertension are not related to the anxiety factor. There is some possibility that either, or both, might be related to an extraversion factor running through nations, but the data are too fragmentary to arrive at any conclusion.

The inquiry turns next to the question of economic growth, and it is shown that there is a strong tendency for the more anxious countries to have high growth rates. It is suggested that one reason for this may be that more anxious people work longer hours. Another possibility is that anxious people tend to be creative, and that the canalisation of creativity into business enterprises could result in a high rate of economic growth.

The question of reproducing the factor among other sets of nations is now considered. Some fragmentary results are presented, but the only major verification of the factor was found among the constituent states of the United States of America. The discovery of the factor a second time would seem to put beyond question the conclusion that the factor is genuine.

Finally, we turn to the question of the influences responsible for these national differences in anxiety. The possibilities of relative affluence, urbanisation, political instability, the strength of Roman Catholicism, and the effects of a high rate of economic growth are considered, but none of them are found plausible.

A stronger case can be made for some climatic factor. The most likely variables are summer heat, solar radiation or storminess (or some correlate of these such as electromagnetic long waves), all of which show reasonable correlations with national anxiety levels. The existence of a climatic factor would also account for the seasonal variations which are well known for suicide and are present in several of the measures of national anxiety level. At the present time, the concentration of electromagnetic long waves would seem to be the most significant climatic factor affecting national levels of anxiety.

A case can also be made for a racial factor in the determination of national anxiety levels. If Ripley's simple classification of the European races into Nordics, Alpines and Mediterraneans is used, the anxiety level of all the countries (except Japan) can be explained reasonably well on the assumption that the Nordics are a lower anxiety race than the Alpines and Mediterraneans. The more elaborate racial classification of Coon produces essentially the same results. There is also a limited amount of experimental data supporting the proposition that such racial differences exist.

In essence, this monograph attempts to reduce the idea of national character to the familiar psychological concept of anxiety. It seeks to establish that there are national differences in anxiety which manifest themselves in a number of ways. At the present stage, it seems most probable that both climatic and racial factors are responsible for differences in national anxiety levels.

REFERENCES

ADAM, J. M. and FERRES, H. M. (1954) Observations on oral and rectal temperature in the humid tropics and in a temperate climate, *J. Physiol.* **125**, 21.

ALBRINK, M. J. (1967) Obesity, in BEESON, P. B. and McDERMOT, W. (eds.), *Textbook of Medicine*, Philadelphia and London: Saunders.

ALEXANDER, F. (1939) Psychoanalytic study of a case of essential hypertension, *Psychosom. Med.* **1**, 139–52.

ALEXANDER, F. (1939s) Emotional factors in essential hypertension: Presentation of a tentative hypothesis, *Psychosom. Med.* **1**, 175–9 (a).

ALEXANDER, L. (1955) Epinephrine–mecholyl test (Funkenstein test), *Arch. Neurol. Psychiat.* **73**, 496–514.

ALEXANDER, L. (1959) Objective approach to psychiatric diagnosis and evaluation of drug effects by means of the conditional reflex technique, in MASSERMAN, J. H. (ed.), *Biological Psychiatry*, New York: Grune and Stratton.

ALEXANDER, L. (1961) Effects of psychotropic drugs on conditional responses in man, in *Neuro-psychopharmacology 2*, 93–123.

ALEXANDER, L. (1962) Differential diagnosis between psychogenic and physical pain, *J.A.M.A.* **181**, 855–61.

ALONSO-FERNANDEZ, F. (1966) Dangerous psychological configuations of the tremulous driver, *Revista de Psicologia General y Aplicada* **21**, 947–60.

ALTMAN, L. L., PRATT, D. and COTTON, J. M. (1943) Cardio-vascular response to acetyl-beta-methylcholine (mecholyl) in mental disorders, *J. Nerv. Ment. Dis.* **97**, 296–309.

ASHLEY MONTAGU, M. F. (1945) *Man's Most Dangerous Myth: The Fallacy of Race*, New York: Colombia Univ. Press.

ATKINSON, R. M. and RINGUETTE, E. L. (1957) Obesity, *Psychosom. Med.* **29**, 121–30.

BANTON, M. (1969) What do we mean by "racism"? *New Society* **341**, 551–4.

BARRON, F. (1963) *Creativity and Personal Freedom*, Princeton: Van Nostrand.

BASOWITZ, H., PERSKY, H., KORCHIN, S. J. and GRINKER, R. R. (1955) *Anxiety and Stress: an Interdisciplinary Study of a Life Situation*, New York: McGraw-Hill.

BEACH, F. A. (1958) Neural and chemical regulation of behavior, in HARLOW, H. F. and WOOLSEY, C. N. (eds.) *Biological and Biochemical Bases of Behavior*, Madison: Univ. Wisc. Press.

BELENKAYA, N. YA (1960) Electroencephaloscopic investigations of paranoid schizophrenics using meratran, *Zh. Nevropat. Psikhiat.* **60**, 224–330.

BELENKAYA, N. YA (1961) The result of an electroencephaloscopic investigation of paranoid schizophrenics under aminazin therapy, *Zh. Nevropat. Psikhiat.* **61**, 218–27.

BERLYNE, D. E. (1960) *Conflict, Arousal and Curiosity*, London: McGraw-Hill.

BIESHEUVAL, S. and WHITE, M. E. (1949) The human factor in flying accidents, *South African Air Force Journal* **1**, 25–31.

BLACK, J. N. (1956) The distribution of solar radiation over the earth's surface, *Arch. Met. Geoph. Biokl.* **7**, 165–89.

BLEULER, E. (1950) *Dementia Praecox or the Group of Schizophrenias*, New York: International Universities Press.

BLEULER, M. (1955) A comparative study of the constitution of Swiss and American alcoholic patients, in DIETHELM, J. (ed.), *Etiology of Chronic Alcoholism*, Springfield, Illinois: C. C. Thomas.

BLOCK, M. A. (1962) *Alcoholism*, London: Day.

BRADLEY, R. M. and HINDMARCH, I. (1968) Research students: time wasters? *New Society*, 28 November.

BRADY, J. V., PORTER, R. W., CONRAD, D. G. and MASON, J. W. (1958) Avoidance behavior and the development of gastroduodenal ulcers, *J. Exp. Anal. Behav.* **1**, 69–73.

BRAIN, W. R. (1948) Some reflections on genius, *Lancet*, pp. 661–72.

BRANDON, S. (1968) Eating disorders in a child population, *Acta Paedopsychiatrica* **35**, 317–23.

BREED, W. (1963) Occupational mobility and suicide, *Amer. Sociol. Rev.* **28**, 179–88.

British Medical Journal (1963) **3**, 853.

BROADHURST, P. L. (1964) Summation of drives: a study of the combined effects of air and food deprivation, in EYSENCK, H. J. (ed.), *Experiments in Motivation*, Oxford: Pergamon.

BROCK, R. B. (1945) The effect of motion pictures on body temperature, *Science* **102**, 259.

BRODY, E. B. and ROSVOLD, H. E. (1952) The influence of prefrontal lobotomy on social interaction in a monkey group, *Psychosom. Med.* **14**, 406–15.

BROOKS, C. E. P. (1950) *Climate in Everyday Life*, London: Ernest Benn.

BURT, C. (1912) The inheritance of mental characters, *Eugenics Review*, vol. 4.

BURT, C. (1915) The general and specific factors underlying the primary emotions, *Brit. Ass. Ann. Rep.* **84**, 694–6.

BURT, C. (1944) *The Young Delinquent*, London: U.L.P.

CALLARD, M. P. and GOODFELLOW, C. L. (1962) Neuroticism and extraversion in schoolboys as measured by the J.M.P.I., *Brit. J. Educ. Psychol.* **32**, 241–50.

CANNON, W. B. (1929) *Bodily Changes in Pain, Hunger, Fear and Rage: an account of researches into the function of emotional excitement*, New York: Appleton–Century–Crofts.

CATTELL, R. B. (1957) *Personality and Motivation Structure and Measurement*, New York: World Book Company.

CATTELL, R. B. (1964) *Handbook for the 16 P.F.*, Illinois: I.P.A.T.

CATTELL, R. B. and BUTCHER, H. J. (1968) *Achievement and Creativity*, New York: Bobbs–Merrill.

CATTELL, R. B. and KRUG, S. (1967) Personality factor profile peculiar to the student smoker, *J. Counsel. Psychol.* **14**, 116–21.

CATTELL, R. B. and SCHEIER, I. H. (1959) Extension of meaning of objective test personality factors: especially into anxiety, neuroticism, questionnaire and physical factors, *J. Gen. Psychol.* **61**, 287–315.

CATTELL, R. B. and SCHEIER, I. H. (1961) *Measurement of Neurotisicm and Anxiety*, New York: Ronald Press.

CAVAN, R. (1927) *Suicide*, Chicago: Univ. Chicago Press.

CHAPMAN, W. P. and JONES, C. M. (1944) Variations in cutaneous and visceral pain sensitivity in normal subjects, *J. Clin. Invest.* **23**, 81–92.

CHRISTENSEN, H. T. and CARPENTER, G. R. (1962) Value-behavior discrepancies regarding premarital coitus in three western cultures, *Amer. Sociol. Rev.*

CLARIDGE, G. S. (1967) *Personality and Arousal*, Oxford: Pergamon Press.

COLLINS, O., MOORE, D. and UNWALLA, D. (1964) *The Enterprising Man*, M.S.U. Business Studies.

COON, C. S. (1939) *The Races of Europe*, New York: Macmillan.

COON, C. S. (1966) *The Living Races of Man*, London: Jonathan Cape.

COON, C. S., GARN, S. M. and BIRDSELL, J. B. (1950) *Races*, Springfield, Illinois: Thomas.

COWIE, V. (1961) The incidence of neurosis in the children of psychotics, *Acta Psychiat. Scand.* **37**, 37–87.

CREED, R. S., DENNY-BROWN, D., ECCLES, J. C., LIDDELL, E. G. and SHERRINGTON, C. S. (1932) *Reflex Activity of the Spinal Cord*, London: O.U.P.

CRITCHLEY, M. (1945) Problems of naval warfare under climatic extremes, *Brit. Med. J.* **2**, 208–12.

CRITCHLEY, M. (1956) Neurological changes in the aged, *Res. Publ. Ass. Nerv. Ment. Dis.* **35**, 198–223.

DAHLGREN, K. G. (1945) *On Suicide and Attempted Suicide*, Sweden: Lund.

DAMARIN, F. L. (1959) Multivariate studies involving the time dimension, *Proceedings Amer. Psychol. Assn.*, Cincinnati, Ohio.

DE RUDDER, B. (1952) *Grundriss einer Meterobilogie des Menschen*, Berlin: Springer-Verlag.

DENIKER, J. (1900) *The Races of Man*, New York: Scribner.

DOBRZHANSKAYA, A. K. (1955) An investigation of the neurodynamics of acute schizophrenia, in *Proceedings of the All Union Theoretical–Practical Conference dedicated to the Centenary of S. S. Korsakov and to Current Psychological Problems*, Moscow: Medgiz.

DOKUCHAEVA, O. N. (1955) The special features of the associative reactions of schizophrenics under the influence of caffeine, in *Proceedings of the All Union Theoretical–Practical Conference dedicated to the Centenary of S. S. Korsakov and to Current Psychological Problems*, Moscow: Medgiz.

DORPAT, T. (1966) Suicide in murderers, *Psychiatry Digest*, pp. 51–55.

DREW, G. C., COLQUHOUN, W. P. and LONG, H. A. (1958) Effect of small doses of alcohol on a skill resembling driving, *Brit. Med. J.* **2**, 993–9.

DUBLIN, L. I. (1965) *Factbook on Man*, New York: Macmillan.

DUBLIN, L. and BUNZEL, B. (1933) *To Be or Not to Be*, New York: Harrison Smith and Haas.

DUFFY, G. (1930) Tensions and emotional factors in reaction, *Genet. Psychol. Monogr.* **7**, 1–79.

DÜLL, B. and DÜLL, T. (1938) Neuer Beitrag zur Erforschung des Bioklimas, *Die Umschau*, 31, Frankfurt.

DURKHEIM, E. (1897) *Suicide: A Study in Sociology*, London: Routledge & Kegan Paul.

DURRET, M. and STROMQUIST, M. (1925) Preventing violent death, *Survey* **59**, 437.

EARLE, A. and EARLE, B. V. (1955) The blood pressure response to pain and emotion in schizophrenics, *J. Nerv. Ment. Dis.* **121**, 132–9.

EKOLOVA-BAGALEI, E. M. (1955) The effect of cocaine on catatonics, in *Proceedings of the All Union Theoretical–Practical Conference dedicated to the Centenary of S. S. Korsakov and to Current Psychological Problems*, Moscow: Medgiz.

ELLINGER, F. P. (1963) Biological effects of ultraviolet radiation, in TROMP, S. W. (ed.), *Medical Biometeorology*, pp. 338–45, Amsterdam: Elsevier.

ERWIN, D. (1934) An analytical study of children's sleep, *J. Genet. Psychol.* **45**, 199–226.

EYSENCK, H. J. (1947) *Dimensions of Personality*, London: Routledge & Kegan Paul.

EYSENCK, H. J. (1952) *The Scientific Study of Personality*, London: Routledge & Kegan Paul.

EYSENCK, H. J. (1953) *Uses and Abuses of Psychology*, Harmondsworth: Penguin.

Eysenck, H. J. (1957) *The Dynamics of Anxiety and Hysteria*, New York: Praeger.
Eysenck, H. J. (1959) *Manual of the Maudsley Personality Inventory*, London: University of London Press.
Eysenck, H. J. (ed.) (1964) *Experiments in Motivation*, Oxford: Pergamon.
Eysenck, H. J. (1965) *Smoking, Health and Personality*, London: Weidenfeld and Nicolson.
Eysenck, H. J. (1965a) *Fact and Fiction in Psychology*, Harmondsworth: Penguin.
Eysenck, H. J. (1967) *The Biological Basis of Personality*, Illinois: Charles C. Thomas.
Eysenck, H. J., and Eysenck, S. B. G. (1964) *Manual of the Eysenck Personality Inventory*, London: University of London Press.
Eysenck, H. J. and Gillan, P. W. (1964) Hand steadiness under conditions of high and low drive, in Eysenck, H. J. (ed.), *Experiments in Motivation*, Oxford: Pergamon.
Eysenck, H. J., Granger, G. W. and Brengelmann, J. C. (1957) *Perceptual Processes and Mental Illness*, London: Chapman & Hall.
Eysenck, H. J. and Prell, D. (1951) The inheritance of neuroticism: an experimental study, *J. Ment. Sci.* **97**, 441–65.
Fedorovsky, Yu. N. (1955) Some electroencephalographic features of schizophrenics during induced sleep, in *Proceedings of the All Union Theoretical–Practical Conference dedicated to the Centenary of S. S. Korsakov and to Current Psychological Problems*, Moscow: Medgiz.
Feldman, M. P. (1964) Pursuit rotor performance and reminiscence as a function of drive level, in Eysenck, H. J. (ed.), *Experiments in Motivation*, Oxford: Pergamon.
Ferri (1887) Variations thermométriques et criminalité, *Archives d'Anth, Criminelle*.
Finegan, A., Hickey, N., Maurer, B. and Mulcahy, R. (1968) Diet and coronary heart disease: dietary analysis on 100 male patients, *Amer. J. Clin. Nutrition* **21**, 143–8.
Finegan, A., Hickey, N., Maurer, B. and Mulcahy, R. (1969) Diet and coronary heart disease, *Amer. J. Clin. Nutrition* **22**, 8–9.
Finn, F., Mulcahy, R. and O'Doherty, E. F. (1966) The psychological assessment of patients with coronary heart disease, *Irish J. Med. Sci.* **6**, 399–404.
Forssman, O. and Lindegard, B. (1958) The post-coronary patient, *J. Psychosom. Res.* **3**, 89–95.
Forster, E. M. (1936) *Abinger Harvest*, London: Edward Arnold.
Frankenhaeuser, M., Myrsten, A. L., Waszak, M., Neri, A. and Post, B. (1968) Dosage and time effects of cigarette smoking, *Report No. 248*, Psychological Laboratories, University of Stockholm.
Franks, C. M. (1957) Personality factors and the rate of conditioning, *Brit. J. Psychol.* **48**, 119–26.
Franks, C. M. (1958) Alcohol, alcoholism and conditioning, *J. Ment. Sci.* **104**, 14–33.
Freed, C. K. (1947) Psychic factors in the development and treatment of obesity, *J.A.M.A.* **133**, 369–73.
Frenkel, G. M. E. (1958) Electroencephalographic investigation of schizophrenics with hypochondriac syndromes, *Pavlov. J. Higher Nerv. Activ.* **8**, 590–615.
Freud, S. (1919) *Totem and Taboo*, London: Penguin.
Freud, S. (1936) *Inhibitions, Symptoms and Anxiety*, London: Hogarth Press.
Friedberg, C. K. (1967) in Beeson, P. B. and McDermot, W. (eds.), *Textbook of Medicine*, Philadelphia and London: Saunders.
Friedman, H., Becker, R. O. and Bachman, C. H. (1963) Geomagnetic parameters and psychiatric hospital admissions, *Nature* **200**, 626–30.
Friedman, M. and Rosenman, R. H. (1960) Overt behavioral pattern in coronary disease, *J.A.M.A.* **173**, 1320–5.

FUNKENSTEIN, D., GREENBLATT, M. and SOLOMON, H. (1951) Autonomic change paralleling psychologic changes in mentally ill patients, *J. Nerv. Ment. Dis.* **114**, 1–18.

FURNEAUX, W. D. (1957) *Report to Imperial College of Science and Technology*.

GABRIEL, E. (1935) *Z. Ges. Neurol. Psychiat.* **153**, 385.

GALBRAITH, J. K. (1958) *The Affluent Society*, London: Hamish Hamilton.

GAMBURG, A. L. (1958) The orientating and defensive reaction in simple and paranoid forms of schizophrenia, in VORONIN, L. G. (ed.), *The Orientating Reflex and Orientating Investigating Activity*, Moscow: Academy of Pedagogical Sciences of R.S.F.S.R.

GAVRILOVA, N. A. (1960) Investigations of the cortical mosaic in different forms of schizophrenia, *Zh. Nevropat. Psikhiat.* **4**, 453–60.

GELLHORN, E. (1956) *Physiological Foundations of Neurology and Psychiatry*, Minneapolis: University of Minnesota Press.

GELLHORN, E. (1957) *Autonomic Imbalance and the Hypothalamus*, Minneapolis: University of Minnesota Press.

GELLHORN, E. and LOOFBOURROW, G. N. (1963) *Emotions and Emotional Disorders*, New York: Harper and Row.

GOOCH, R. N. (1963) The influence of stimulant and depressant drugs on the central nervous system, in EYSENCK, H. J. (ed.), *Experiments with Drugs*, Oxford: Pergamon.

GOTTESMAN, I. I. and SHIELDS, J. (1966) Schizophrenia in twins: sixteen years consecutive admission to a psychiatric clinic, *Brit. J. Psychiat.* **112**, 809–18.

GRAHAM, J. D. P. (1945) High blood pressure after battle, *Lancet* **1**, 239–40.

GRESSEL, G. C., SHOBE, F. O., SASLOW, G., DuBOIS, P. J. and SCHROEDER, H. A. (1949) Personality factors in essential hypertension, *J. Amer. Med. Ass.* **140**, 265–71.

GRIMAK, L. P. (1959) Reproduction of emotional states of a parachutist under hypnosis, *Vop. Psikhol.* **5**, 139–41.

GUTTMACHER, M. (1960) *The Mind of the Murderer*, New York: Farrar, Strauss and Cudahy.

HAAS, A. (1923) Ueber Schlaftie fenmessungen, *Psychol. Arb.* **8**, 228–64.

HAGEN, E. E. (1962) *On the Theory of Social Change*, Illinois: Dorsey.

HAMILTON, J. A. (1942) Psychophysiology of blood pressure: I. Personality and behavior ratings, *Psychosom. Med.* **4**, 125–33.

HARBURG, E., JULIUS, S., McLEOD, J. H., McGINN, N. F. and HOOBLER, S. W. (1964) Personality traits and behavioral patterns associated with systolic blood pressure levels in college males, *J. Chron. Dis.* **17**, 405–14.

HARDY, J. D., HAMMEL, H. T. and NAKAYAMA, T. (1962) Observations on the physiological thermostat in homoiotherms, *Science* **136**, 326–9.

HAYASHI, Y. (1925) On the sleeping hours of school children aged 6–20 years, *Jido Jatshi*, p. 296.

HAYEK, F. A. (1964) The theory of complex phenomena, in BUNGE, M. (ed.), *The Critical Approach to Science and Philosophy*, New York: The Free Press.

HEIMSTEA, N. W., ELLINGSTAD, V. S. and DEKOCK, A. R. (1967) Effects of operator mood on performance in a simulated driving task, *Percep. Motor Skills* **25**, 729–35.

HEMMERLE, W. J. (1965) Obtaining maximum likelihood estimates of factor loadings and communalities, *Psychometrika*, p. 30.

HENDERSON, D. and BATCHELOR, I. R. C. (1962) *Textbook of Psychiatry*, London: O.U.P.

HERZBERG, A. (1929) *The Psychology of Philosophers*, London: Kegan Paul, Trench and Trubner.

HOAGLAND, H. and FREEMAN, H. (1959) Some neuroendocrine considerations, *Res. Publ. Ass. Nerv. Ment. Dis.* **37**, 183–203.

HOAGLAND, H., MALAMUD, W., KAUFMAN, I. C. and PINCUS, G. (1946) Changes in the EEG and in the excretion of 17 Ketosteroids accompanying electro-shock therapy of agitated depression, *Psychosom. Med.* **8**, 246–51.

HOFLING, C. K. (1963) *Textbook of Psychiatry for Medical Practice*, Philadelphia: J. B. Lippincott.

HOLLINGSHEAD, A. B. and REDLITCH, F. C. (1958) *Social Class and Mental Illness*, New York: Wiley.

HORTON, D. (1943) The functions of alcohol in primitive societies: a cross-cultural study, *Quart. J. Stud. Alcohol.* **4**, 199–220.

HUENEMANN, R. L. (1968) Consideration of adolescent obesity as a public health problem, *Public Health Reports* **83**, 491–5.

HUNTINGTON, E. (1938) *Season of Birth*, New York: John Wiley.

HUNTINGTON, E. (1945) *Mainsprings of Civilisation*, New York: John Wiley.

INNES, G., MILLAR, W. M. and VALENTINE, M. (1959) Emotion and blood pressure, *J. Ment. Sci.* **105**, 840–51.

JONES, C. H. (1956) The Funkenstein test in selecting methods of psychiatric treatment, *Dis. Nerv. Syst.* **17**, 37–43.

KAHN, M. W. (1965) A factor analytic study of the personality, intelligence and history characteristics of murderers, *Proc. 73 Ann. Conv. Psychol. Assoc.*, pp. 227–8.

KALDOR, N. (1954) The relation of economic growth and cyclical fluctuations, *The Economic Journal* **28**, 67–71.

KALLMAN, F. J. (1951) Twin studies in relation to adjustive problems of man, *Trans. N.Y. Acad. Sci.* **13**, 270–5.

KANNEL, W. B., LeBAUER, E. J., DAWBER, T. R. and McNAMARA, P. M. (1967) Relation of body weight to the development of coronary heart disease, *Circulation* **35**, 734–44.

KANTER, V. B. and HAZELTON, J. E. (1964) An attempt to measure some aspects of personality in young men with duodenal ulcers by means of questionnaires and a projective test, *J. Psychosomatic Research* **8**, 297–309.

KARLSSON, G., KARLSSON, S. and BUSCH, K. (1962) Sexual habits and attitudes of Swedish folk high school students, *Research Report No. XV*, Sweden: Uppsala University.

KELLOGG, W. N. (1932) The effects of emotional excitement upon muscular steadiness, *J. Exper. Psychol.* **15**, 142–66.

KELVIN, R. P., LUCAS, C. J. and OJHA, A. B. (1965) The relation between personality, mental health and academic performance in university students, *Brit.J.Soc. Clin. Psychol.* **4**, 244–53.

KESSEL, N. and GROSSMAN, G. (1961) Suicide in alcoholics, *Brit. Med. J.* **4**, 1671–2.

KESSEL, N. and MUNRO, A. (1964) Epidemiological studies in psychosomatic medicine, *J. Psychosom. Res.* **8**, 67–72.

KEYS, A. (1963) *Atherosclerosis and its Origin*, New York: Academic.

KIMBLE, G. A. (1961) *Hilgard and Marquis' Conditioning and Learning*, New York: Appleton–Century–Crofts.

KINSEY, A. C., POMEROY, W. B. and MARTIN, C. E. (1948) *Sexual Behavior in the Human Male*, Philadelphia: Saunders.

KLEITMAN, N. (1945) The effect of motion pictures on body temperature, *Science* **101**, 507–8, **102**, 430–1.

KLEITMAN, N. (1963) *Sleep and Wakefulness*, Chicago: University of Chicago Press.

KOSTANDOV, Z. A. (1955) The neurodynamics and the special interaction of the cortical signal systems in the paranoid form of schizophrenia, *Trud. Inst. Vyssh. Nervn. Deyatel.* **1**, 26–27.

KROEBER, A. L. (1948) *Anthropology*, New York: Harcourt, Brace.

LACEY, J. I. (1950) Individual differences in somatic response patterns, *J. Comp. Physiol. Psychol.* **43**, 338–50.

LAIRD, D. A. (1934) Seasonal changes in calcium metabolism and quality of sleep, *N. Y. Med. Res.* **139**, 65–67.

LANGWORTHY, O. R. and RICHTER, C. P. (1939) Increases in spontaneous activity produced by frontal lobe lesions in cats, *Amer. J. Physiol.* **126**, 158–61.

LANSING, R. W., SCHWARTZ, E. and LINDSLEY, D. B. (1959) Reaction time and EEG activation under alerted and nonalerted conditions, *J. Exp. Psychol.* **58**, 1–7.

LAZARUS, R. S., TOMITA, M., OPTON, E., and KODAMA, E. (1966) A cross-cultural study of stress reaction patterns in Japan, *J. Pers. Soc. Psychol.* **4**, 622–33.

LECKIE, E. V. and WITHERS, R. F. (1967) Obesity and depression, *J. Psychosom. Res.* **11**, 107–15.

LEITCH, A. (1961) Alcoholism and mental health, *Int. J. Soc. Psychiat.* **7**, 19–32.

LEMERE, F. (1953) What happens to alcoholics, *Amer. J. Psychiat.* **109**, 674.

LENNARD, H. L. and GLOCK, C. Y. (1957) Studies in hypertension VI., Differences in the distribution of hypertension in Negroes and whites, *J. Chron. Dis.* **5**, 186–96.

LINDSLEY, D. B. (1951) Emotion, in STEVENS, S. S. (ed.), *Handbook of Experimental Psychology*, New York: Wiley.

LITMAN, R. W. and TABACHNICK, N. (1967) Fatal one-car accidents, *Psychoanalytical Quarterly* **36**, 248–59.

LIVI, R. (1896) *Antropometria Militare*, Rome.

LYNN, R. (1959) Two personality characteristics related to academic achievement, *Brit. J. Educ. Psychol.* **29**, 213–16.

LYNN, R. (1962) Ageing and expressive movements: an interpretation of ageing in terms of Eysenck's construct of psychoticism, *J. Genet. Psychol.* **100**, 77–84.

LYNN, R. (1963) Russian theory and research on schizophrenia, *Psychol. Bull.* **60**, 486–98.

LYNN, R. (1966) *Attention, Arousal and the Orientation Reaction*, Oxford: Pergamon.

LYNN, R. (1969) Personality characteristics of a group of entrepreneurs, *Occup. Psychol.* **43**, 151–2.

LYNN, R. (1969) An achievement motivation questionnaire, *Brit. J. Psychol.* **60**, 529–34.

LYNN, R. (1971) *National Differences in Anxiety*, Dublin: E.S.R.I.

LYNN, R. and EYSENCK, H. J. (1961) Tolerance for pain, extraversion and neuroticism, *Percept. Mot. Skills* **12**, 161–2.

MACLEAN, P. D. (1960) in FIELD, J., MAGOUN, H. W. and HALL, V. E. (eds.) *Handbook of Neurophysiology*, Washington: American Physiological Society.

MACMAHON, B., JOHNSON, S. and PUGH, T. F. (1963) Relation of suicide rates to social conditions, *Public Health Reports* **78**, 285–94.

MCCLELLAND, D. C. (1961) *The Achieving Society*, Princeton: Van Nostrand.

MCGINN, N. F., HARBURG, E., JULIUS, S. and MCLEOD, J. M. (1964) Psychological correlates of blood pressure, *Psychol. Bull.* **61**, 209–19.

MCKENZIE, J. C. (1969) *Obesity and Disease*, London: Office of Health Economics.

MACCOBY, E. E., NEWCOMB, T. M. and HARTLEY, E. L. (1959) *Readings in Social Psychology*, London: Methuen.

MAGOUN, H. W. (1963) *The Waking Brain*, Illinois: Thomas.

MALMO, R. B. and SHAGASS, C. (1949) Physiological study of symptom mechanisms in psychiatric patients under stress, *Psychosom. Med.* **11**, 25–29.

MANHEIMER, D. L. and MELLINGER, G. D. (1967) Personality characteristics of the child accident repeater, *Child Development* **38**, 419–513.

MARCUSSEN, R. M. (1950) Vascular headache experimentally induced by presentation of pertinent life experience: Modification of the course of vascular headache by alterations of situations reactions, *Res. Publ. Ass. Nerv. Ment. Dis.* **29**, 609–14.

MARKHAM, S. F. (1942) *Climate and the Energy of Nations*, London: O.U.P.

MASSERMAN, J. H. and YUM, K. S. (1946) An analysis of the influence of alcohol on experimental neurosis in cats, *Psychosom. Med.* **8**, 36–52.

MEDNICK, S. A. (1957) Generalisation as a function of manifest anxiety and adaptation to psychological experiments, *J. Consult. Psychol.* **21**, 491–4.

MEDNICK, S. A. (1958) A learning theory approach to research in schizophrenia, *Psychol. Bull.* **55**, 316–27.

MENNINGER, K. (1938) *Man against Himself*, New York: Harcourt, Brace.

MERRETT, A. J. (1968) *Executive Remuneration in the U.K.*, London: Longmans.

MEYER, A. and MCLARDY, T. (1948) Posterior cuts in prefontal leucotomy: a clinico-pathological study, *J. Ment. Sci.* **94**, 555–64.

MILGRAM, S. (1961) Nationality and conformity, *Scientific American* **205**, 45–57.

MONROE, R. R., HEATH, R. G., HEAD, R. G., STONE, R. L. and RITTER, K. A. (1961) A comparison of hypertensive and hypotensive schizophrenics, *Psychosom. Med.* **23**, 508–19.

MONTANDON, G. (1935) *L'Ethnie Française*, Paris.

MORGAN, C. T. (1959) Physiological theory of drive, in KOCH S. (ed.), *Psychology: A Study of a Science*, New York: McGraw-Hill.

MORGAN, C. T. (1965) *Physiological Psychology*, New York: McGraw-Hill.

MORRIS, C. and JONES, L. V. (1955) Value scales and dimensions, *J. Abnorm. Soc Psychol* **51**, 523–35.

MORRIS, T. and BLOM-COOPER, L. (1967) Homicide in England, in WOLFGANG, M. (ed.), *Studies in Homicide*, New York: Harper & Row.

MORSELLI (1879) *Il suicidio*, Milan.

MOWRER, O. H. (1950) *Learning Theory and Personality Dynamics*, New York: Ronald.

MYERSON, A. and NAUSTADT, R. (1939) Influence of ultraviolet radiation upon the excretion of sex hormones in males, *Endocrinol.* **25**, 7.

NANDI, D. N. and BANERJEE, S. (1958) Adrenocortical function in some mental diseases, *Proc. Soc. Exper. Biol. and Med.* **99**, 187–9.

NEBYLITSYN, V. D. (1964) in GRAY, J. A. (ed.), *Pavlov's Typology*, Oxford: Pergamon.

NELSON, R. and GELLHORN, E. (1957) The action of autonomic drugs on normal persons and neuropsychiatric patients, *Psychosom. Med.* **19**, 486–94.

NESTURKH, M. (1963) *The Races of Mankind*, Moscow: Progress Publishers.

NORVIG, J. and NEILSON, B. (1953) A follow up study of 221 alcoholic addicts in Denmark, *Quart. J. Psychiat.* **109**, 633–42.

ØDEGAARD, O. (1961) Current studies of incidence and prevalence of hospitalised mental patients in Scandinavia, in HOCH, P. H., and ZUBIN, J. (eds.), *Comparative Epidemiology of Mental Disorders*, New York: Grune and Stratton.

PACKARD, V. (1968) *The Sexual Wilderness*, London: Longmans.

PALMER, R. S. (1937) The factor of mental stress in essential hypertension, *N. Engl. J. Med.* **216**, 689–93.

PALOLA, E. G., DORPAT, T. L. and LARSON, W. R. (1962) Alcoholism and suicidal behaviour, in PITTMAN, D. J. and SNYDER, C. R. (eds.), *Society, Culture and Drinking Patterns*, New York: John Wiley.

PARRY, M. H. (1968) *Aggression on the Road*, London: Tavistock.

PAVLOV, I. P. (1955) *Psychopathology and Psychiatry*, Foreign Languages Publishing House.

PAYNE, R. W. and HEWLETT, J. H. G. (1960) Thought disorder in psychotic patients, in EYSENCK, H. J. (ed.), *Experiments in Personality*, London: Routledge & Kegan Paul.

PETRIE, A. (1952) *Personality and the Frontal Lobes*, London: Routledge & Kegan Paul.

PETRIE, A. (1960) Some psychological aspects of pain and the relief of suffering, *Ann. N.Y. Acad. Sci.* **86**, 13–27.

PFEIFFER, J. B. and WOLFF, H. G. (1950) Studies in renal circulation during periods of life stress and accompanying emotional reactions in subjects with and without essential hypertension: Observations on the role of neural activity in the regulation of renal blood flow. *Res. Publ. Ass. Nerv. Ment. Dis.* **29**, 929–53.

PHILIP. A. E. (1969) Personality factors involved in suicidal behaviour. *Bull. Brit. Psychol. Soc.* **22**, 146.

PIEDMONT, E. B. (1961) A review of prevalence estimates for alcoholism, *Int. J. Soc. Psychiat.* **7**, 11–14.

PITTARD, E. (1926) *Race and History*, London: Routledge & Kegan Paul.

PITTMAN, D. J. and HANDY, W. (1964) Patterns in criminal aggravated assault, *J. Crim. Law, Criminol. Polit. Sci.* **55**, 462–70.

PITTS, F. N. and WINOKUR, G. (1964) Affective disorders. III: Diagnosis correlates and the incidence of suicide, *J. Nerv. Ment. Disease* **139**, 176–81.

POPHAM, R. E. (1966) *Indirect Methods of Alcoholism Prevalence Estimation: a critical evaluation*, Toronto: Addiction Research Foundation.

POPHAM, R. E. (1969) Personal communication.

POPOV, E. A. (1955) On some of the pathophysiological peculiarities of schizophrenia, in *Proceedings of the All Union Theoretical–Practical Conference dedicated to the Centenary of S. S. Korsakov and to Current Psychological Problems*, Moscow: Medgiz.

PORTER, R. W., BRADY, J. V., CONRAD, D. G., MASON, J. W., GALAMBOS, R. and RIOCH, D. (1958) Some experimental observations on gastro-intestinal lesions in behaviorally conditioned monkeys, *Psychosom. Med.* **20**, 379–94.

POTTER, S. (1947) *Gamesmanship*, London: Rupert Hart Davis.

QUASTEL, J. H. and WALES, W. T. (1938) Faulty detoxication in schizophrenia, *Lancet* **235**, 301–5.

RADZINSKI, J. M. (1959) The American melting pot, *Amer. J. Psychiat.* **115**, 873–86.

REES, L. (1950) Body build, personality and neurosis in women, *J. Ment. Sci.* **96**, 426–34.

REITER, R. (1952) Verkehrsunfallziffer und Reaktionzeit unter dem Einfluss verschiedener meteorologischen, komischen und luftelektrischen Faktoren, *Meteorol. Runschau* **5**, 14–17.

REITER, R. (1953) Neure Untersuchungen zum Problem der Wetterabhängigkeit des Menschen, *Arch. Meteorol. Geophysik u. Bioklimatol.*, Ser. B, **4**, 327.

REITER, R. (1956) *Einfluss des Wetters auf die Häufigkeit von Unfällen im Untertagebetrieb*, Arbeitsschutz, Koln, pp. 133–4.

RENBOURN, E. T. (1960) Body temperature and pulse rate in boys and young men prior to sporting contests, *J. Psychosom. Res.* **4**, 149–75.

RICHTER, C. P. and HAWKES, C. D. (1939) Increased spontaneous activity and food intake produced in rats by removal of the frontal lobes of the brain, *J. Neurol. Psychiat.*, Chicago, **24**, 231–42.

RIPLEY, W. Z. (1899) *The Races of Europe*, New York: Appleton.

ROBINS, E., SCHMIDT, E. and O'NEAL, P. (1957) Some interrelations of social factors and clinical diagnosis of attempted suicide, *Amer. J. Psychiat.* **114**, 222–4.

ROBINSON, J. D. (1959) A study of the relationship between blood pressure and certain aspects of personality, *Bull. Brit. Psychol. Soc.* **37**, 5A. (Abstract.)

ROHDEN, H. (1933) Einfluss des Föhns auf das körperlichseelische Befinden, *Arch. Psychol.* **89**, 605.

ROOK, A. (1959) Student suicides, *Brit. Med. J.* **1**, 599–603.

ROSEN, E. and GREGORY, J. (1965) *Abnormal Psychology*, Philadelphia: W. B. Saunders.

ROSTOW, W. W. (1960) *The Process of Economic Growth*, Oxford: O.U.P.

ROSVOLD, H. E., MIRSKY, A. F. and PRIBRAM, K. H. (1954) Influence of amygdalectomy on social behavior in monkeys, *J. Comp. Physiol. Psychol.* **47**, 173–8.

RUBIN, L. S. (1960) Pupillary reactivity as a measure of adrenergic–cholinergic mechanisms in the study of psychotic behavior, *J. Nerv. Ment. Dis.* **130**, 386–400.

RUBIN, L. S. (1962) Patterns of adrenergic–cholinergic imbalance in the functional psychoses, *Psychol. Rev.* **69**, 501–19.

RUDIN, S. A. (1968) National motives predict psychogenic death rates 25 years later, *Science* **160**, 901–3.

RUNQUIST, W. N. and ROSS, L. E. (1959) The relation between physiological measures of emotionality and performance in eyelid conditioning, *J. Exp. Psychol.* **57**, 329–32.

RUSKIN, A., BEARD, O. W. and SCHAFFER, R. L. (1948) Blast hypertension: elevated arterial pressure and victims of the Texas City disaster, *Amer. J. Med.* **4**, 228–36.

RUSSELL, C. and RUSSELL, W. M. S. (1968) *Violence, Monkeys and Man*, London: Macmillan.

SAARMA, YU. M. (1955) On the changes in the neurodynamics of schizophrenics during insulin therapy, in *Proceedings of the All Union Theoretical–Practical Conference dedicated to the Centenary of S. S. Korsakov and to Current Psychological Problems*, Moscow: Medgiz.

SAINSBURY, P. (1955) *Suicide in London*, London: Chapman & Hall.

SAINSBURY, P. and BARRACLOUGH, B. (1968) Differences between suicide rates, *Nature* **220**, 1252.

SAMUELS, I. (1959) Reticular mechanisms and behavior, *Psychol. Bull.* **56**, 1–25.

SARGANT, W. and SLATER, E. (1963) *An Introduction to Physical Methods of Treatment in Psychiatry*, Edinburgh: Livingstone.

SAUL, L. A. (1939) Hostility in cases of essential hypertension, *Psychosom. Med.* **1**, 153–61.

SAUL, L. A., SHEPPARD, E., SELBY, D., LHAMON, W., SACHS, D. and MASTER, R. (1954) The quantification of hostility in dreams with reference to essential hypertension, *Science* **119**, 382–3.

SAWREY, W., CONGER, J. and TURRELL, E. (1956) An experimental investigation of the role of psychological factors in the production of gastric ulcers in rats, *J. Comp. Physiol. Psychol.* **49**, 457–61.

SAWREY, W. and WEISS, J. D. (1956) An experimental method of producing gastric ulcers, *J. Comp. Physiol. Psychol.* **49**, 269–70.

SCHMID, C. (1933) Suicide in Minneapolis, Minnesota: 1928–32, *Amer. J. Sociol.* **49**, 47.

SCHUBERT, D. S. (1965) Arousal seeking as a central factor in tobacco smoking among college students, *Int. J. Soc. Psychiat.* **11**, 221–5.

SCHULZE, V. E. and SCHWAB, E. H. (1936) Arteriolar hypertension in the American Negro, *Amer. Heart. J.* **11**, 66–74.

SEGAL, YU. E. (1955) Clinical-physiological investigations of the destruction of the internal analysers in schizophrenia, in *Proceedings of the All Union Theoretical–Practical Conference dedicated to the Centenary of S. S. Korsakov and to Current Psychological Problems*, Moscow: Medgiz.

SEIDEN, R. H. (1966) Campus tragedy: a study of student suicide, *J. Abnorm. Psychol.* **71**, 389–99.

SELTZER, C. C. (1967) Constitution and heredity in relation to tobacco smoking, *Annals of the New York Academy of Science* **142**, 322–30.

SHAGASS, C. (1957) A measureable neurophysiological factor of psychiatric significance, *Electroenceph. Clin. Neurophysiol.* **9**, 101–8.

SHAPIRO, A. P. (1960) Psychophysiologic mechanisms in hypertensive vascular disease, *Ann. Intern. Med.* **53**, 64–83.

SHATTOCK, F. M. (1950) The somatic manifestations of schizophrenia, *J. Ment. Sci.* **96**, 32–142.

SHAW, L. and SICHEL, H. S. (1961) Reduction of accidents in a transport company by the determination of the accident liability of individual drivers, *Traffic Safety Research Review* **5**, 2–12.

SHEARD, M. H. (1958) Responsivity of adrenal gland in schizophrenia to corticotropin, *Arch. Neurol. Psychiat.* **79**, 727–9.

SHIELDS, J. (1962) *Monozygotic Twins*, London, O.U.P.

SHIELDS, J. and SLATER, E. (1960) Heredity and psychological abnormality, in EYSENCK, H. J. (ed.), *Handbook of Abnormal Psychology*, New York: Basic Books.

SILVERSTONE, J. T. and SOLOMON, T. (1965) Psychiatric and somatic factors in the treatment of obesity, *J. Psychosom. Res.* **9**, 349.

SINKEVICH, Z. L. (1955) An experiment investigating conditioned disinhibition in schizophrenia, *Trud. Inst. Vssh. Nervn. Deyatel.* **1**, 11–25.

SLONIM, A. D. and SCHERBAKOVA, O. P. (1954) Observations of night sleep in monkeys, in BOGORAD, S. I. (ed.), *The Sleep Problem*, pp. 312–19, Moskva: Medgiz.

SPENCE, K. (1960) *Behavior Theory and Learning*, New Jersey: Prentice Hall.

STANISHEVSKAYA, N. N. (1955) A plethysmographic investigation of catatonic schizophrenia, in *Proceedings of the All Union Theoretical–Practical Conference dedicated to the Centenary of S. S. Korsakov and to Current Psychological Problems*, Moscow: Medgiz.

STENGEL, E. (1964) *Suicide and Attempted Suicide*, Harmondsworth: Penguin Books.

STERNBACH, R. A. and TURSKY, B. (1965) Ethnic differences among housewives in psychophysical and skin potential responses to electric shock. *Psychophysiology* **1**, 241–6.

STORR, A. (1968) *Human Aggression*, London: Allen Lane.

STRANGE, J. R. (1965) *Abnormal Psychology*, New York: McGraw-Hill.

STRELTSOVA, N. L. (1955) The characteristics of some unconditioned reflexes in schizophrenics, in *Proceedings of the All Union Theoretical–Practical Conference dedicated to the Centenary of S. S. Korsakov and to Current Psychological Problems*, Moscow: Medgiz.

STRÖM-OLSEN, R. and WEIL-MALHERBE, H. (1958) Humoral changes in manic-depressive psychosis with particular reference to the excretion of catecholamines in urine, *J. Ment. Sci.* **104**, 696–704.

SWINSCOW, D. (1951) Some suicide statistics, *Brit. Med. J.* **1**, 1417–22.

TARANSKAYA, A. D. (1955) The effect of certain drugs on hallucinations, in *Proceedings of the All Union Theoretical–Practical Conference dedicated to the Centenary of S. S. Korsakov and to Current Psychological Problems*, Moscow: Medgiz.

TEPLOV, B. M. (1964) in GRAY, J. A., *Pavlov's Typology*, Oxford: Pergamon.

TERMAN, L. (1925) *Genetic Studies of Genius*, Stanford: Stanford University Press.

THOLUCK, H. J. (1942) Selbstmord und Wetter, *Beiträge Gerichtl. Med.* **16**, 121.

TRAUGOTT, N. N., BALONOV, L. YA., KAUFFMANN, D. A. and LUCHKO, A. E. (1958) On the dynamics of the destruction of orientating reflexes in certain psychotic syndromes, in VORONIN, L. G. (ed.), *The Orientating Reflex and Orientating Investigating Activity*, Moscow: Academy of Pedagogical Sciences of R.S.F.S.R.

TREKINA, T. A. (1955) The clinical manifestations and course of schizophrenia with the maniacal syndrome, in *Proceedings of the All Union Theoretical–Practical Conference dedicated to the Centenary of S. S. Korsakov and to Current Psychological Problems*, Moscow: Medgiz.

TROMP, S. W. (1963) *Medical Biometeorology*, New York: Elsevier.

TUCKMAN, J. and LAVELL, M. (1959) Emotional content of suicide notes, *Amer. J. Psychiat.* **116**, 59–63.

TURSKY, B. and STERNBACH, R. A. (1967) Further physiological correlates of ethnic differences in responses to shock, *Psychophysiol.* **4**, 67–74.

ULETT, J. and ITIL, T. M. (1969) Quantitative EEG in smoking and smoking deprivation, *Science* **164**, 969–70.

UTERS, M., HOFSCHLAEGER, J., ANTON, H. U. and ZIMMERMAN, W. (1951) Die 17-ketosteroidsausscheidung als Anzeigen für die Beringlussung des organismus durch meteorologische Faktoren, *Deut. Med. Wochschr.* **76**, 1408–9.

VALLANCE, M. (1965) Alcoholism: a two-year follow-up study of patients admitted to the psychiatric department of a general hospital, *Brit. J. Psychiat.* **111**, 348–56.

VENABLES, P. H. (1960) The effect of auditory and visual stimulation on the skin potential response of schizophrenics, *Brain* **83**, 77–92.

VENABLES, P. H. (1964) Input dysfunction in schizophrenia, in MAHER, B. A. (ed.), *Progress in Experimental Personality Research*, New York: Academic Press.

VERTOGRADOVA, O. P. (1955) Conditioned and unconditioned vaso-reflex in schizophrenia, in *Proceedings of the All Union Theoretical–Practical Conference dedicated to the Centenary of S. S. Korsakov and to Current Psychological Problems*, Moscow: Medgiz.

WARWICK, K. M. and EYSENCK, H. J. (1963) The effects of smoking on the CFF threshold, *Life Sciences* **4**, 219–25.

WATANABE, G. I. (1958) Climatic effect on the packed red-cell volume, *Brit. J. Haematol.* **4**, 108–12.

WEBER, M. (1904) *The Protestant Ethic and Spirit of Capitalism*, translated by T. Parsons (1930), New York: Scribner.

WILKINS, J. (1967) Suicidal behavior, *Amer. Sociol. Rev.* **32**, 286–98.

WOLF, S., PFEIFFER, J. B., RIPLEY, H. S., WINTER, O. S. and WOLFF, H. G. (1948) Hypertension as a reaction pattern to stress: Summary of experimental data on variations in blood pressure and renal blood flow, *Ann. Intern. Med.* **29**, 1056–76.

WOLFGANG, M. (1958) An analysis of homicide-suicide, *J. Clin. Exper. Psychopathology* **19**, 208–18.

WOLPE, J. (1958) *Psychotherapy by Reciprocal Inhibition*, Stanford: Stanford University Press.

YESSLER, P., GIBBS, J. and BECKER, H. (1961) On the communication of suicidal ideas II. Some medical considerations, *Arch. Gen. Psychiat.* **5**, 12–29.

ZBOROWSKI, M. (1952) Cultural components in responses to pain, *J. Soc. Issues*, **8**, 16–30.

INDEX